The Courage to Lead

Transform Self, Transform Society

R. BRIAN STANFIELD
for The Canadian Institute of Cultural Affairs

NEW SOCIETY PUBLISHERS

In memory of Lyn Edwards Mathews, a founder of ICA, a social pioneer and a signal presence.

Oh, for the wonder that bubbles into my soul,
I would be a good fountain, a good well-head,
Would blur no whisper, spoil no expression.
D.H. Lawrence

Cataloguing in Publication Data:

A catalog record for this publication is available from the National Library of Canada.

Copyright © 2000 by The Canadian Institute of Cultural Affairs.

Editors: Ronnie Seagren and Brian Griffith.
Design and layout: Ilona Staples.

Printed in Canada on acid-free, partially recycled (20 percent post-consumer) paper using soy-based inks by Transcontinental/Best Book Manufacturers.

New Society Publishers acknowledges the financial support of the Government of Canada through the Book Publishing Industry Development Program (BPIDP) for our publishing activities, and the assistance of the Province of British Columbia through the British Columbia Arts Council.

Paperback ISBN: 0-86571-425-8

Inquiries regarding requests to reprint all or part of *The Courage to Lead: Pioneering Social Change* should be addressed to New Society Publishers at the address below.

To order directly from the publishers, please add $4.00 shipping to the price of the first copy, and $1.00 for each additional copy (plus GST in Canada). Send check or money order to:

New Society Publishers
P.O. Box 189, Gabriola Island, BC V0R 1X0, Canada

New Society Publishers aims to publish books for fundamental social change through nonviolent action. We focus especially on sustainable living, progressive leadership, and educational and parenting resources. Our full list of books can be browsed on the worldwide web at: http://www.newsociety.com

Copublished by

NEW SOCIETY PUBLISHERS
Gabriola Island BC, Canada

The Canadian Institute of Cultural Affairs (ICA Canada)
579 Kingston Road, Toronto, ON Canada M4E 1R3

Contents

SECTION A Relation to Life

SECTION B Relation to the Self

SECTION C Relation to the World

SECTION D Relation to Society

ACKNOWLEDGEMENTS

This book has been a team effort from the beginning, even though one name is ascribed to the writing. So the acknowledgements are many. I have to acknowledge first of all those graduates of ICA courses who kept on coming back to ICA Canada for course after course. They kept asking us the same question, "What lies behind all these courses? What is ICA hiding from us?" It was questions like these that really pushed us at ICA Canada to get this book written. Our Board asked similar questions. They said, "There are things you know that many other people in the world need to know. You have to publish a book to get your foundational wisdom more widely known." And so a book was commissioned. Without those questions there would have been no book. We are grateful to those who kept pushing us to publish.

In particular we must acknowledge the constant urgings and support of Board members, Shelley Cleverly, David Dycke, Daphne Field and Board Chair Judy Harvie. David remained steadfastly convinced of the importance of getting a book written. Judy throughout has been a wellspring of practical wisdom. Daphne kept asking hard questions, Shelley has shepherded the book along from the beginning every step of the way. From beginning to end, she was the iron pillar that kept on convincing everyone that this book was possible.

On behalf of ICA Canada, I must express particular thanks to those new and old colleagues who put money up front to defray the publication costs, especially to the David and Anne Patterson family, and the Phil and Margaret Devor family.

Acknowledgements must be made also to the team of ICA people who gave up time to meet the forty times it took to brainstorm and design the content of the book, and to critique each chapter as it came off the computer. Those forty or so Monday morning meetings were invaluable in focusing the book and revealing the potholes in the text.

A number of international people with long ICA experience played a critical role. They were invited to form an advisory group to read each chapter and make suggestions. We especially want to mention Bill and Barbara Alerding, John Epps, Gordon Harper, and Betty Pesek for their reading of the chapters and their wise advice, encouragement and cautions. The chapters are saner and richer for their contributions.

Special thanks to Sheighlah Hickey who has cared for ICA Canada's archives and kept them in excellent order, making the research task comparatively easy.

This opportunity must be taken to thank those who prepared the first CD-ROM, Golden Pathways, on selections from ICA's global archives. Without that CD-ROM, that provided instant access to thousands of archival files of ICA wisdom, the task of assembling the book would have been incredibly more difficult.

ICA Canada Director Duncan Holmes throughout has been an invaluable mentor to the writer and has also put up with the latter's strange working hours without comment.

The editorial team of Brian Griffith and Ronnie Seagen excelled themselves in their painstaking devotion to tightening and sharpening the text, and in helping the author avoid fatal blunders.

The writer is personally grateful to the ICA Canada staff who were willing time and time again to make themselves available as a resource to provide many different kinds of data.

Finally, I must express my appreciation to my wife, Jeanette, who allowed herself to be a sounding board for all kinds of ideas related to the book, at any hour of the day or night.

BRIAN STANFIELD

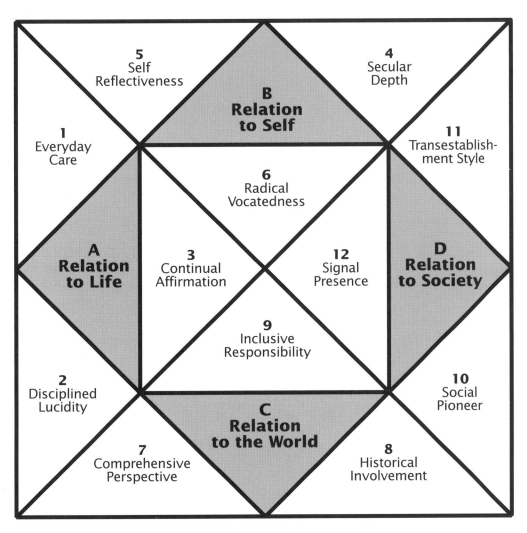

Matrix Diagram

This is the matrix from which the structure of *The Courage to Lead* derives. The matrix covers the four basic relationships leadership must have to be authentic: the relationship to LIFE, to the SELF, to the WORLD, and to SOCIETY. Each relationship has a basis: the relationship to life is based on a faith in reality as it is; the relationship to self is grounded in consciousness and its intensification; the relationship to the world is grounded in the triad of space, time and relationships; the relationship to society is grounded in a compassionate commitment to creating new human images and new social structures that care for all. Each relationship is expressed through three stances, or postures, as shown in the three interior triangles in the matrix. These 12 stances are the stuff of the 12 chapters of this book.

 ## INTRODUCTION

I cannot be less than the most I can be, otherwise I would be spitting at God. If I've
been given this much talent and this much intelligence, then I'm obliged to use it.
MAYA ANGELOU

A fine wind is blowing the new direction of Time.
If only I let it bear me, carry me, if only it carry me!
D.H. LAWRENCE

HOW LIFE QUESTIONS GET RAISED

Authentic leaders have always tangled with the key questions of life and rendered their
own answers in the integrity of their own being as they have confronted the situations
that life has placed them in. Those who have not heard life's questions tend to be lost,
emotionally numb, and vocationally unengaged. Part of a leader's authenticity is the
willingness to engage daily in dialogue with the events and situations life throws at us.

When I was growing up in Australia, my parents lost a lot of money in the great
depression, so in 1936 we sold our hotel in Sydney and made the car trip to a little seaside town in New South Wales. They leased a small hotel right by the water. I lived a halcyon life, swimming, surfing, bicycling. In the school holidays, hotel guests who were
friends of the family took me fishing up the river, or surfing. Life seemed to be a breeze.
One day at the end of fourth grade, when we were spinning our wheels in class after

annual exams were over, Sister Emmanuel got us started making a scrapbook. My first page was silly. I put in a full page ad for toothpaste. The next day was the attack on Pearl Harbour. So, my second page had the classic shot of US warships ablaze on battleship row. I filled up the scrapbook and five more with the history of World War II.

One day these two worlds—my carefree life by the seaside and the war—came together for me. I was down on the bayside beach near our hotel, when I noticed a launch approaching. It stopped just a few feet from where I was building sand castles. Five men were taken out of the launch. I saw that they were covered in oil and badly burnt. A butter ship had been torpedoed just a few miles off shore by a Japanese submarine, and these were the survivors. They were temporarily made at home in the lobby of our hotel until an ambulance could come.

The sight of those terribly burned men brought the suffering of war home to me in a way that none of the Movietone newsreels, or war movies could. Perhaps, in retrospect, I began wondering how these two worlds—terrible suffering, and days without care—could exist side by side.

The next day my father got me out of bed, and said, "We're going to pick up some butter." But butter was rationed. Where were we going to get butter from? As our truck made its way out along the southern beaches, I was told that the butter ship's cargo was washing up all along the shores. Boxes of butter lay everywhere. We joined the townsfolk who were strung along the beach salvaging the butter crates among the seaweed. We stacked crate after crate of butter in the truck, and then went back for more to stock our hotel freezer. The hotel dining room, to guests' amazement, had butter on the table all through the war. But at the time I was stunned—a ship gets torpedoed, and we get butter! How can disaster and suffering live side by side with such possibility?

Well, my days of not a care in the world quickly came to an end as all the young men in the town went off to war. It was impossible to hire male help.

At ten, I became my dad's "right-hand man", filling up quarts of "draught" from the firkins (nine gallon barrels) and kilderkins (18-gallon barrels), sweeping out the bar every morning, working side by side with him for the "victory [vegetable] garden" in our back yard. I had joined the working class.

In the back of my mind, a question was forming, something like, Is life really like this? A roller coaster ride with terrible suffering and mysterious boons? I think for the next thirty years I struggled with those questions. What was the relationship between the religion I was taught in Catholic school and real life? How could life contain such opposite experiences? Which part of life was real? Was it the halcyon days of not a care in the world, or the godawful suffering and hard work associated with "the War". I think it would be bizarre to suggest that at age ten or eleven I was mature enough to ask these questions. But I do believe that life raised them, and I felt them, willy nilly.

Of course, there were other struggles, too. My dad and I were always at loggerheads about how much free time I should get. I always wanted more; but, with so much work to do, he figured there was less. Sometimes I just sneaked away to hang out with the "Kenny gang", as we called ourselves, to go out on the bay in aircraft drop tanks, to ride ponies, or to throw rocks at the public school kids. So, how much work was fair for me to do?

Later, when I thought that I had solved my life questions by joining a religious order, these childhood questions were only exacerbated. We delved into tomes on moral theology, ascetical theology, church history, hagiography, until we knew all the big words, with not an idea in the world of how they applied to everyday life. As I passed through the training and began teaching religion in a Catholic school, I noticed the sheer boredom of the kids when there was talk of "transubstantiation", "the hypostatic union", "the beatific vision". After a while, in desperation at not being able to make any sense of it, or apply it to life, we would start talking about "practical issues": social issues, work, getting a job, dating, euthanasia, and so on. Much more interest in all that. But still there was no connection between the theological big words and real life.

I began going to conferences to look for clues there. I went to meetings of the Society which studied the works of Roman Catholic theological heavyweight, Thomas Aquinas. At every one of these Aquinas Society meetings at Sydney University, the same man got up and said something like: " Søren Kierkegaard presents a totally different theological approach to life. We should be hearing what he has to say." (Søren Kierkegaard was a 19th century philosopher-theologian from Denmark—the first of the existentialists, who, among other things, posited faith as an alternative to existential despair.) After this man spoke, all hell would break loose. I did not have enough background at the time to really understand what was going on. But that Kierkegaardian knew that the study of Thomas Aquinas without any grounding in real life was pure abstraction, however valuable.

It is strange that for every new piece of technology, we get a manual on how to use it. Except for humans. We come into this world to face the puzzles of existence without any manual called, How to Be a Human Being. If we buy a car, computer, refrigerator, or even a digital watch, we get a manual of operations. But no one passes out instructions when we are born, not to us or our parents. Later on in life we may encounter the Bible, the Koran, the Eightfold Path, or Bill Bones' *Pathways on Life's Journey*. But, without good teachers who know how to use these great books, they often remain impenetrable, sometimes a source of one more fundamentalism.

Yet, everyone needs a big picture of the way life is, a good map to navigate the rapids of life and skills for the journey. For life initially comes to us as "one great big buzzing confusion", as the psychologist William James put it. Later on, as we get more scientifically literate, we may refer to it grandly as "chaos dynamics". Or, more simply, as the Latin American author Ortega y Gasset put it: "Life comes to us as pure problem." Not whether to order a steak or a salad for lunch, not just the practical daily problems associated with the workplace or the family or spouse or kids, not just a few ethical problems, like whether to divorce or not, to abort or not. But pure problem: Why am I here at all? Who am I? What do I do with my life? Or, how do I style my existence in the world? These questions never go away.

So I started reading like one possessed, but found nothing that helped relate theology to real life. At one stage, it seemed that Vatican II was going to be the answer, but the conservative forces won out and, except for a few victories, the glow of Vatican II died. We were left with the same old disrelation to real life. Finally, the time came when I left the religious order, joined the peace movement, began raising hell in the press about the Catholic Church's abuse of authority, its approach to birth control, its radical conservatism and much more. I was going deeper and deeper into despair.

One day, a woman by the name of Carol Pierce called from the Ecumenical Institute in Sydney and invited me to attend a course. I said I couldn't bear one more course. Half an hour later, she called again and with the same schpiel. I declined. Half an hour later she called a third time, and went through it all again. I said to myself: "This is some woman, and she doesn't take no for an answer." I couldn't find it in myself to say no again. Carol and her husband, Joe Pierce, taught the course about what life was really like in the 20th century and what its possibilities were, and it was right up my alley. That course, experienced and lived for the next 30 years actually forms the basis of Chapters 2, 3, 9, and 10 of this book.

The course solved none of my life struggles for good; in a sense, it raised more questions than it answered, but it was a new set of questions that set me on a journey of discovery, and gave me names and handles for things.

As you read, you may want to reflect back on your life as I have done above to see where the big life questions were first raised for you. These questions arise many times in the course of a lifetime, but the answers do not all pop out neatly in one place. These days, the questions seem to turn up early in people's lives; for example, those youth who graduate from university with a bachelor's degree, or even a doctorate, and can't find work related to their training.

So how do we enable young, middle-aged or older people to face up to the three fundamental questions of life:

1. *Who am I?* (What is a human being? Who am I as Mary, Vikash or Vincente? Who am I really?)

When life picks me up in its wave, and then dumps me on the beach so that my head burrows a hole in the sand, it raises the question, who am I? Do I rejoice at those ups and downs because that's how life is? Do I give up surfing the waves of life just because I got dumped? Has this experience enlarged me or diminished me? Am I a lover or hater of life? And then the big one: how do I relate to the fact that I am going to die?

2. *What do I do?* Why was I born? Why am I in the world? What is my life about? What is my vocation in life? What do I want to do with my once-around-the clock life? How can I make a difference to the world and its social structures?

For many of us this question was raised when we left the regular structures of school life, and attended our ceremony of graduation. Suddenly we realized that the next years of our lives seemed like a yawning abyss. In our own ways, each of us faced our life opening before us. If my life is to have structure or purpose, it is up to me to create it. So what am I going to do with the whole rest of my life?

3. H*ow do I style my life?* How am I going to live my life? How do I style myself as a human being? How do I be who I am to the fullest? How do I relate myself to myself to others and to the depths of my being? How do I live fully in whatever situation I find myself?

When my mood hits rock bottom as I encounter life's vicissitudes and soars like a rocket when life is good to me, I am experiencing something quite normal. As I face life's questions, I have the opportunity to develop a constancy, a centeredness in my relationship to life. I create what it means for me to be a leader in the real situations I face.

We all have to tangle with these questions as we live. But it is not so easy. In fact, any time we are confronted with one of these questions, as we shall see in chapter 2, our response is generally some kind of paralysis.

LEADERSHIP AND PARALYSIS

The title of this book attempts to join two ideas. First, there is an overwhelming radicality to the stance of living a full human life. Second, we don't need to be paralysed by all the issues and questions in our lives. We can begin to deal with them as social innovators in our own household, around the kitchen table, at the coffee klatch, round the water cooler, wherever we are. We don't need to put up barricades and start a revolution. We can lead by instigating small changes wherever we are—once we deal with the paralysis bugaboo.

There are times in everyone's life, when we feel that something overwhelmingly different is demanded of us. It is as if life is a great marriage feast to which we are invited. Something in us wants to say, "yes, yes, I want to participate." Maybe we wake up in the middle of the night and experience a sudden yearning for something different—to go on a great adventure; to get involved in our local community; to give up the rat race for one weekend and go on retreat; to abandon our career as hotshot market trader and go work in Central American villages for a year and see what happens. But the possibility leaves us paralysed: we start coming out with our excuses. There is an old gospel song about it:

> I cannot come, I cannot come to the wedding,
> I have married a wife, I have bought me a cow,
> I have fields and commitments that cost a pretty sum.
> Pray hold me excused, I cannot come.

The concern of this book is that people do not seem to be aware of their own ability to act. From time to time they wake up to their freedom to make choices and take charge of life's meaning. They experience an overwhelming drive to do something, try something, but they are paralysed. This book challenges people to take charge of their own internal quest for meaning in life. It encourages them to move out of paralysis by acting powerfully wherever they are.

In that great old movie *Auntie Mame*, there is a scene in which the heroine has invited some guests to a feast in her house. The guests are standing round listlessly, not partaking of anything, when Mame begins her walk down the grand staircase to meet them. Suddenly she pauses on the stairs to look down at the scene below. Moved by a sudden inspiration, she yells out to them: "Life is a banquet, and all of you poor suckers are starving to death!"

All of us, at times, have this experience. We are invited to a banquet, and yet our own paralysis and indecision has afflicted us with spiritual anorexia. Underneath this is a sense that someone else is in charge of our future—not we ourselves. Richard Critchfield wrote a great book on village development in the early 1980s. In it he says,

> The great divide in the world today is not so much between the rich and the poor, the educated and the illiterate, the healthy and malnourished, but between those who think that humans can shape their own destiny and those who still believe that personal fate is decided by outside forces.

This paralysis is nowhere more obvious than when we come up against social issues. Someone dumps their garbage in a vacant lot, or toxic chemicals in the creek. "Someone should do something about that!" Mrs Jones is housebound and can't get out anymore. "Her relatives should attend to that!" There are accidents on this particular corner every month. "They should put up traffic lights."

Our paralysis always seems to invoke some other party as the one responsible: the government, relatives, other people in the community. Yet the issues mentioned here are not major issues. But we seem to grow faint at the very thought of intervening, of doing something, anything at all, to deal with the problems. No wonder that when we come into contact with the big ones, for example, when the global economy dominates over national governments (as in the proposed Multilateral Agreement on Investments Treaty (MAI) issue, or the poor quality of education, or inequities in the health care system, or youth gangs, or the void of meaning in people's lives, we all start running for cover.

Sometimes we feel the same paralysis ourselves.We all reach points in our lives when we get so flustered, rushed, overwhelmed by everything that's coming at us, that we say to ourselves, "I need to stop, go aside, and think about what's going on in my life, and decide how I can deal with all this complexity." But, no, we are afraid to stop, because we think, if we do, everything will only get worse. If we leave the office or workplace to itself for a few days, the sky will fall in. We are paralysed by the very need to reflect, we do nothing about it, and our stress level continues to rise. Or we reach a certain momentum in our work: we are working fourteen hours a day, leaving our partner and the kids to fend for themselves. Our work has become everything. People expect us to keep producing at this pace, and we like the kudos we're getting. We know we're headed for a heart attack or stroke or something, but we are addicted to work, and life rushes by us. We are too busy to see those moments when life turns transparent and the awe breaks through. Work has become the meaning of our life. What we hoped to accomplish for society in that work has been forgotten.

We are all subject to this paralysis in our own ways. We know its name, and how it feels. We are in charge of our own lives, we can pick up responsibility and deal creatively with issues from our own standing point.

OUR SOURCE: LIVED EXPERIENCE

On leafing through this book, you may ask where all this content comes from? This book relies heavily on many of the foundational understandings behind the work of the Institute of Cultural Affairs (ICA) spread over nearly 40 years. The author, Brian Stanfield, is really a figurehead representing the people who worked as staff or volunteers with ICA over the years in its work of social pioneering on several continents.

You will find ideas in this book that are unfamiliar, and parts of it may be difficult to handle. Some of the language with tendencies to jargon may irritate you. But the content of this book come from lived experience, from forty years of programming in cities, towns, communities and tribal villages on every continent, with all age groups and every sector of society. This broad base of experience gives a certain authenticity to the book. Even beyond the track record, ICA staff have done their homework on the dynamics of social change and the depths of the human spirit. (See Appendix for more on the history of ICA)

The heart of this book is life experience and the constant dialogue with life itself. My colleagues and I believe that life prepares us for leadership by plunging us into many different kinds of experience that raise foundational questions for us. Often, life questions appear long before we have the resources to come to terms with them. The test of this book for you is this: is this book talking about my real life experience? Is it talking about the way life is?

WHO IS THIS BOOK FOR?

1. The original impetus for writing this book was to satisfy the curiosity of those who, having taken ICA's courses or participated in its consultations, sensed something deeper below the surface. Many recent course grads have had the impression of something more profound behind the technologies of participation (ToP™ methods). They pestered their teachers to pull back the curtain. This book is written for them.

2. We also think the book has a much wider application for those who are concerned about living fully wherever they show up in the social framework. This book can be useful to teachers, mothers, CEOs, and professional people, as well as to social entrepreneurs, community development practitioners and social change agents.

This is a book that ties together life's knowing, doing and being. It attempts to lay out a picture of unmitigated human living and courageous leadership. It is about how we care in our homes and neighborhoods, and for ourselves and for the world. It looks at how we find purpose in life. It is about clambering onto the stage of history and deciding to take responsibility for things from where we are. It's about caring for society in a way that beckons to other people.

WHAT IS A STANCE?

This book presents these foundational understandings by describing twelve stances. The dictionary defines stance as a way of standing, especially the way one places one's feet in certain sports. So there is a fencing stance, the stance of the batter, the wrestler, the archer, and so on. These stances are readily recognizable. But what about the stance of being a social pioneer? a social entrepreneur, a change agent? There is a lot more to those stances than where you place your feet and arms although when it comes to implementation, feet and arms are relevant. A stance is the way we present our deepest convictions through a style of being that integrates the knowing, doing and being of our lives. A stance shows a particular perspective on life. It represents a conscious choice about how we will live our lives.

When we talk about stance, we don't mean social posturing—presenting ourselves as more than we are. We don't mean charisma or chutzpah or dramatic poses to win admiration. We mean a deep inner conviction about life that manifests itself externally. So, for example, the stance of care derives from the belief that the life of the leader has to do, in the first instance, with care for other people rather than absorption with oneself. It manifests itself in expressions of concern for others—words, gestures, actions. A stance involves a basic decision about the direction of life and one's mental preoccupations. A stance is an inner posture manifested externally in how we live.

This book deals with twelve such stances. Three are about our relationship to life as a whole, three about our relation with ourselves, three about our relation with the world, and three about our relation to society.

HOW TO USE THIS BOOK

There is no law that you have to start a book at the beginning and proceed right to the end. You may want to try another approach.

- All twelve stances express important dimensions of living with integrity. You might want to read the introduction and then the introductions to each of the four sections and then decide which section really captures your attention. Then plow in wherever your attention is grabbed.

    - To focus more on the *"Who am I?"* question, look at chapters 1, 2, 4, 5, and 9.

    - To examine *"What do I?"* questions, read chapters 6, 8, 10, and 11.

    - To explore *"How be I?"* questions, Chapters 1, 3, and 12 would be of interest.

- You could scan the book quickly, then read each chapter in depth. When you finish each chapter, do the exercise provided or answer the reflective questions.

- If you're the kind of reader who's not even going to look at the content before you've seen its intellectual pedigree, then read the Introduction and Appendix on the history of ICA.

Exercise

You can use this exercise to decide intentionally how to use this book:

1. Run your eyes down the table of contents. Mark the chapters that look interesting.

_____

_____

2. Which chapters are you least interested in?

_____

3. Which chapters do you really think you most need to read in terms of your current situation?

_____

4. In the light of your answers, write down the order in which you want to read the chapters, beginning with the introduction.

_____

5. Write this order of chapter numbers to serve as a reminder on something you can use as a bookmark.

_____

_____

6. What do you intend to do about the exercises at the end of each chapter?

☐ Deal with them as they come up?

☐ Do them all on a weekend retreat?

☐ Pick out the ones you need to do most and do them first?

☐ Invite a group to which you belong to do the exercises together?

☐ Tackle the exercises after you have read the whole book?

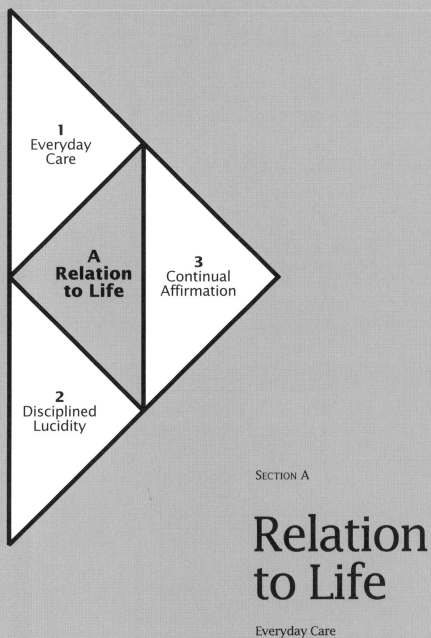

1
Everyday Care

A
Relation to Life

3
Continual Affirmation

2
Disciplined Lucidity

Relation to Life

Everyday Care

Disciplined Lucidity

Continual Affirmation

Introduction to Section A

All of us have to grapple with a response to the way life is. For everyone the question gets raised: how should I respond to the people I meet? How should I react to what I read in the newspaper? Do I think about what my experiences mean? Or am I too busy having a good time, or trying to keep my head above water? Do I just say "Whatever!" and tackle the next task on my to-do list?

The quest for meaning in life is the deepest of all human quests, far deeper than the quest for money, sex, status, or power. It is the contention of this book that meaning is found precisely in the midst of living life in all its varied situations. These are generally not the the situations we want, or would choose if it were up to us.

When we thankfully acknowledge both the tragedy and the possibilities in the midst of a given situation, rather than a better one over the next hill, then we are related authentically to life.

Leaders relate authentically to life when they are clear that it is their care, not their happiness, that gives life its significance. In the first instance that care is simple, everyday care. While we do what our care drives us to, we see life's tragedy and possibility. Without this lucidity, we are like children, babes in the wood, relative to the realities of life. Our lucidity exposes us to the question of how we relate to the realities of life, whether we curse them or accept them. We see the possibility of affirmation, of saying a yes to all of life.

These three, everyday care (Chapter 1), disciplined lucidity (Chapter 2), and continual affirmation (Chapter 3) express our authentic relationship to life.

CHAPTER 1

Everyday Care

Care is Everywhere

Give and it shall be given unto you
is still the truth about life.
But giving life is not so easy.
It doesn't mean handing it out to some mean fool,
or letting the living dead eat you up.
It means kindling the life quality where it was not
even if it's only in the whiteness of a washed pocket handkerchief.

D.H. LAWRENCE

It is care which gives life its significance.

RUDOLPH BULTMANN

CARE IS INESCAPABLE

Care is inescapable. It is everywhere we look. There is care for our work, there is structural care that cares for a whole group, there is symbolic care, there is the question of care in human encounters. Finally, there is the cost of care. The first stance of a leader has to do with being fully aware of her care, not escaping it.

There was a time in my life when I tried to escape care. In my mind, life was about having fun and doing what you wanted to do with the time you had: swimming, bike riding, or reading the comics. Then there was a time in my life when cares seemed to multiply, and I had to be clever to find enough time to still do what I wanted to do. Later still, I came to see that life is caring and caring is life, and then I had to make sure to carve out enough time so that I could take care of myself in order that I might better care for others. At one time I thought that only a few people did the caring: mothers, nurses, priests, nuns. Then my image shifted. I saw that everyone cares: parents care, kids care (even though they spend a lot of time pretending not to), bus drivers care, cabbies care; the panhandler cares. Cynics care, complainers care, and all those in the caring services (what some have called the uncaring services) care. People care even when they say they don't. "I just don't care" is a statement of care. So is "I couldn't care less." When you walk on the other side of the street to avoid someone, you care. When you turn off the TV set because you can't stand the news, you care. To refuse to participate in care is to be really dead. Care touches our humanness at depth.

We tend to take for granted the network of care that sustains each of us in life: our parents who gave us life; our relatives who have cared for us in many ways; our friends and support circles that encourage us, keep us wised up, cheer us on in our endeavours; the bus, streetcar, and subway drivers and systems that transport us from place to place; the weather service that helps us decide on what to wear, the crossing guard who gets our kids safely across those yellow bars to the other side; the family doctor; the people who tend public parks; those who repair the roads; the mentors who give us professional advice, on and on and on. Sometimes we resent paying so many fees and taxes—and taxes can be too high—but we often forget the infrastructure of everyday care that they provide.

Care is a two-way thing. We care, and we are cared for. We live off the deaths, the physical or psychological energy expenditures of people, just as other people live off our deaths. Everyday, people spend their life energy and others benefit.

If we stop to reflect, we realize how much we care every day about everything around us. As I rode along a bike path beside a creek one day, a young man, splattered with mud, stood in the middle of the creek trying to manhandle a shopping cart that someone had dumped in. He was pulling it out of the creek. As I got off to help him get it out, he said to me, "I just wish I didn't care as much as I do." I told him I knew exactly what he meant. It might make a good movie title, *The Man Who Cared Too Much*.

I ride my bike three kilometres to and from work each day. Even on my familiar ride, I realize how many things I care about. At a red light at the first intersection a car stops on the pedestrian crossing; making it more dangerous for people to walk across the street. Care. On the other side of the street, I notice the new supermarket going up. I'm wondering if the new one will be better laid out than the old one. Care. I do hope they put some trees around it. Off now into the railway underpass which needs a good painting. Care. On the other side of the tracks, another supermarket is to being built. Three supermarkets within 300 yards. Is this overkill? Care. Good lord, look at that huge ad. "World War III! World Soccer Finals on Channel WZX." That is irresponsible, knowing what we know about European soccer fans. Care. And I'm only a third of the way to work.

At this stage I pay attention to what's going on, and notice that I do care about it. I am concerned. Rather, I am concern. I *am* my care. What *I do* about it is another matter.

CARE IS EVERYWHERE

You too are aware of the deluge of everyday cares: making the kids' lunches, getting breakfast, dressing right for the office, listening to the concerns of a fellow worker, getting Johnny to the doctor, buying a gift for Jane's birthday, picking up the dry cleaning, and some veggies for dinner, checking the e-mail, making a list of things to do for tomorrow, starting a grocery list for the weekend, helping Johnny with his homework.

At work, people keep lists of things to do. They add items that don't get done to the next day's list. Eventually, the lists are thrown away and a new list is begun. Regardless of how we deal with our cares, care is multitudinous, ubiquitous, never-ending. Sometimes people think that, if they didn't have all these cares, they could really enjoy living. But, as German philosopher Rudolph Bultmann remarked, "it is care which gives life its significance." The daily cares are our real life.

Most of us wear several hats. There is our householder hat: we need to keep our dwelling clean, repaired, and all its tools and equipment maintained. As parents, we deal with children, schools, teachers, sports, doctors, dentists, all their clothes, equipment, and tools. Then there is our work hat, and the tasks related to our job. Finally, our citizen hat, with obligations and duties to vote, keep ourselves informed, be active in our community, serve on the boards of voluntary agencies.

Care consumes us. Some days we feel that we have been thrown into a large bowl full of piranha fish, pecking, pecking, biting, snapping, rending our very flesh away. At the end of the day, we may feel like mere skeletons, eaten alive by daily care. Then the question arises: how do we take care of ourselves so that we can do our everyday care?

I spent almost all my life living in institutions, or apartments, where the responsibility for my environment belonged to someone else. Since I bought a condominium seven years ago, finding out just how many things and processes have to be cared for has been a revelation. Everything has to be serviced: the bike; the car; the plants; batteries; climate control; the stove; light bulbs; the computer; the ceiling fan; the heat pump.

James Hillman, in *Kinds of Power*, asks that we alter our perspective on efficiency and growth and calls for less demeaning images of maintenance and service. Objects, he says, have their own personalities that ask for attention. When we treat things as if they had souls, carefully, with good manners—that's quality service…Things then become subjects rather than mere objects. When they are neglected, they reveal more and more toxicity. Hillman's sort of care treats each particular thing as if its value is in the thing itself, and not only its operational effectiveness. He goes on to say that perhaps this kind of quality care is only possible when we treat things as if they are alive.

Many feel that maintenance is a pain in the neck—a distraction from the real agenda of life. It wastes good time that could be spent with people, or writing a book, or watching the game of the week. It's more than "just maintenance," this stuff is our lives. What would it mean for us to see the maintenance of the things in our lives as more of a gift than a chore, as if attending to our property is also a gift to the things themselves. Of course, this may imply not having more than we need.

CARE FOR OUR WORK

People who worry when they fly in commercial aircraft say they don't worry a lot about the pilots. Who they worry about is the ground crew who maintain and service the aircraft: have they done their job carefully? Likewise, people who know the car business tell us that cars produced on Monday often turn out to be lemons. The theory is that after the relaxation of the weekend, it takes time to develop the attention to the job demanded for quality work. The pace of modern life puts such an emphasis on speed that getting a job done efficiently becomes more important than doing it with care.

Part of the challenge in doing our work with care comes from the many demands on our time. It is astonishing how many things we can be asked to do in a week, many of which have nothing to do with our actual jobs. If we are not careful, we find ourselves running around accomplishing everything except our "real" job.

Even good workers—housekeepers, factory workers, clerks, executives, managers—can be guilty of what might be called spiritual laziness. We do our work; we do what is asked of us. No one could blame us by almost any rational criterion for laziness. We do our work at a certain level of acceptability. However, we stop short of real quality. It isn't that we don't have the time or the ability. Could it be that we were lazy—spiritually lazy—all day yesterday and again today, not in the sense that we are sit around doing nothing, but that we refuse to think or push through our tasks to a level of excellence that makes us proud of our work?

Life is so complex. It's having four pots boiling on the stove at the same time, the phone's ringing, then the doorbell starts ringing, and you really wanted to think about the speech you're making tomorrow morning. In that overwhelming complexity, you run from pot to pot, from doorbell to phone. Somehow, you need to learn how to say NO to that telephone, NO to pot number one, NO to pot number two, NO to pot number three, and NO to pot number four. Then you can say YES to the doorbell from the bottom of your being and just let the four pots wait! You let the telephone ring its silly head off or take a message. You go to the door and decide to be totally present to this door experience.

I remember a time when I was so consumed with getting everything done, that I ran around like a chicken with its head cut off. One day a friend said to me out of the blue, "Brian, have you ever heard of putting brackets around certain things, so that you can focus on doing the one thing that is necessary right now?" There's a right time to deal with everything. When we are beset with multiple things to care about, all of which demand instant attention, we need to bracket. It doesn't mean you won't deal with it later, but you are not going to attempt to handle it now. So you put it on the calendar for next Wednesday, and deal with that problem then. If you don't bracket, you end up not doing anything well.

There is much wisdom available these days from people like Stephen Covey who discuss the importance of balancing the most urgent tasks with those tasks most related to one's vision of the future. What is the most urgent is not always what needs your attention. What needs your attention now may be something that is going to happen in two years' time. All of this has to do with doing our work like human beings, not as robots or slaves.

It is astonishing to me how some innocent-looking tasks develop into real monsters. As you start to do a simple task, its ramifications start to unfold endlessly, and before long you are smothered in details which tax your care to the limit. Three years ago, I switched to a four-day work week. My wife still worked a five-day week. In a moment of magnanimity I said to her, "Now that I have some extra time, why don't I take on the kitchen: food procurement, the kitchen organization—the works. Of course, she agreed. I thought that food shopping was a matter of a three-minute walk to the nearest supermarket, bringing home a basketful of goods, and stashing them away. Oh my, Oh my! After two years at it, I bow my head in homage to that great tribe of people, many of them women, who have done this task with such apparent effortlessness over the centuries.

After my first few kitchen efforts I learned that you just can't pick anything off the shelf. There are values to consider: do you want organic, do you want to buy peas from this frozen food company that is turning Mexican peasants off their land? Then there are brand names we are committed to because of their quality, or the air miles attached to their purchase. So on Friday mornings when my wife is going off to work, I'd say cheerily, "I'm off to do the food shopping this morning." Afterwards, the food had to be put away. So I stuck a third in the freezer, a third in the cupboard, and a third in the fridge. Well, that prompted a little lecturette from my wife on what went in the big freezer and what in the small freezer in the fridge, and what needed to be refrigerated and what could go on the shelf. I said to myself, "Lord, I'm 65 years old. How could I have missed all this?"

Well, the upshot was that on my shopping day, I would get up early to make the shopping list, plot them on my map of the stores, clean out the fridge and the cupboards, recycle the bottles, cans and plastics. Then I checked the list again to make sure I had the right brand names, and had considered Air Miles specials or any bulk bargains. Three years later, I'm a real pro. But it was a major growth experience in my life. And I'm still astonished at how complex a kitchen system can be, and the amount of care that goes on in the kitchens of the world whatever the circumstances.

A similar thing can happen when you are asked to do a favour. It may seem simple, but as you take it on, the layers of complexity begin to unfold. Each layer takes more and more time. You feel like the fisherman who got his hook into the tail of the whale, and was being dragged out of the boat, down, down into the depths of the ocean. That simple task takes you down into the depths of humanness and tests every bit of "right stuff" you have. You realize the cost of your care.

STRUCTURAL CARE

It was a revelation to me when I discovered the power of structural care. I had always associated care as a psychological thing, somehow related to sensitivity training. But a course I took with ICA really destroyed that illusion. Joe Pierce thundered, "The poor care nothing for your sympathy or the degree of your empathy for them: what they demand is structural justice: a place to sleep at night, a health center that will deal with them seriously, education to fit themselves for a job. They need structural care." My liberalism was really dealt a blow and so I have come to see that, in the first instance, everyday care for other people is structural. A good government, for example, doesn't go round trying to hold everybody's hand to show how sympathetic and caring it is. It shows its care by setting up and maintaining the structures that will enable people to know what they need to know, to do what they need to do, and to be what they need to be. So it establishes a network of libraries and information services. It builds transportation, education, legal, health and social service structures. It supports the arts so that cultural and artistic events can nurture the public imagination and spirit. It creates parks where people can go to breathe and recreate themselves. It sets up emergency and defence structures to maintain domestic tranquillity.

So, in the home, workplace, or associations we belong to, the most foundational and effective way to care for everybody is structural. You don't need empathy, sympathy, the gift of gab, a degree in counselling or psychology, or even a good listening ear, although these may be valuable assets. You simply need to pick out one structure that needs caring for, and work with it. You also need to ensure that you don't trip over someone else's operation. An executive walks into the office after a holiday in the Caribbean, and realizes that the space feels like a morgue. The walls are white, devoid of colour or decor. He creates a plan, checks with the managers, gets input from the staff, and together they recreate their working space so that it is inviting, inspirational, and a joy to work in. Such structural care works for everybody.

An assignment structure is structural care. When a family creates an assignment structure for meal preparation, it is caring in an equitable way for the sustenance of the family. The opposite procedure is for one member of the family, probably Mom, to arbitrarily assign whoever's available to do the next meal. "Well, I did Monday's dinner—it's someone else's turn." Instead of arbitrarily dishing out orders, the family meets to discuss meal preparation and create a month's worth of assignments for breakfast and dinner on the refrigerator door, then no one is in control. The whole family is responsible for the assignment structure. And there is flexibility. If someone can't do the assignment one day, they are responsible for arranging a swap. Younger people in the family know they have structural responsibility, but they still have freedom. It is not a matter of telling kids or spouse what to do every minute of the day. Below is an example of meal prep assignments for the older members of a family:

Figure 1.2   **MEAL PREP ASSIGNMENTS FOR THE VIKRAM FAMILY**

July: Week 1	Mon 3	Tues 4	Wed 5	Thu 6	Fri 7	Sat 8	Sun 9
Bkfst	John	Joan	Mom	Dad	John	Joan	Dad
Dinner	Mom	Dad	Joan	John	Mom	Dad	Joan

(This week, Dad and Joan have four assignments. But next week the rotation will ensure they have only three, while Mom and John have four. Similar assignment structures could be used for doing the laundry, mowing the lawn, taking the garbage out. Over a year the assignments could be rotated.)

Going out to get snacks for an office staff meeting is an act of structural care. Ensuring the workplace and the home are kept secure, clean, and graciously appointed are structural ways of caring for everyone. Preparing meals is structural care, as is cleaning the toilets. Structural care is the practical expression of concern by creating or maintaining a structure that cares for everybody day after day, without any spoken expression of concern or solicitude. Economist Hazel Henderson refers to these expressions of care as "the love economy": a vast system of services performed in the home without pay and done out of love, or care. This unofficial economy includes doing the laundry, shopping for food, preparing meals, doing the dishes, changing diapers, vacuuming and cleaning, taking kids to all their activities, caring for grandmas and grandpas and grandchildren, on and on and on. Without this "love" economy, the world would dissolve into chaos.

Objectivity in care needs to be emphasized over the notion that talking about your problems will be beneficial. This has got many people in trouble because somebody helped them get their problems out in the open. Commiserating over your problems does not necessarily care for yourself or anybody else. It is so easy to turn into a sympathy junkie, or fall into the ranks of the permanent victims or, to use Carol Myss's phrase, "the permanently wounded." There is a role for psychology and counselling in the world: helping people find ways to push their experiences through to the center, drain the meaning from them, decide on proactive ways to deal with problems, and get life moving forward.

RITUALS OF CARE

Rituals are almost as objective as structures. Saying "Good morning" when you meet co-workers for the first time each day is an important everyday ritual, even if there has been a falling out with a colleague on the previous day. Such rituals keep the wheels of civilization well oiled. And they say, "I care about your well-being. I might have said the wrong thing to you yesterday, or unconsciously snubbed you in some way, or you may have done it to me, but we are still colleagues and we agree that what happened yesterday is forgiven." "Good morning" is a way of getting that said.

In a team or department, someone may want to collect the day of everyone's birthday, so that none go uncelebrated. Below is an example of the kind of conversation that has been used to honor the birthday person.

BIRTHDAY CONVERSATION

We are all used to birthday celebrations. Staging a birthday party is a caring ritual by which we can celebrate the mystery, depth and greatness of a person, and the miracle that they made it into history. The ordinary birthday party with cake and candles can be usefully amplified by asking just a few questions, such as:

- How old are you? (when appropriate)
- What were some key events of the past year?
- What are you looking forward to in this next year?

Before planning a personal celebration, get permission from the person—especially the first time you do it. The conversation can be very short. Five minutes is adequate. If you are leading the conversation, be ready to give answers to the reflective questions and start the wishes in order to avoid awkward silences.

Celebrations are rituals of care. A workplace may have half-yearly and yearly celebrations. These are times to celebrate the accomplishments of the previous time period, and celebrate everyone's contribution to the mission of the organization. Such events become caring celebrations when they are planned beforehand and have a basic structure or program.

Couples may celebrate wedding anniversaries yearly, and major public events at intervals. These are opportunities to go out to dinner and reflect on their past year or years together. Some couples I know associate anniversaries with a ritual of accountability, for which the question may be: Have you been faithful to your covenant of marriage over the past year? If others are present, someone else may ask the partners individually. This ambiguous question of accountability covers many perspectives and aspects of being a couple. So, rather than answering either "yes" or "no", they respond with either "yes and no" or "no and yes". "Yes and no" communicates: "As I look back it seems to me that, on the whole, I was more faithful than unfaithful to the covenant. And vice versa for "no and yes". These couples are clear that the question of accountability always need to be accompanied by a ritual of absolution. It is appropriate for the asker to respond with something like, "In spite of the objective failures to honor the covenant, this marriage is still full of possibility, and the future is wide open." Absolution is a ritual of forgiveness that pronounces that the past is approved and the future is open. It is appropriate as a response to accountability at many other points in life.

There are many other opportunities for celebration. At retirement it is possible to go beyond the traditional gold watch presentation, and stage an event that remembers and appreciates and celebrates the retiree's contribution to the company, the work and associates, and claims promises for her future. Winning an important victory, getting a major contract, pulling off some extraordinary deed are all occasions for celebration.

One of the most common caring rituals is sending a card. The greeting-card shops have this down to a fine art with all the different types and styles of cards. It is not a major decision to go to a shop, buy a card, and write something on it specifically for the person, but it's often a struggle to make it a priority. But taking time to give form to our care has an effect on the lives of relatives, friends and colleagues.

SYMBOLIC CARE

Symbolic care brings depth intention to formal events and meetings. When you take exquisite care, the group is honored. Life is basically two-dimensional: practicality and significance. Ordinary living is enlivened with elements of practical care that point beyond themselves to significance and meaning. I know families who at Thanksgiving take exquisite care to set the table for dinner, restaurant style, with the colours and symbols of harvest time as a centerpiece, and an artform on the wall that communicates what each one is thankful for. The dinner table become a place of awe.

Symbolic care can mean attending to the space of group or community gatherings. I know facilitators and meeting conveners who make it a point to inspect the meeting room at least an hour ahead of time. They usually end up rearranging the furniture to provide a venue that announces to the participants as they arrive, "Something significant is about to occur here." They usually have to provide decor that highlights the focus of the gathering so that when the minds wander, as they surely will, they wander to something related to the topic rather than to something unrelated. During the breaks, they make a point of straightening up the place so that, on reentry, participants see the focus again. They also fill space with sound—music—during breaks to create a mood of relaxation in the midst of work.

Being on time for a meeting is symbolic care. A consultant friend in Japan tells of a 10.30 a.m. appointment with seven executives of a major Japanese corporation. He got there early so that he could arrange the room as he wanted with the right number of chairs, the slide projector, an artistic centerpiece, and water for each person. At 10:25, he started to get worried—he was the only one there. He began to watch the clock. At 10:27, still no one. He started to wonder if he had the date right. But at 10.29, seven executives walked into the room, sat down in the seven chairs, arranged their papers and looked expectantly at the consultant. It was exactly 10.30. The Japanese capacity for this kind of intentionality is well-known, but the consultant was blown away by their style.

Starting a meeting on time is another expression of symbolic care. I remember sitting in a car with my father waiting for an acquaintance to show up. We waited. After a time had passed, my father turned to me and said, "This man is late. He does not take his life seriously," after which we drove away. Some people make punctuality into an absolute, just as others make latecoming part of their style. Facilitator colleagues of mine acknowledge that they walk a tightrope here. They tell me that allowing too much time beyond the declared starting time does not honor those who made the effort to be on time; while starting on time honors the punctual ones, but dishonors those who are still coming. They say it often helps to discuss when to start with those who are present.

CARE IN HUMAN ENCOUNTERS

Let's say that everything up to this point is doable, with some basic good will and gumption. Let's go further; let's say that in human encounters some aspects of care seem relatively easy. But let's put ourselves in an average day in the home or workplace, and we are likely to witness human encounters that make us blanch.

The question here is not how we maintain basic courtesy between humans, although basic courtesy is good. Rather, the question is: How can we, in every encounter, let our care shine forth? Or better: how, in our everyday work, can we take the time to honor a colleague who comes into our office when we are pushing to meet a deadline? We can treat the colleague as an interloper, an unwanted intruder, or an automaton. Our whole manner may say, "Can't you see you're interrupting me? I have important work to do. Even when completion of the work is urgent, it takes only 20 seconds to say, "Hey, John, I'd love to chat, but I just have to have this ready by noon. Could we have lunch?".

In the movie *As Good As It Gets*, Jack Nicholson's Mr Udall is a very successful writer working on his sixty-second book. He is also a manic depressive. But what is more obvious is that he has a hard time caring for other people. His door has five locks on it. But life has a way with locked doors. After his neighbor has been robbed and attacked, he is asked if he would take the neighbor's dog for a walk. At first, of course, he refuses, saying he cannot be disturbed ever for any purpose. But, something gets under his defences, and he ends up taking the dog for a walk. This is the same dog he had thrown down the garbage chute earlier because of its habit of peeing in the hallway. That small act of care in a strange way liberates him for more. He feels impelled to assist a waitress's son who needs urgent medical treatment. Eventually he decides to take his wounded, broke neighbor, an artist and a homosexual, into his own home. Once even a small chink is opened in a human being's defences, care sneaks in. It proceeds to possess that human being like an alien power, enabling his care to go from strength to strength.

What does it take to put "the life quality", as D.H. Lawrence refers to it, in our relations with other human beings? It could mean taking the three minutes more it takes to be human in dealing with another's question or request, when every nerve in your body is saying,"Keep going at your own work. You're falling behind!" Everyone knows the difference between being treated as a human being, and being shunted off to a sidetrack, or treated like a robot.

A nurse friend of mine tells this story:

> During my second year of nursing school our professor gave us a quiz. I breezed through the questions until I read the last one: "What is the first name of the woman who cleans the school?" Surely this was a joke. I had seen the cleaning woman several times, but how would I know her name?

> I handed in my paper, leaving the last question blank. Before the class ended, one student asked if the last question would count toward our grade. "Absolutely," the professor said. "In your careers, you will meet many people. All are significant. They deserve your attention and care, even if all you do is smile and say hello."

> I've never forgotten that lesson. I also learned her name was Dorothy.

The level of energy with which we respond to others makes a world of difference. If we are busy, we can still take the the time and effort to deal with other people as human beings by turning and facing them, acknowledging their humanity. To continue typing away and looking at the computer screen while you reel off a standard answer is not a high-energy encounter, although sometimes it may be the best you've got. The level of energy we put into our encounters with people communicates whether we regard them as human beings or pests.

Consider forgiveness as a basic form of caring for others. Everyone carries around a burden of guilt. Forgiveness stops the constant lengthening of those guilt lists. When a colleague accidentally bumps into me, and says, "Pardon me," I can look offended and say nothing; or I can look offended and say boorishly, "Next time look where you're going." Or I can say, "No problem!" Workplaces, homes, communities, life on the street rely on this twin ritual of apology and absolution.

At times, a breath of compassion is needed. Recently, I was in line at a supermarket checkout counter. The checkout clerk looked like she was in pain. The people in the line looked like they were under sedation. Suddenly a man coming through the next checkout point made his way over and said to the clerk, "How's your husband doing?" Immediately she smiled a painful smile, and said that his cancer had worsened and he was in intensive care. The man hugged her, talked a little more, and went off. As each person made their purchases, they were moved to express their sympathies as well. She was deeply touched. Some raw humanness had appeared and moved us all.

A friend went to get her driver's licence renewed recently. Standing in line, she noticed a deadening mood in the office. People answered questions in monosyllables; the clerks seeemed to treat their customers as unwanted intruders; their voice tones were flat; it seemed more like a morgue than a place of business. The customers were automatically adapting their mood to that of the morgue workers. When my friend's turn came, she said in an intentionally loud and cheerful voice to the clerk, "Good morning! And how are you today?" The head of every clerk snapped up as if spring-propelled to search out the source of that voice. Something shifted in the whole place. Then, it was as if a realization hit everybody at once. It didn't have to be the way it was. People in the line-ups started talking to each other. The clerks dropped their sepulchral tone of voice and begain talking a little more like human beings. Something had changed.

This kind of caring looks for what may be holding energy back. Larry Ward, a consultant to many large and small corporations, explains how he decides what kind of care an organization needs:

> I use a particular practice with some clients. I arrive early and spend five minutes walking through the facility. It's amazing what wisdom can emerge when you do this. I took the entire management team of a medical company on a walk through their organization—in silence. When we returned, we wrote down what we had noticed. Now this organization made medical equipment—instruments you see in doctor's offices, surgeries and hospitals. There was not a single picture of a human being on the wall. Not one. The only thing on the wall was metal equipment. Today they have art throughout the facility, with testimonials from patients and customers, and thank-yous from those who underwent successful surgery and thanked the company for the quality of their products and services. Now, when employees at that company come to work, they are connected to the way users and patients experience the technology they create, and they feel proud to contribute in that way to people's lives. The managers noticed other things on that first walk. Now that company is so different! There is energy, excitement, pride, and a heart connection. My insight in walking through there was that the staff had lost the heart connection to their product.

THE COST OF MY CARE

Sometimes people who care greatly for others do not allow others to care for them. They develop what Carol Pearson calls the Suffering Martyr syndrome in *Awakening the Hero Within*. This type feels that she or he is always giving to others and never getting enough back. Usually, martyrs have difficulty receiving perhaps because they have learned "it is more blessed to give than receive" or they fear being obligated to others.

But we cannot maintain the combination of quality care for our tasks and depth care in our human encounters unless we discover how to care for ourselves. For caring has a cost. It can be bone-wearying. Taking care of ourselves is not the same as pampering ourselves; it is caring for the body, mind and spirit through stopping, resting and, especially, reflecting on our lives. More on this in a later chapter.

Recent books focus on people who sacrifice too much to be caring. And no doubt some do spend too much time caring for others, and not enough time taking care of themselves. But care does require expenditure. People constantly make claims on our time and energy, beyond the normal demands of work and home. Someone on the other side of the world wants a current photo of our family. The next-door neighbor wants us to take care of their kids when they go out. Our club or church wants us to volunteer at the next bake sale. Our relatives in Kamloops want us to come and celebrate their 25th anniversary. Our workplace wants us to put in extra hours. A simple response of well-meaning people to all the demands on their lives is to try to do all the cares, to fulfil all the requests.

But it is important to ask, "What does it mean to really care in this situation?" To respond caringly is not invariably to say yes to every request, but to respond seriously and caringly. I heard recently of a corporation which had a fund for special projects. It was administered by a wonderful, caring woman, named Lyn. When people in the organization got an idea that could use some seed money, they would explain to Lyn their project and the money it needed. Lyn would listen very carefully and ask a lot of objective questions about the project. Often she would say yes, often she would say no. She was so gracious, understanding, and honoring of the person and the request, that, afterwards, the petitioner felt like a million dollars, even when refused. In fact, they really experienced a yes to their being, despite the no to their request. Lyn embodied profound care for the being of the other.

Albert Camus revived the myth of Sisyphus in a way that speaks to courage, especially in situations where we finish with one job of care, and must immediately start all over again on another. Camus reminds us that the gods had condemned Sisyphus to ceaselessly roll a rock to the top of a mountain. When he got to the top, the stone would fall back of its own weight. The gods had thought, with some reason, that there is no more dreadful punishment than futile labor. Camus pictures the labors of Sisyphus:

> One sees the whole effort of a body straining to raise the huge stone, to roll it and push it up a slope a hundred times over; one sees the face screwed up, the cheek tight against the stone; the shoulders bracing the clay-covered mass, the foot wedging it, the fresh start with arms outstretched, the wholly human security of

two earth-clotted hands. At the very end of his long effort the purpose is achieved. Then Sisyphus watches the stone rush down in a few moments toward that lower world whence he will have to push it up again toward the summit. Sisyphus is a hero of the absurd. He and the absurd are two sons of the same earth. They are inseparable.... Sisyphus' fate belongs to him. His rock is his thing. The absurd man says yes, and his effort will henceforth be unceasing. Sisyphus concludes that all is well. Each atom of that stone, each mineral flake of that mountain in itself forms a world. The struggle itself towards the heights is enough to fill a man's heart. One must imagine Sisyphus happy.

That last sentence is the real shocker. Every day, for the caring one, is a matter of rolling that rock to the top to see it come tumbling down again. Next day it has to be rolled up again.

The courage to care is the foundation of the courage to lead. Dag Hammarskjöld was Secretary-General of the United Nations in the 1960s. His care took him all over the world, to many trouble spots like the Congo, where he died in a plane crash. He wrote of the deep weariness that comes to people who care:

> Tired and lonely
> So tired
> The heart aches ...
> It is now,
> Now that you must not give in.

In that deep weariness that comes from having one's care all poured out, there is a transformation, a strange new life.

Exercise

1. How do you experience the dynamics of care?

_____

2. Which kinds of care do you find difficult? Or tend to shy away from?

_____

3. Which do you find relatively easy?

_____

4. What are the different ways you see people relating to their cares?

_____

5. When do your cares make you angry? Or make you rebel against having so many of them?

_____

6. What do you do when you want to escape from your care?

_____

7. What difference does it make whether you care or not in particular situations?

_____

8. In what arenas of your life do you need to show more care?

_____

9. Name 10 specific acts of care (beyond the usual) that you need to do in the next week.

_____

_____

10. How, in the future, are you going to make sure you take care of yourself, that you may continue to care for others?

_____

CHAPTER 2

Disciplined Lucidity

Acknowledging Life As It Is

> It is the world's one crime that its babes grow dull.
> Not that they sow, but that they seldom reap.
> Not that they serve, but that they have no god to serve.
> The tragedy is not death,
> The tragedy is to die with commitments undefined,
> with convictions undeclared and with service unfulfilled.
> VACHEL LINDSEY

This chapter presupposes that a leader needs a very clear idea of the way life is. As Mathew Arnold put it, "It is a matter of seeing life clearly and seeing it as a whole."

THE WAY LIFE IS

Joe Pierce was a rural development consultant; travelling between projects in West Africa, where airlines at that time had a reputation of flying by the seat of their pants. He used to be a radio DJ and had a good command of the language and of life. On the flight into Abidjan, the DC-8 had flown through a highly unstable air mass, falling and rising a couple of hundred feet every so often. On the Lagos leg, the plane had developed a fire in the engine which the pilots extinguished by going into a nose dive, which spilt hot coffee all over Joe's pants and the report he was writing. There was no lunch on the plane; it had been left on the tarmac. All in all, Joe had a roaring headache. At the Lagos airport, he deplaned in a filthy mood, but very lucid about the contrariness of life.

At Customs, the official asked, "Mr. Pierce, do you have anything to declare?" Suddenly, all the experiences of the last 24 hours coalesced in Joe's mind into a truth about life. Taking the official's ritual words literally, he said in a level tone, "Yes, I do indeed have something to declare!" Raising his voice, he declaimed to the startled official and anyone in earshot: "I declare that life is a son-of-a-bitch. It's a son'v a bitch! Once you realize that, you can either sit in a corner for the rest of your life and suck your thumb or you can take a relationship to the life you have, and decide to live it to the full. Yes, I do indeed have something to declare!" The response of the customs official went unrecorded, but he had heard a cry from the heart of one who had fallen through one of life's dread-filled trapdoors and come out of the experience with an insight into life.

This chapter is about how we come to see through our experience of life to what's real. *Lucidity* is an unusual word, but it is difficult to find one ordinary word that communicates clarity about the way life is. I guess a more normal way to say it would be *living in reality. Disciplined* indicates that we are interested particularly in the habit or stance of being clear about the way life is and deciding to live the life we are given. The lucid person deals with what *is*—the way life actually is, not the way life *ought* to be. This awareness of *life as it is* with inherent limits and possibilities is required to live with any degree of wholeness.

THE CRUNCH

Living between the assault of our limitations and our possibilities is living "in the crunch" or, what has been called, "the big squeeze."

The crunch describes how we are driven into life and at the same time cut off from it. We are indebted to the German philosopher Rudolph Bultmann for his description of how the crunch works.

First, he says, we are driven by care, which in the first instance, is care for the morrow, through provisioning, procuring and preparation—sustenance. We feel impelled to shop for food and prepare at least two good meals a day. We care for our future through putting money aside for our childrens' education and our own later years. This care is never-ending, whether for ourselves or others. But we can never make life secure by all this

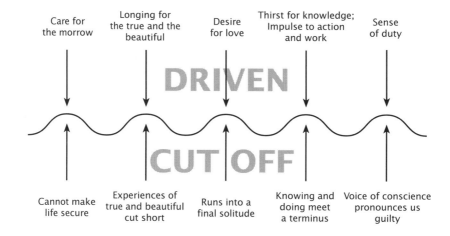

care for the morrow. Sustenance is never satisfied. We can shop till we drop but we all know, in the end, that there is no final satisfaction. Even when our amassed wealth, our cleverness, or our strength seem to endow us with financial security, we discover that we cannot really make life secure. There is something in life—some have called it the Mystery—which limits us, even when we think we are our own master. Perhaps we run into a stock market crash, or a tornado, or a really sharp confidence man. The result is the same.

It is this care which really gives life its significance. However we refuse to see it as such. Life is driven by a longing for the fantastic human experience or what Bultmann has called "the true and the beautiful": a great art collection, a movie, a great rock concert, a perfect barbecue, three scoops of your favorite ice cream, a job well done, a peak performance of a great orchestra, an afternoon at the races when all your horses come home, a well decorated room, an amazing South Sea Islands cruise. When we do have one of those experiences, we want it to last forever. But all of them, without exception, come to an end—the movie, the concert, the cruise, the races, the barbecue. And after three scoops of icecream, you're full. There is a Mystery in the midst of life which ends or even cuts short these experiences.

Or again, says Bultmann, life is driven this way and that by the desire for love—for a great romance, great sex, for friends who understand us and speak our language, for the perfect marriage, for people at work who appreciate us as human beings. But even the greatest love encounters a final solitude: there are critical points in even very good marriages where spouses are not on speaking terms, where a tension-filled silence reigns. There are times at work when even the most appreciative of our friends cannot help us. And there are times when even sex reaches its limits. And even if we have loads of friends all through our life, we die alone.

Then again, life is motivated by the thirst for knowledge and the impulse to action and work. We are innately curious; we are driven to know everything about the times, literature, computers, Cajun cooking, baseball scores, and the latest celebrities. Some people can't keep themselves away from bookstores and libraries. They have an obsession to know it all. But over 1000 books are published in English alone every day, and the more you read, the more you forget. There is a mysterious power that sets a limit to knowing. Then we are driven to act, to work for our livelihood, to begin and complete great projects, to get the house really clean, to work overtime to please the boss, or simply because the work itself fascinates us. Some become workaholics. But just as knowledge is cut off, deeds are not completed, miscarry, or do not satisfy. Again we run into the mystery that puts a terminus to our doing.

Finally we are driven by the sense of duty— by all life's "oughts". We think we ought to be able to do them all. For most of us, that would bring great satisfaction, because it would demonstrate that we have mastered ourselves. So we strive mightily to get all our work done on time, to take the kids to sports and lessons, to do all our chores at home, to be honest, decent, pure, thoughtful, kind and use our time well.

But we have all discovered that mastering ourselves is a struggle, and so we beat ourselves up because we watched too much TV, slept too long, went to the races instead of taking Johnny to Little League or Peewee Hockey. We didn't fix the garage door as promised, and we were really catty to the new woman at work. Conscience begins to beat the living daylights out of us by pronouncing "Guilty!" on our lost opportunities, our wasted time and laziness. Conscience here acts as the limit.

So, there it is: our daily care, our reaching out for love, our seeking a knowledge that will wrap up the universe, our concern to do something lasting. Then we realize with a clear conscience that there is never any solution to our daily care or to all our indefinite longings. Lucidity sees that there is no lasting comfort. As for love, no one can ever love us the way we need to be loved. There is no kind of intellectual solution. Not only will the little nitty-gritty things pass away, but the great and magnificent things will also pass as history flows on by. As for duty, we will never have easier consciences, no matter how much we resolve or grow.

And so, in the diagram on page 34, our concerns for making life secure encounters the limit of death (the first set of arrows); our desire for fantastic human experiences encounters something that will not allow them to last (the second set of arrows); our desire for love runs into a final solitude (the third set); our drive to knowledge, action and work runs into the limits of time and energy (the fourth set), and our desire to do it all right runs into a guilty conscience (the fifth set).

So, where are we in this picture? We know we are caught right in the middle, where the curly line is. When? We really need to answer this out of our own life experience, but probably most or all the time though we may not be aware of it day to day. We are most conscious we are there when, for example, we encounter an intense drive or motivation and find ourselves cut off from achieving it. I have half an hour to drive to an office to nail down the biggest contract of my career, and my car and my cellular phone break down at the same time. To say I'm frustrated is putting it mildly. My name is Fury, I am like a wild beast, a seething mass of anger, I mouth expletives I never thought I knew. I am experiencing the crunch. I curse the German car company, the telephone company. Why me? Why today? Well, life is a son of a bitch.

Developing a consistent stance towards the contrariness of life is a struggle. But the question is, What is a human response to these "blows of fate"? To call life a "son of a bitch" because it tripped us up is to believe somehow that we are in control of what happens; perhaps because we have a right job, the perfect marriage, the right appearances, bright children, an understanding boss. These things simply ought not happen to us, because we have life under control. Not so. No doubt Princess Di thought she had the bases covered: a great divorce settlement, a new beau, the yacht, the right cars, the right hotels, but she was not in control. As Shakespeare put it in *Cymbeline*:

> Golden lads and lasses
> All must, as chimney sweepers,
> Come to dust.

In the Atlantic Maritime Museum in Halifax, Nova Scotia, an exhibit on the Titanic shows all kinds of memorabilia associated with the ship going down. It includes the famous utterance by the Titanic's purser. A female passenger about to board the ship asked the purser whether it was quite safe to travel on the Titanic. In an often quoted reply, the purser said comfortingly, "Madam, not even God could sink this ship." As it turned out, all it took was one decent-sized iceberg. No matter how rich, how smart, how pert, how cool, how big you are, no one is spared life's contingencies. Many good jokes illustrate this, like this transcript of an actual radio conversation between a U.S. navy ship and Canadian authorities off the coast of Newfoundland, as released by the Chief of Naval Operations, 10-10-97:

US: Please divert your course 15 degrees to the north to avoid a collision.
Can: Recommend you divert your course 15 degrees to the south to avoid a collision.
US: This is the captain of a US Navy ship. I say again, divert your course.
Can: No. I say again, you divert your course.

US: This is the battleship USS Missouri. We are a large warship of the US Navy. Divert your course now.

Can: This is a lighthouse. Your call.

Every time human beings become control freaks, either through setting up a fortress to protect themselves, or a system, or a style or fashion, or worldview, they eventually encounter the Mystery of life that is really in control. We want to believe we have an inside track: that we know how things are going to work out. When it doesn't turn out that way we say, "That's wrong; that's too bad." We don't see the new situation, only the fact that life left us in the lurch. When something happens—our picnic is rained out, our computer crashes—and all we can say is, "That's terrible." We have a hard time seeing that life's "No"s, are full of possibility, if we can be patient and reflective.

Control freaks eventually encounter the great wrecking ball that renders our bulwarks against contingency vulnerable. Some just give in, when they realize what's happening. But, Tracy Goss reminds us of another approach, in *The Last Word on Power*: "Accepting that you can't control the outcome is not the end of action—it is the opening for the boldest and most daring action. You can accept total responsibility for your choices and action. You are free to play full-out in creating and implementing an extraordinary future for yourself and your organization."

THE LIMITS AND THE POSSIBILITIES IN LIFE

Life seems to come to every human being as both dread and fascination, as the Great "Oh No!" when we encounter dread, and the Great "Oh Yes!" when possibility opens up. When I was a young man, this kind of thing drove me crazy. I used to try to live in such a way that I was never surprised by adversity or possibility. Of course, it was like performing a lobotomy on myself. It drove me nuts. Finally, I had to say yes to the fact that life was just this way. It picks you up and then it lets you down—as Frank Sinatra used to sing:

> Riding high in April
> And shot down in May.

No way to control it, no way to nail it down or wrap it up. Life is sheer mystery. Yet how we deal with the limits and possibility determines our stance in life.

The 20th century has played out this roller-coaster experience on a grand scale. the great fear of nuclear annihilation throughout the Cold War was followed by the ecstatic breaking down of the Berlin Wall in 1989, followed by US-Russian cooperative space ventures. We watched the pounding of Iraq during and after the Gulf War, and the wonder of the Wye River Peace Agreement between Israel and Palestine, and the return of Kosovo to its citizens.

THE FINAL LIMIT

Over and over we run into the fact of contingency. The dictionary defines *contingency* as the quality of being dependent on something which may or may not occur. You and I may be alive tomorrow, or we may not. Our job may stand us in good stead, or we may be fired, and find ourselves on the street. People have nightmares about this. But it is a fact of life. We are not in control, much as we might like to think we are. Something else is in control, something we can only refer to as the mystery of life.

Life is also tragic. That young people in the prime of life can face disease and death is tragic. It is distressing that people have to live on the streets, that thousands are wiped out every year by fires, floods, tornadoes and earthquakes. It is a pity that those with great gifts don't get the opportunity to develop them, that millions of Jews died in the gas chambers of the concentration camps, that we are all going to die. That everything finally passes away is both tragic and absurd. You don't hear people talking about this dimension of life at parties. It is something we are taught to evade, to put under the carpet, until such time as it is flung into our face.

Of course, when someone dies, there is always the need for a cycle of mourning, for dealing with the grief of a life completed, and for celebrating that life. But the pendulum always moves us from death to life, from the encounter with limits to a meeting with possibility, and back again.

One of Thornton Wilder's characters in *Our Town* describes the shortness of life:

> You know how it is: you're 21 or 22 and you make some decisions; then whisssh! you're 70: you've been a lawyer for 50 years, and that white-haired lady at your side has eaten over 50,000 meals with you.

It is no wonder that the encounter with death, contingency and limits, pushes us back into a longing for more life.

Do we readily come to terms with our mortality? Ask how many people in your office or your circle of friends have made their wills. A recent survey showed that only forty per cent of Canadian adults had wills. To make a will, you have to stare your death in the face. A lot of people don't like to do that.

Instead we look for some kind of security, some Linus blanket that will stave off contingency and our sense of creatureliness. We seek security in various bunkers: "that ol' time religion" bunker; or the "big bucks" bunker, or having a lot of friends. But something always seems to crack open our security bunkers: the minister is caught with his hand in the till; the currency is drastically re-valued; or all our friends leave us when we contract AIDS.

Once you realize that anxiety and insecurity are normal, and not some kind of mental disease you've picked up, a certain relaxation and openness to life takes place. Jack Nicholson's Mr. Udall in the movie, A*s Good As It Gets*, uses extraordinary means to fend off "germs" which might endanger his health: his bathroom cabinet is full of cakes of soap lined up in military formations. When he washes his hands, he uses a cake of soap, then throws it away; then he washes his hands again, and throws away the second cake. When he visits the same restaurant each day, he always takes his own set of plastic ware with him. He walks sideways down the street to avoid contact with passers-by. But one day, life comes knocking at his triple-locked door, and everything changes. Life embraces him and saves him from his exaggerated fear. He discovers that life can be beautiful.

E.E. Cummings has a darkly witty way of saying how all through history, integral human beings have conveyed the facts of life which everyone has to face. Sometimes, he says, it takes a "made-in-Japan" piece of elevated railway" falling on his head:

> it took
> a nipponized bit of
> the old sixth
> avenue el
> in the top of his head:
> to tell him.

During the war in Vietnam, I had a friend in Australia who would knock on my apartment door in the middle of the night. I would stumble out of bed, open the door, and there would be Chris, looking wild and bedraggled, with his sunglasses still on. He wanted to talk. I invited him in and got my lick in first:

"Chris, you've got to settle down: you can't live like this. You've got to calm down!"

He would say, "I can't calm down. I won't calm down."

"Why don't you go back home and get some sleep?"

"I can't sleep. I won't calm down. I can't sleep. I won't settle down!"

"For God's sake, Chris, if you keep on like this, you're headed for a mental breakdown!"

"How can I calm down? Women and children are being napalmed in Vietnam. B-52s are bombing the tripe out of a whole people. There are hundreds of millions of hungry people in the world; my sister has cancer of the throat; my father died a month ago of alcoholism; I'm $20,000 in debt, I feel like shit, and you ask me to calm down? I want to live, but how can I live in a world like this?"

That for many is the question: How can I live in a world that has so much pain and suffering in it? An existential crisis like Chris's leaves us insecure, restless, and uncertain. Life has become a cruel game. We feel we're suffocating and cry out: "I want to live!" It is in this kind of internal crisis that the question comes, "Now, who am I? How can I possibly relate meaningfully to a life that is like this?"

When I first encountered this question in a philosophy class, I assumed it was an intellectual question, to be answered in an intellectual way: "I am an ontological entity operating in a phenomenological field and related systemically to all that is."—whatever that means. Then I thought it was a psychological question to be answered by my skills sub-sets, or perhaps my net worth (what net worth?) or my Meyers-Briggs profile. This existential question is related to every human's depth struggle with life. My mentor Joe Pierce brought home to me that I can only answer this question when I face my death. This life question is prompted by a sudden consciousness of the inevitability of death. Answering the question lucidly means acknowledging the fact that death is inevitable; death is a part of life. And so in the face of that, who am I? As soon as we become conscious of that question, no, a half-minute before we become conscious of it, we are already in full flight. We do not take the time to figure out the obvious answer: I am a dying entity, who is, nevertheless, free. We run as fast as we can.

Let me play out Kierkegaard's formula further: the escape part, or running from the question, that preoccupies our mind. Traditionally, if we are honest with ourselves, you and I have two main ways of running from this question: we hang on to the past, or we hide from the question. We find a new religion: we may get into the car religion, the shopping religion, or take on physical fitness for 40 hours a week. Or we may turn charismatic, or born-again, switch from United Church to Icelandic mysticism, as if any of that will deal with the question. Or we find a new lover or partner, and pretend that that is somehow the answer. Maybe we join a therapy group and find new psychological security, or we redo the cottage to make an even more comfortable getaway.

Rather than excape, sometimes we hide from the question, We keep out of the line of fire. We stay away from anyone who might rock our boat; we make sure our friends are dull enough that no serious questions get raised in our presence; we may keep away from funerals; read only shallow books, and watch only vapid TV programs, so that no serious life questions are ever raised. If we are busy enough, entertained enough, distracted enough, serious questions about life will stay out of our way.

We can also hide from the question by deciding to be happy. We read books about happiness; we pin on Smiley badges, and try to make sure everyone else is happy too. Many years ago, I spoke about happiness as an escape in a course. Suddenly a woman burst out: "Don't you say those things! How dare you say those things about happiness!

I'm happy! I'm happy! I'm happy!" and then burst into tears. The other teacher invited her outside for a glass of water, and she never returned. She didn't see that happiness is a by-product of caring for the world; that it is a decision, a sense of fulfilment that follows our engagement, not a permanent emotion.

But the question is insistent. Who am I? After I have dug through the fairy floss of wishdreams, clouds with silver linings, I see with blinding lucidity that I am a dying human being, who is, nevertheless, free to live his life in spite of that. The paradox is that the very key to life is accepting death as part of life. As Joan Baez put it: "You don't get to choose how you're going to die. Or when. You can only decide how you're going to live, now."

Joe Pierce once thundered out to me in a lecture, the paradox is that, until we come to terms with the fact that we are going to die, we can never take life seriously. But also: until we come to terms with what we are going to do with our death, we will never take life seriously.

Carlos Castaneda advises us to put death always on our left shoulder, and let it be one of our key advisors. The challenge is to *embrace* our death, to make it our best friend, because it always tells the truth, if we listen.

THE POSSIBILITIES OF LIFE

Just as we meet limits in the midst of life, we also find possibility, the undiluted freedom to create and live our lives. Everyday the sun rises is a new day full of possibilities. We do not have to approach today in the same way as we approached yesterday. Every week is a new week with a new set of tasks, demands, adventures, any of which reveal brand new possibilities. At work, we are asked to use new tools which open up new possibilities. My old computer's capacity was 80 megabytes; I had to back files up on larger computers. Now my new computer has a hard drive with 4.5 gigabytes of memory and that's no longer considered big. It holds all my 7000 files and maybe 500,000 more. I can do so much more with this computer.

Every time one dares to risk, new possibilities seem to open up. An ICA Canada consultant, Bill Staples, really thought he was going over the edge when he got his first $20,000 consulting contract. But that gave him courage to raise his sights higher. The next one was for $115,000. Possibilities unfold each time we stand in our death, take our courage in both hands and venture forth.

This can be especially clear in a health crisis: when the doctor says you have three years to live, or one year, or a few months. There is still possibility. We have all seen people appraise their situation, affirm it, and then decide what they want to accomplish in their remaining time.

Possibility can emerge when we least expect it, in the middle of the darkest night and blackest despair. No one predicted the fall of the Berlin Wall. Few predicted that the Iron Curtain would be torn up about the same time. No one predicted the end of apartheid in South Africa, although Shell Oil's scenarios forecast what would happen if apartheid did not end. If we live in a time of terrible global suffering, we also live in an age of miracles. Test-tube fertilization is now routine, as are surrogate fathers and mothers. A camel herder in sub-Saharan Africa can speak on a pocket-sized cellular phone to a suburban commuter in Vancouver. Future shock is yesterday. History seems to have jammed its foot down hard on the accelerator. Evolutionary change was once measured in millions of years. William Irwin Thompson warned us in *Pacific Shift*, that the acceleration of history will shortly bring about a situation in which major transformative events will occur all at once or within a time frame of months and weeks rather than decades and years.

Through the Internet we can have friends and contacts across the planet, set up our own Web site, and buy a suit or book from a digital store. Knowledge is doubling every six months. It seems that every school in North America will be wired into the Internet in the near future. We can get cash from machines, do our banking by computer. We can create our own business, and work from home, if we like. We can book a transit to the moon, or Mars. Nanotechnology is experimenting with bacteria-size machines. Cryonics can suspend patients in liquid nitrogen awaiting future medical treatment. We are on the verge of the next stage of life's evolution where life takes control of itself. We get surprised by these new technological developments as we become aware of them, till someone says,

"Oh, that's old news. Have you heard about the whiffle-woofler?"

Christopher Dewdney says in *Last Flesh* that we are about to enter the trans-human age, in which we will surpass our current biological limitations—such as a fleshly body. There are those who say that, in time, every part of the human body could be replaced with artificial or hi-tech prostheses. We can now reach into the genetic structure and rearrange the molecular basis of life. We are on the verge of the next stage of life's evolution where life takes control of itself. Teilhard de Chardin said 40 years ago, "Man is now at the tiller of evolution."

We can have whatever kind of family fits our need: traditional, single parent and child, homosexual, cohabiting couple, married couple, living in different places, on and on. We can get ourselves cloned. Women in the West are experiencing a degree of freedom that even a couple of decades ago was unheard of. There are not only women politicians, but women policemen, women in the armed forces, women in the fire brigade. It is possible that a woman could be elected US President. (Of course, in other parts of the world, such as Afghanistan, women are being ground into the ground, still lacking elementary human rights.)

Children, likewise, sense the possibility. They have made themselves at home in the world of technology and may talk over internet with friends around the world. They feel at home with space and technology in a way that their elders may never approach.

The exploits of young people like Canadian Terry Fox both thrill and beckon to people. Cancer had left him with a wooden leg, but he saw he could use the wooden leg as a gimmick to raise money for cancer research. Starting in Newfoundland, he walked on his wooden leg half way across Canada before his cancer caught up with him. Another young man, Rick Hanson, a paraplegic who used to be an athlete, pushed himself across the 5000-mile width of Canada in a wheelchair, and subsequently around the world, on behalf of spinal-cord research. Imagine all the people who told them, "You can't do this."

The possibilities are endless. And it is the same with the creativity that is breaking loose all over. People who are unhappy with current economics are creating their local trading systems; those who have become disenchanted with the nine-to-five job are creating new cottage industries at home; some very rich people, like Ted Turner, are working to give a lot of their money back to the world where it is needed, for the United Nations or to create open societies. Camcorders document abuses of power and become a force for emancipation. More people seem to be setting out to do the impossible. Some sail round the world on their own. Mount Everest has a garbage problem on its summit, through the sheer numbers of successful climbers; even fifteen-year olds are preparing to climb it. US and Russian spacecraft have cooperated in space exploration further into our galaxy. Everything is up for grabs and open-ended at the same time. Just make up your mind what you want and start experimenting or pushing. If you want a child, but you think getting married is for the birds, you can arrange for a donor. If you're the kind of person who is always getting lost, you can buy yourself a small global positioning instrument to tell you where you are.

We easily become intoxicated with the miracles of technology that keep emerging, but technological advancement on its own without an ethical framework can be counterproductive. Is the integral development of the human being advancing at the same pace? What are we going to do about the hundreds of nuclear devices rusting out in the Soviet Union? Who is taking responsibility for all that nuclear waste? It is one thing for the wunderkind to create these technological wonders and monsters. It is another to think through a long-term plan for them. We have marvelled at the wonder of test-tube babies and the creation of embryos. But more than 25, 000 frozen embryos are waiting in US laboratories for people to decide about their future: to use them or trash them. It seems that there are big decisions waiting to be made in every one of the arenas we have mentioned. The lucid ones know that the future comes to all of us as crushing demand. It will constantly call on us to attempt the impossible.

There was a time in my life when I became a fanatic amateur futurist and read every book I could find on new things being developed and the kind of future they would create. One day I spouted on about it all to some friends over a beer. I told them that you know, all this flesh and bone could disappear and we could turn into a set of more efficient artificial prostheses, including heart and brain. As soon as I had said it, one of my friends asked with some feeling, "You think being a tin man would be great? Is that the kind of human being you want us to become?" I said that I had not thought about it personally, to which he responded, "Look, Brian, it's fine to get excited about all this, but someone's got to take responsibility for all these new inventions. We need to get to a consensus on this quickly, or certain scientists will have us all clanking around like tin men. It is fine to get intrigued about the many different forms of marriage and partnership today and the end of the nuclear family, but we've got to decide what form of the family is really going to care for people, children and society?" I said nothing further, just sipped my beer. His point was too obviously true to deny.

There are so many other cases: what shall we do about the Palestinian-Israeli impasse? What needs to happen in the former Yugoslavia? What is the key to turning Central, West, and East Africa around? How do we get a truly participatory governing system here, in which the economic, political and cultural dimensions of society are held in balance, without the cronyism between business and government ? How can we enable full rights for Aboriginal people? How are we going to change schools into places where people really learn how to live life and make a life? Who is going to recreate vital local health systems? Local community? Who are going to be the champions of the environment? Everywhere we look we see what needs to be done. Nothing has to remain the way it is.

It is the same with us. We can become whatever we decide. We are in charge of creating our own future (although we are not in control.) Many of the limits we create for ourselves are just that—self-imposed limits. In *Chicken Soup for the Soul at Work*, Canfield and Co. give the example of Azie Taylor Morton, past United States Treasurer. Her mother was deaf and could not speak. She didn't know who her father was. Her first job was picking cotton. Later in her life she witnessed to possibility:

> Nothing has to remain the way it is, if that's not the way a person wants it to be. It isn't luck, and it isn't circumstances, and it isn't being born a certain way that causes a person's future to become what it becomes. Nothing has to remain the way it is, if that's not the way a person wants it to be. All a person has to do to

change a situation that brings unhappiness or dissatisfaction is answer the question: How do I want this situation to become? Then the person must commit totally to personal actions that carry them there.

Whoopi Goldberg made a similar witness in *The Whoopi Goldberg Book*. She says she looks on acting as such a joyous thing because it is shot through with possibility. Anything can happen:

> As I write this, I'm appearing eight times a week, on Broadway, in a part originally written for a man, but you'd never know, right? If you come to a thing with no preconceived notions of what that thing is, the whole world can be your canvas. Just dream it, and you can make it so. I believed a little girl could rise from a single-parent household in the Manhattan projects, start a single-parent household of her own, struggle through seven years of welfare and odd jobs, and still wind up making movies. So yeah, I think anything is possible. I know it because I have lived it. I know it because I have seen it. I have witnessed things the ancients would have called miracles, but they are not miracles. They are the projects of someone's dream, and they happen as the result of hard work.

We hear of such examples, and say, "Yes, I see that. Yes, that's wonderful for them. But my situation is different, you see." Now our problem is not insecurity or emptiness, but overwhelming possibility. The problem is that life is too full, like a double-yoked egg. To decide which way our life is going to go, which ditch we are going to dig, which issue to aim it at, seems absurd, when there are so many. ICA Canada director Duncan Holmes tells about when he was a kid and ice cream parlours sold 12 varieties of ice cream—that was something. His mother took him in and invited him to pick an ice cream. Confounded by the magnificence of all the offerings, he could opt only for the tried and true vanilla. Upon hearing "vanilla", his mother said loudly, dogmatically and in a tone that would brook no opposition: "Duncan, you are not going to stand there and choose vanilla. I simply will not allow it! Choose something different!"

There's a bookstore in Toronto, called appropriately The World's Biggest Bookstore, over half a block big and two stories tall. It is absolutely packed with books. To decide to buy anything there is a real achievement. Often I walk around for two hours and leave empty-handed—just can't decide; it's too much.

Many of those who have made it in life had to break through impossible blocks, but they trusted in the possibility in life and did the impossible. A well-known recording company wrote in a note to the Beatles: We don't like your sound, and guitar music is on the way out." Fortunately, the Beatles persevered. A well-known computer company said to Steve Jobs when he sought funding for Apple computers, "Hey, you haven't gone through college yet." English novelist John Creasey got 753 rejection slips before he published 564 books. Many of the great social reformers, from Emily Pankhurst to Gandhi and Nelson Mandela, were imprisoned for their pains. But that only made their determination stronger.

LIFE QUESTIONS AND ESCAPE PATTERNS

In this situation we tend to say, "Too much". Faced with overwhelming possibility and overwhelming demand, the question is "What do I?" What am I going to do with my whole life? Which of the many possible furrows am I going to plough? Which social demand will I commit to? This is not an economic question related to job or income, but a question of one's historical thrust. But as soon as we ask it, we want to take a nap. Like Scarlett O'Hara in *Gone With the Wind*, we tend to say, "I'll think about that tomorrow." Or, "I need more data to be able to decide. It's not all that clear. And after all, there's no urgency; I have my whole life before me." Or, when we do assign ourselves time to think about our future, we sit down with fingers on the computer keys, and nothing comes. Yet, even as we postpone the decision, our life clock is ticking away, one heart beat at a time—ker BOOM, ker BOOM, ker BOOM; *life* and *death* and *life* and *death*; de-*cide*, de-*cide*, de-*cide*. Samuel Beckett, in *Waiting for Godot*, puts such delaying tactics into the mouths of Vladimir and Estragon:

> Vladimir: Well? What do we do?
> Estragon: Don't let's do anything. It's safer.
> Vladimir: Overnight we can travel: Let's wait and see what he says.
> Estragon: Godot.
> Vladimir: Good idea.
> Estragon: Let's wait until we know exactly how we stand.

Everyone gets only once around the clock in this lifetime. No one gets a second chance. This is it. Even as we postpone the decision, our lives are ticking away. We long for some quick solution to put an end to the demand on our lives, an end to our own procrastination. The irony is that when possibility breaks out all round us, we find ourselves longing for death. Camus put it this way in *The Myth of Sisyphus*:

> There is but one truly serious philosophical problem, and that is suicide. Judging whether life is or is not worth living amounts to answering the fundamental question of philosophy. All the rest—whether or not the world has three dimensions or the mind has nine or twelve categories—are games. One must first answer... One must follow and understand this fatal game that leads from lucidity in the face of

existence to flight from light.... Killing yourself is merely confessing that life is too much for you.

There are many ways of committing suicide beside the drug overdose, slashed wrists, or hanging. I had a friend, a brilliant guy with a Ph.D. in microbiology and too much money, who slept about the same amount of time as a cat: sixteen hours a day. The rest of the time he drove all over the place in his car with no shortage of energy.

We flee from the question of *Who am I?* by hiding from it. We escape from the question, *what do I?*, by floating. It's as if we were up there with those round-the-world balloonists. We look down at the passing scenes on the world below. The balloon passes over people picking up food from garbage dumps, and we exclaim, "Gee, that's terrible—someone really ought to do something about that!" But the balloon moves on, and we see the forests in the Amazon burning, and we say, "Look at that: good rainforest going up in smoke—that's ecologically indefensible. Someone ought to stop that!" But the wind takes the balloon on and now it's over what remains of Yugoslavian communities: we catch scenes of internecine strife; people digging mass graves and shovelling the dead into them; explosions, machine gun fire, old and young being cut down. "Terrible! Shocking!" is our response. "They need someone to take responsibility for that situation." Then the balloon moves on, and we witness slave labor and the terrible living conditions of the New York garment workers, but the balloon moves inexorably on and on. It never lights down. Just floats and floats, on, and on round the world, until maybe it just flops down in the ocean and sinks.

Cynicism is another escape. We denigrate life, hoping to excuse ourselves from serious engagement, because "life is really a pile" or "people are just no damn good—you can't trust anyone these days." Or, show up at a meeting with a "grenade" in our back pocket. As soon as it looks like a creative proposal might go somewhere, out comes the grenade to bring the creative flow of energy to a grinding halt: "Hey, we tried that three years ago, and it didn't work!"

Yet each of us has the chance to live one great life and die one great death. Life is like one of those Roman candles: we light the Roman candle and someone sings out, "Hey, shoot it this way!" And we turn round and aim it in that direction, until someone else says, "Hey, over here!" And we shoot it that way, and another way. Then someone says, "Shoot it over here!" And we turn the candle that way. Suddenly, oops! No more sparks. The candle is finished. Like that Roman candle, a human is just a burst of energy. The question is always where to direct it.

So each of us is faced with the option: Do I choose my destiny and grasp it every day of my life or do I spend my life waiting for it?

THE DISCIPLINED STANCE OF LUCIDITY

Lucidity about reality is not like learning to ride a bike: once learned,we never forget. Lucidity as a stance that has to be recapitulated day after day, so that we are not being constantly smashed by the way life comes to us. Hence the need to discipline our lucidity. We need to know how to stay grounded in our actual situation, and live in reality day by day. This is no snack, as T. S. Eliot reminds us: "Human kind cannot stand very much reality."

Some people I know start each day like this after climbing out of bed:

> Life is never the way we want it.
> We refuse to accept its promise.
> Nevertheless we are free to live.
> Be it so.

Tracy Goss has this summary:

> Life does not turn out the way it "should".
> Nor does life turn out the way it shouldn't
> Life turns out the way it does.

These are good mantras to use every now and then. These rituals can be the equivalent of rubbing the sleep out of our eyes. They remind us of both the limits and the possibility that life is and set one's course for the day. I know people who start the day by sitting on the floor and doing some yoga exercises. Some people go to Mass to rehearse the way life is; in monasteries, they make sure they get their stance straight by chanting the office of Lauds at 3 a.m. These are highly specific ways of starting the day. For some of us, the act of taking a shower may be the ritual by which we say to ourselves, "I'm going to stay awake today to life as it is. Other people sit down fully dressed to make out their "Do list" for the day and state their intention to remain grounded in the realities of their situation.

There are many other ways to keep ourselves grounded in reality. One is exposing ourselves to the full spectrum of reality through the movies we watch, the news we decide to listen to or read, the places we go. If we note that the last half-dozen movies we have seen are all romances, we might want to try a serious drama. If we notice that our TV watching focuses a lot on talk shows, we might want to watch the six o'clock news for a while.

Others like to immerse themselves in the experience of the four seasons: the burst of new possibility in the spring; the full flowering and growth in the summer; the wonderful colors and browning in the fall, the cold and death of winter, followed by the quickening and then the explosion of life in the spring. This for them is a rehearsal of life as it is.

Life is full of things that ease this sense of being in "the big squeeze"—alcohol, drugs, possessions, illusions—that take away our sense of limits or our belief in possibility. This is why lucidity is a discipline that every leader needs. It is never acquired once and for all, but has to be rehearsed every day.

The final question here is how we relate to life: that is, how we name it. We all know people who say: "Life is a bitch and then you die." We can relate to the crunch as cynics, or romantics, or we can relate to it as *good* and decide to dance the dance of life. Which brings us to the question of affirmation, the subject of the next chapter.

Exercise

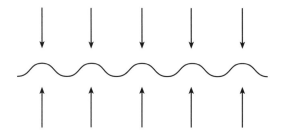

1. When recently did you experience yourself in the middle of the crunch?

_____

2. What was it you wanted to do or have happen?

_____

3. What was the limit that was being placed in your way?

_____

4. How did you react? What was your state of being?

_____

5. Did you realize you were in the crunch?

_____

6. If you realized you were in the crunch, what was it that enabled you to do so?

_____

7. What name did you put on this experience at first?

_____

8. What name did you, perhaps, put on it later?

_____

9. What is the possibility in the midst of that limitation?

_____

CHAPTER 3

Continual Affirmation

The Yes to All of Life

> I walked in a desert,
> And I cried
> "Ah God, take me from this place!"
> A voice said, "It is no desert!"
> I cried, "Well, but . . .
> The sand, the heat, the vacant horizon..."
> A voice said, "It is no desert."
> STEPHEN CRANE
>
> Life is good, and we can shout,
> With the sun and the moon and the stars.
> FIFTH CITY, CHICAGO, PRESCHOOL SONG

The preceding chapter raised the question of how we relate to life. Those who take a sour relationship to life, we are likely to call cynics. Those who take life's blows with a stiff upper lip, we call stoics. What do we call people who relate to life as good. Maybe we could call them the people of the "Yes" stance.

WHAT AFFIRMATION IS

There are times when one's job or family turns into a desert, and we cry, "Oh get me out of this," but inside, we may hear a voice saying, "This job, this family is no desert—it's your actual life." And we feel the voice urging us to say yes to that life as it is. We are being invited to "affirm" it, to develop an appreciation of the possibilities it contains.

This kind of response is no Pollyanna thing. It is an approach based on a "yes" to life, in spite of what we know about our struggle with our lives, our jobs, our families, our physical well-being. This book refers to this "yes" to life as *affirmation*—the decision to celebrate life just as it is, limits and possibilities.

WHAT AFFIRMATION IS NOT

Affirmation is not a romantic vision of life. It is not seeing the grass as greener on the other side of the mountain. It is not rose-coloured glasses. It is daring to affirm life just as it is, without any attempt to pump up the volume or get some good vibes.

Affirmation is not an escape from life's problems. It is the acceptance of pain, struggle, and joy as part of life.

Affirmation is not optimism. Affirmation does not say that every cloud has a silver lining. Affirmation says that the cloud is the silver lining.

Affirmation is not the forced visualization of a better life. Emile Coué, a French psychologist, popular earlier in the 20th century, used optimistic auto-suggestion and got people chanting, "Every day, in every way, life is getting better and better." This is not to discount the value of what Louise Hay and others call "affirmations". But, as a standing point, the stance of affirmation says that life is good right now. It may or may not get better in the future, but whatever happens, it's still good, just as it is.

Affirmation is not mere cheerfulness, although we welcome cheerfulness when we encounter it. But affirmation is more than an attitude; it's a decision, a deliberate choice we make in life, when to be optimistic would seem an escape.

This affirmation is an unusual response with many aspects. First of all, it happens as an *event*, an intrusion in the midst of life and things are different after the experience. Second, affirmation comes as a *wave of light* in the midst of darkness and despair. In that light we become aware of life's basic goodness. As a result, the self is reconciled with itself and with all of life.

Finally, affirmation is a *life style*, an everyday stance of saying yes to life, even dancing to life.

ILLUSIONS

To be human is to be filled with dread, defined by the dictionary as "a great fear or apprehension." Many people live with this permanent sense of insecurity about dying, or the fear that something terrible might happen any time—what was referred to in the last chapter as contingency. Because we find this dread intolerable we manufacture illusions. These illusions, we believe, will shield us from the realities of life and protect us from the dread.

An illusion is like a little universe within which we live, protected from reality. Those who boarded the *SS Titanic* for its maiden voyage were under the illusion that the ship was unsinkable. When the ship struck the iceberg, the band played on. Such is the power of an illusion. We've all heard of people with great wealth and a magnificent household who are under the illusion that being rich will protect them from most of life's pains and inconveniences. Until the day they discover that their children are drug addicts, and one of them has just slit his wrists.

Others think they can get through life with just a few smarts, enough to hold life at bay while they, as captain of their soul and master of their fate, live life on their own terms. In Australia, I had a friend Chris who had such an illusion. One day, when he was skimming along the straight stretch into Penrith in his Lamborghini, the tires hit a little oil spill on the road. I visited him in hospital. His time in traction gave him a lot of time to re-evaluate just how smart he was, and to what degree he was master of his fate.

A. THE EVENT OF AFFIRMATION

THE INTRUSION

One by one, life intrudes on our illusions; events crash in upon our reduced images of living. Someone—it could be a friend, co-worker, boss, or partner, says something that pierces our illusion about life. It can happen anywhere in our ordinary life. Our whole perspective is called into question. We sense that our self-image is in danger, and that we might have to change. When we feel the threat to our way of life, we try to defend our shattered life by destroying the intrusion. Each of us has a metaphorical dagger hidden in our back pocket or bag to use against the intruder. But the intrusion will not go away. It happens something like this.

When my wife and I were first married, I was quick to get our lives in order, organizing our space and our finances. There were aspects of Jeanette's daily living I couldn't understand, but, eventually, what chagrined me most was her tissues. She had the habit of keeping them up her sleeve, where gravity ensured that they would make a fairly quick exit to the floor, from which, of course, *I* had to pick them up. One day, about six months after we were married, I happened to chide her about the tissues. "Jeanette," I said, "About these tissues. Couldn't you pick up your own tissues? It would make our life so much more orderly."

Several seconds elapsed. Did I imagine it, but was she fuming a little? And then the floodgates burst. "Tissues? Tissues! You worry about tissues? Tissues are not the problem in our marriage. The problem in our marriage is that you are such a crushing bore. Why are you turning every aspect of our marriage into opportunities for order and control? It's boring! Boring! There's more to life than rationality and order!" And she stalked out of the room. I was quick to follow her, sensing grave danger to my story about life. Out came my dagger. "Now just a minute. You call me boring? You seem to forget I've taken you to the movies every Monday night for the past six months. That's not boring! And you're not exactly a big bundle of fascination, with your endless doodling and journal writing every evening. She said nothing more. She knew her words had struck home as I rose to my defense.

But, I said to myself, I'm really an exciting, with-it kind of guy—I tell jokes—people think I'm funny; I do bring her flowers sometimes. Me, boring? No. And yet her words stuck. I noticed I was getting more and more restless. Her words pushed me to the edge of my self-understanding.

I saw that I had a choice. I could either face this new life we were building and the demand on me to change, or I could build another illusion. I could see that to face it, would require me to surrender my old self, the self that preferred control to love and change. This was a crisis, for I was now in despair about my old boring orderly self. I had just had the carpet ripped out from underneath me.

In different situations, this kind of intrusion happens to all of us over and over. Often, after the heat subsides, we put it behind us and go on with our lives pretty much as they were. But sometimes, in the midst of such events, something else happens.

B. THE WAVE OF LIGHT

At the moment when I feel most restless and threatened, when the question, "Who am I?" is like a prickly pear in my armpit, a strange kind of revelation can sneak up on me. Philosopher Paul Tillich put it this way:

Sometimes, at that moment, a wave of light breaks into our darkness, and it is as though a voice were saying, "You are accepted. *You are accepted*, accepted by that which is greater than you, and the name of which you do not know. Do not ask for the name now; perhaps you will find it later. Do not try to do anything now; perhaps later you will do much. Do not seek for anything; do not perform anything; do not intend anything. *Simply accept the fact that you are accepted*"!

I AM RECEIVED

In the light of this acceptance, I see that I am received by life just as I am. I may be big or small, Down's Syndrome or an IQ of 160, a size 2 waistline, or a size 18, but I'm still received. There is nothing in me that can be an excuse for not living my life. Of course, it's one thing for Mohammed Ali to say "I'm the greatest!" with all his boxing brilliance. Other people have a bigger struggle to accept their greatness, but the experience of acceptance happens at times to everybody, no matter who they are. As Matthew Fox puts it: "The sun rose this morning and blessed all of us. It didn't give us a test first about our orthodoxy, about whether you're going to legitimize your life today by making money, or getting a good grade; it just shines on all of us; it's been doing it all the time."

ALL IS GOOD

In the light of this acceptance, you can relate to all of life as good: both the evil and the good. The external situation is never the real problem. It's how we relate to that situation that's important. In the light of this acceptance, not war, nor the genocide of six million Jews, nor environmental destruction can excuse us from living our own lives. Events like these brought civilization to where it is today. Some people live in a kind of permanent pout because their world is not the way they would have constructed it. Other people embrace life just as it is, genocide, environmental problems and the rest— just as it is. Of course, there is still the question of responsibility for social change but, without the capacity to affirm life as it is, social responsibility easily devolves into angry cynicism. Leaders, above all, have to be able to say a big "yes" to life as it is.

An Australian doctor, Liz Banks, once flew to India for a meeting. As her plane approached Bombay (now Mumbai), the captain's voice came over the intercom: "Ladies and gentleman, something is seriously wrong with the nose wheel of the plane. It won't lock into landing position. We may have trouble landing. So please take off your shoes and glasses, and take up the position for a crash landing. We have to land in fifteen minutes." Bent over, like everyone else, their knees knocking together loud enough for everyone to hear, the passengers wondered what on earth was going to happen. Well, the plane crash-landed. The front of the aircraft caught fire: it took twenty minutes for the rescuers to get everyone out. After Dr Liz shot down the rescue chute to the tarmac, she reflected, "Life is nothing but sheer gift. I could have skipped through the streets of Bombay, taking every beggar by the hand and declaring: 'Whether you like your life or not, it doesn't matter. Life is a sheer gift." Later, she added, "Ever since that crash landing, I have been driven to declare that we have just one life to live, and it can be lived every day with gratitude. Every day, this memory keeps me affirming life."

THE PAST IS APPROVED

This message of acceptance has amazing impact. It says that the past, my past, and the past of civilization, is approved. I want to say at this point, "But what about that really mean thing I did to Jimmy Jackson at school, when I ate the whole cake that we had both won on a shared raffle ticket?" Yes! What about those events I've never told anyone about, not even my wife? Yes. Do you mean that time when I yelled out to my friend, Bobby Johnson, "Hey, Bobby, you're father's dead. Ha, ha, ha." Yes, that one, too. Nothing in your past ever needs to be a block again. Your guilt is erased. In the movie *The Eraser*, the US marshal runs a witness protection program that sets up events that erase people's past, and fixes them up with everything they need for a brand-new identity. Well, that's not quite what happens here; we still have our identity, and our past is not erased, but all the guilt and shame related to deeds in our past are wiped out, in the light of this event. We can begin anew without the albatross of that guilt and shame around our neck, preventing us from moving into the future.

American poet laureate Maya Angelou has undergone almost every crisis known to womankind. She was raped by her mother's lover at eight, became a single parent at sixteen, worked as a prostitute, waitress and singer. For five years after she was raped, she was mute. Her mother's partner was lynched the next day and the shock robbed Maya of speech. Yet she says,

> I can't segregate all my senses, but I do think my respect for human beings comes from that period of muteness when I learned how to concentrate. I imagined my whole body as an ear and as a result I've been able to learn languages [she speaks seven fluently] by just giving myself over to the sound. I cannot be less than the most I can be, otherwise I would be spitting at my maker. If I've been given this much talent and this much intelligence, then I'm obliged to use it.

The very experiences that might have embittered many people for life opened up for Maya Angelou a new possibility. When someone asked her once how she got from her impoverished rural Arkansas background to being America's poet laureate, she said simply, "By being grateful."

The past is approved. Wars, slavery, all kinds of skullduggery by religious and secular leaders, the Great Plague, colonialism— all approved. The world today would not have got to where it is without that special history. Of course, neither you nor I approve of events like the Holocaust, and we don't want to repeat them. But the mystery of life embraces the totality of the past and offers us the possibility of approving it. All those historical events are "endorsed by life itself", in spite of our personal or collective opinion about the horrors related to these deeds.

THE FUTURE IS OPEN: ALL IS POSSIBLE

In this realization, sometimes we see that the future is open and all is possible. Yet, it seems that only when we are in deep personal crisis are we open enough to hear that all is possible. Yes, it's true that tomorrow I could get run over by a car, but today, nothing is blocking me. Nothing at all. I can move mountains. If the doctor tells me I have cancer with six months to live, then I have six months to live fully—with cancer.

John Cock is a clergyman and author who has always believed that everything is possible. Every time he runs into a problem, he asks, "What would it take to deal with this issue? It must be possible to deal with this, because everything is possible." Once, when he was living in Kansas City, he had to fly to Chicago to officiate at a wedding. The plane was late, and by the time he picked up his luggage from the carousel, it was 9:45 a.m. and the wedding started at 10:00. No standard means would get him there on time, since it was twenty-two miles from the airport. Rev. Cock had a black patch over one eye which he had lost in an accident. He also had a winsome way about him. On realizing the situation, his first thought was, "It must be possible," so he looked around for a clue. His eyes fastened on a police car idling at the curb. "This could be the window of opportunity," he said to himself, and sidled up to the officer in the driver's seat. He explained his situation, and asked his standard question to the officer: "What would it take...to get me to the church on time?" For whatever reason, the policeman said, "Hop in!" He turned on the siren and proceeded to pass every car on the freeway, making it to the destination with a minute to spare. As Henry Ford put it, "Whether you believe you can, or whether you believe you can't, you're absolutely right." In the face of the blocks life throws at us, we never have to be victims.

The future is open. We don't relish walking into an open future with arms wide open to embrace it. It scares us. As soon as we encounter something out of the ordinary, we tend to lose our nerve and run back to the safety of the familiar. When we step on the waters of life, and see the waves running high, it is difficult to remember the openness of the future. We easily lose our nerve. But if all is possible, we can all step out on the uncertain waters of life with confidence in the openness of the future, like the anonymous Vietnamese woman who wrote in 300 AD:

> I shall ride the storm
> tame the waves
> slay the sharks
> I shall drive away the enemy
> to save our people
> I shan't be content
> with the customary fate of women
> to bow their heads as concubines.

So this is the message we find:

In spite of the pain and tragedy of life, life is good just as it is. In spite of all my neuroses and faults, I am received. In spite of all the pain I have brought to others in the past and my own foul-ups, that past is approved. And the past of the whole human race is approved, in spite of the wars and genocide. And in spite of all its ups and downs. And in spite of my own fears, the future is wide open. I can do the impossible.

My wife Jeanette went to see Maya Angelou performing in Toronto and wrote this reflection:

> Maya came onto the stage—genuine Maya without pretense—just her body and her being alive. She proceeded to talk, sing, tell stories, share poetry, and do some spontaneous dance, and the two hours were gone—just like that. I was caught up the whole time with this tall black woman. In fact, I noticed at the end that I literally felt taller than when I came into that room. I felt fully human and fully alive and it was 12:30 at night on a weeknight! Why did this happen—not just to me but to my friend Sandy, and many others? The audience asked for two encores and could have taken more. Sandy and I reflected on the way home that Maya Angelou is living, talking, breathing affirmation. She affirms life as it is. I knew from her autobiography what she had been through. She knew what "in spite of" is all about.

In this evening in her 60s, she was honoring the pain and struggle of all the ancestors who went before, not only the history of black people—although certainly
that—but also of Asians, Europeans, Native people. She announced to all of us,
"You have been paid for—your ancestors have all fought the good fight—you have
been paid for." I heard, "You don't have to prove yourself. You don't have to earn
affirmation or pay any more dues. You are accepted as you are. There are no criteria, except your willingness to say yes to the universe's own yes on your life." And
I felt my back getting straighter by the minute.

THE OFFENSE AND THE DECISION

Well, once I have heard this word, no problem, right? Not so: The message of acceptance
shakes up my life/ It picks me up and shakes me, as a dog might a kitten, or a cat a
mouse. It questions my universe and demands a life answer. It is an offensive message.
First, it offends me intellectually. I want to say, "What do you mean—all of life is good? If
you really knew me, you couldn't say that my life is accepted. Tell me why." Well, there
are no good reasons. What's required is a leap of faith, not rationality. It also offends me
emotionally. People can get quite angry when you tell them that life is good just as it is
and outraged when you put concreteness on it like Chernobyll, or genetically engineered
foods. I have to make a major decision about this, to say yes to it, to accept all of life.

Life asks me to say no to my illusions, to pick up my life exactly as it is and to live
it to the full, warts and all. Life asks me to die to my old illusions about life, and to
embrace life as given in all its goodness.

DEATH AND NEW LIFE

There was a professor who worked part-time as a university counselor. Every month or
so, a student came to tell him all her problems. The thing about her was that she had a
very long neck and tried to camouflage it by draping her long hair all round it, wearing
high-necked clothes, and walking with a stoop. The counsellor got tired of her tale of
woe every month. On one occasion, the counsellor was having a bad day. There sat this
student in front of him one more time, with her hands over the back of her neck and her
elbows resting on the desk, something snapped inside him, and he saw with sudden
clarity what her problem was, and just blurted it out, "Melissa, you know what your
problem is? You are a long-necked girl, and you just cannot stand being the long-necked
girl that you are!" No sooner had he spoken, than she raked her nails across his face,
stalked out of the room, darted across the quadrangle and disappeared. The counselor

didn't see her for a long time. But one day, as he was looking idly out the window, he saw an apparition: Melissa was walking across the quad with the presence of a queen. She wore high heels and an attractive dress, and her head was held high, so that her neck seemed even longer than usual. And she was smiling. "Wow," he asked himself, "what happened to you?" Melissa, after considerable struggle, had managed to say yes to having a long neck. With that yes, everything else changed. She had become a different human being.

This is the stuff of change and transformation, of death and resurrection. This is what Melissa had passed through in the weeks between scratching her counselor's face and showing up looking like an African queen. She had died to her old understanding that she couldn't live her life with a long neck. She now understood that her long neck was a personal badge of honor, and that she could live her life to the hilt as a girl with a long neck. One of E.E. Cummings' poems gets hold of the experience:

> I who have died am alive again today,
> and this is the sun's birthday, this is the birth
> day of life and love and wings, and of the gay
> great happening illimitably earth
> now the ears of my ears are awake
> now the eyes of my eyes are opened

It is one thing to hear that life is good, your life is received, the past is forgiven and the future is open. It is another thing to let all that get to you. It destroys all excuses for not living fully, and releases the possibility of engaging creatively in what previously seemed an impossible situation.

To die is to live is an ancient truth about life. When we die to our illusions about life and embrace the essential goodness of life as it is, we are freed up to live fully in the moment, rather than wishing for some future that is risk-free and secure. To live fully is to risk. This is why we need to hear others talk about the possibilities they see.

In the first instance, affirmation is passive. It happens when we are in darkness and despair. It's as if the sun starts shining again after a long eclipse. It's like experiencing the universe smiling just at you. You experience you have been "yessed". In your turn, you say "yes" to that experience. In the light of this event, everything is different.

C. AFFIRMATION: A WAY OF LIFE

Affirmation is not only an event that can happen in anyone's life. It is also the habit of saying yes to all of life: past, present and future. It is the habit of affirming everything that happens not only to me personally, but to others and to the world. It is the acceptance of the universe's "yes" to my personal past as well as to the history of civilization as what brought us to this point. It is affirming ourselves personally, our neuroses, gifts, uniquenesses and the things we don't want anyone to know about. It is the yes that opens up our future as sheer possibility. It is one thing to say our yes once. The challenge is to do it every day of our lives.

Now the question is: how do we get this yes into every part of our own lives and the lives of others.

To investigate what a lifestyle of affirmation might look like, let's look at the life of Peter Frumusa, wrongfully convicted of two murders and sentenced to 25 years in a federal penitentiary. Something enabled him to give up being angry about his imprisonment. He chose to walk alone, and refused to align himself with any cliques. He decided that the prison was where his real life was happening: "I had to make prison my world. Once you start thinking about the outside world, you lose it." Because he would not accept the guilty verdict, he was denied any self-help programs. He was told he was in denial. So he found work as a cleaner in the center dome of the prison, then in finance and administration working for the warden. Eventually he won the respect of all the inmates. When other inmates told him it was too difficult to give up drugs while in prison, he would counter by saying that, if they could stay clean in prison, doing it for the rest of their lives would be simple. Meanwhile, outside his parents were spending everything they had in legal fees, fighting for his release.

It would have been easy for him to spend his time feeling sorry for himself, and cursing those who had placed him there. But feeling sorry for ourselves gets us nowhere. DH Lawrence seems to say that it's not even natural:

> I never saw a wild thing
> sorry for itself.
> A small bird will drop dead from a bough
> without ever having felt sorry for itself.

Sometimes we are shocked at the creativity of people who find ways to affirm a difficult situation. Judy Harvie, a retired president of a careers management company, tells the story of a man who, at the apex of his career, lost his voice box to surgery. Instead of feeling sorry for his loss, he found unusual ways to express his ideas and feelings and great sense of humour. He used a combination of mime, exaggerated gestures, and a child's quick-erase doodleboard. At parties and social gatherings, when there was a story to be told or a point to be illustrated he would jump up and start a pantomime, something like a charade, to make the point or tell the story. Through actions, eyes, gestures, smile or frown, he could express himself almost with greater clarity than with words. He was no longer a talking head. Now his whole being infused each idea with meaning, emotion and movement. Ideas flowed, connections were felt, laughter, joy and sorrow were shared, all without words. Others would be telling stories, when suddenly he would put a deeper spin on what had just been told by simply writing a one or two-word metaphor on his board that brought everyone up short and got them chuckling, or finding deeper meaning in it. He could also cut off the conversation when it grew unkind by standing up and drawing a big X in the air; then he smiled and changed the subject with his doodleboard. People like him embody the possibility of affirming turning whatever happens to us to advantage.

THE STRUGGLE TO AFFIRM

Affirmation does not come naturally to us, because we are immersed in a culture of complaint. It is almost considered virtuous to complain. The slightest irregularity provides an excuse for complaining: lumbago, the computer that crashes, the car that won't start. There is reason to complain if the weather is hot, cold, cool, rainy, foggy, windy, stormy, cloudy or humid, sunny, or if the UV index is too high. We complain about our spouse, our kids, our mother-in-law, our relatives. We complain about taxes, traffic, and long line-ups.

Recently, I was in the supermarket at a busy time. Not all the check-out clerks were on duty. In the unwieldy lines, carts, baskets, people in the line, and people passing by got mixed up. Shoppers kept swapping check-out lines, gambling on which one would move faster. I waited ten seconds. I knew it was going to happen—someone would open up. It was the guy behind me: "I can't understand why they can't put on enough clerks...all these people waiting. It's a real pain in the neck." I felt like agreeing with him, but I caught myself, and I said to the complainer, "You know life is a banquet, but most of us can't see it, because we're too busy complaining." He looked puzzled, then a sheepish grin came over his face. People who had heard us started talking about the weather, a new baby, their last picnic, all kinds of things. So I said to him, "You know, if there were enough check-out clerks, we wouldn't be having such a good conversation in this line." He hesitated, then grinned, "You know, you're probably right."

The second cousin of the culture of complaint is the culture of victimhood. In one of Bill Watterson's comic strips, Calvin and Hobbes are discoursing on responsibility:

> CALVIN : Nothing I do is my fault. My family is dysfunctional and my parents won't empower me! Consequently I'm not self-actualized!
> HOBBES: scratches his head and says nothing.

CALVIN : My behaviour is addictive functioning in a diseased process of toxic codependency. I need holistic healing and wellness before I'll accept any responsibility for my actions.
HOBBES : One of us needs to stick his head in a bucket of ice water.
CALVIN : I love the culture of victimhood.

In recent years people in the mainstream have tended to see themselves as victims of a situation or a system, as powerless people. Psychological explanations have played into a disempowering relationship to self, world and the historical process, which leads easily into the paralysis: "There's nothing I can do about this":
In his inaugural speech, Nelson Mandela put our victimhood in another light:

Our deepest fear is not that we are inadequate; our deepest fear is that we are powerful beyond measure. We ask ourselves, "Who am I to be brilliant, gorgeous, talented and fabulous?" Actually, who are you not to be? You are a child of God. We are born to manifest the glory of God that is within us. It's not just in some of us, it's in everyone.

"I Am Always Falling Down" is a preschool song sung to the tune of "London Bridge Is Falling Down":

> I am always falling down,
> But I know what I can do,
> I can pick myself up and say to myself,
> I'm the greatest too.
> It doesn't matter if I'm big or small
> I live now if I live at all,
> I am always falling down
> But I know what I can do.

The way of affirmation, however, doesn't mean letting life or other people roll right over you, while you are busy affirming your situation, life, and them. Affirmation is not the opposite of self-assertion and freedom. Affirmation is really about the everyday: accepting the self as is and the rest of the world as is, while you figure out what you are going to do about your situation, the future, and the people who are rolling over you.

Those who pride themselves on their rationality may have a difficult time with affirmation. You're getting dressed fast in the morning to get to work early, and your shoelace snaps. The tendency is to get all rational about it, and start asking "why" questions. "Why does this have to happen this morning, of all mornings? Why does it have to happen to me?" Then we universalize: "Why is this always happening to me?" And then we may start quoting Murphy's Law. On this little snapped shoe lace I burn up scads of psychological energy I may need later on in the day. I may also ask, "Why didn't I notice earlier that the lace was getting frayed, and change it?" As one who embraces all of life as good you see this as a moment for proactiveness—putting another shoelace on.

The affirming life style also demands a vigilance about destructive self talk. Mohammed Ali knew what he was doing with his ritual, "I'm the greatest!" Through our own self-defeating stories we become our own worst enemy. Many mornings I get up at 3:00 a.m. to write. My computer hutch is in a corner of the kitchen. It's quiet. The only sounds are those of the fan, and the kettle on the stove. There are no interruptions. Concentration is easy. Most mornings, the first thing I do is to read over my work of the day before. This has the effect of putting me into a blue funk: "Look at this stuff. *I* can't write this book! It's too complex, too many people have a stake in it and will watch every goof-up I make. There are too many values to hold. I don't have enough data. I'm getting too old for this...on and on and on. At some point, I become aware of what's happening— I'm having a blue funk attack. So I have to pick myself up and say to myself, like that preschool kid, "I'm the greatest, too!" or "Nevertheless, in spite of all that, it is still possible." Martin Luther used to say that, when that kind of funk attack happens, you have to stop what you're doing and throw your ink pot at the devil. So I have to stop and remind myself of the truth about life, then write a few more words, and the demons vanquished, I can continue my work.

There are also times we find ourselves saying, I feel rotten. I'm no damn good. Sometimes other people have to pick up the task of affirmation, as in this story told me by Del Morrill, now a hypnotherapist in Tacoma, Washington:

> One day I went to a dentist in Chicago. I had an abscessed tooth. I felt rotten. I had on my old green raincoat with torn pockets and hanging and missing buttons. I hadn't washed my hair in days. My head was hanging pretty low. I saw the dentist and he said I was not only going to have to have this abscessed tooth dealt with but that I also had pyorrhea and would need it operated on. Well, I'd gone through that pain before, and when I walked back home, my nose was scraping the pavement. An old bum leaning against the wall called out, "Hey lady." I thought, "Oh, God, I don't want to have to think whether I should give this guy a dime or not." So I kept on walking; and he called out again, "Hey, lady! You have fantastic kneecaps!" Now, in all my years of marriage my husband has not even noticed my kneecaps. And in my forty-six years, I haven't really even noticed my kneecaps—in fact, I never considered them one of my redeeming features. But, I tell you, I walked home that day in a different way! My head was up and my back straight and proud.

We all need all the affirmation we can get, although it is not something we go through life looking for; otherwise there is question of whether we truly have accepted our acceptance and said yes to our own greatness. As D.H. Lawrence put it,

> Those that go searching for love
> only make manifest their own lovelessness
> and the loveless never find love,
> only the loving find love
> and they never have to seek for it.

We can play with that poem a little, replacing love with "affirmation":

> Those who go searching for affirmation
> Only make manifest their own lack of affirmation
> And the unaffirming never find affirmation
> Only the affirming find affirmation
> And they never have to seek for it.

Sometimes life plays no and yes games with us, to test us. It dumps us into a dark abyss and just when we are ready to throw in the towel, it lifts us up and affirms us beyond all reason. Duncan Holmes, Director of ICA Canada, tells a story in this connection:

> I had just been through an incredibly horrid year of work in Ottawa. Everything I did turned to dust in my hands. It was my first leadership position in ICA. I felt so bad that I had decided I would never lead a group of people again—I was not equipped for this kind of role. Well, I was in the process of leaving for a new position in India, when I received a call from a previous employer. The president of the organization asked if I would return as CEO of a large health care institution. He related the history of the organization since I left and the problems they had experienced. They rehearsed for me all the reasons I might not want to return and all the solutions they were prepared to take to remedy those concerns, including firing several people they thought I did not get along with. While, on reflection, I realized that this person didn't really know me, it came through to me loud and clear that people needed me, appreciated what I had to offer, and were prepared to go out of their way to get my services. I experienced the telephone call as an external objective affirmation on my life that I could not escape from.

At certain marking points, people benefit from special affirmation: birthdays, anniversaries, retirements. These are days when the mystery, uniqueness, depth and greatness of a human being or partners can be celebrated.

Some things in life take time to heal—the death of a loved one, the loss of personal reputation, a home that has been wrecked by storm or tornado. We may have to do our grieving before healing can take place. Finding the courage to keep going in the process may create the space for affirmation to happen.

AFFIRMATION IS A DECISION

These examples remind us that it is entirely up to us how we face each day. We can choose to be a victim in the face of everything that's happening, or we can choose to tackle our problems and gain insight from the process. We can choose to stand passively by while someone dumps their complaints on us, or we can actively encourage people to look at things in a life-affirming way. For life is all about making decisions about life. When we strip every situation down, it's all about our decision. We decide how we are going to react to situations. We choose how people will affect our mood. We choose to be life-affirming, or the opposite. Our stance toward life is in our hands, not in those of the weather.

Suffering is the real test of our degree of affirmation. The journey towards being able to affirm suffering is a long one for most of us. The actor, Christopher Reeves, who played the role of Superman for so long, suffered a spinal cord injury during an equestrian competition and is now a quadriplegic who operates his wheelchair by breathing through a tube. He is now a popular hero because of his non-victim relationship to his suffering, and has gone on to direct a film. Suffering often makes the sufferer bitter. Martin Luther King who suffered more than most as leader of the United States Civil Rights Movement in the United States recalls his decision:

> As my suffering mounted, I soon realized that there were two ways in which I could respond to my situation—either to react with bitterness, or seek to transform the suffering into a creative force. I chose the latter.

The power of the affirming story about life is astonishing. Ruth Waldick, a young doctoral student in biology at McMaster University in Hamilton, Ontario, was in Manaus, Brazil, researching primates in the Brazilian forest. As she strolled down the street on Sunday morning, a drunk driver passed out at the wheel and drove up onto the sidewalk. He rammed Waldick head on, leaving her with one kneecap broken, the other dented, a concussion, a lost front tooth and lots of cuts and bruises. Four weeks later, she returned to her primate research in the Brazilian rainforest. Although surveying techniques for monkeys had always required slow walking, her pace was even further reduced by the inability to bend her knees. Walking painfully on legs that would not bend, she listened for the cries of howler monkeys. "Some people think I had the worst luck," she said. "But no, if I had the worst luck, I'd be dead. I have the best luck. I'm alive."

In fact, there is no situation in which life cannot be lived and affirmed. A development consultant told me of a visit he made to India—the place of so many realizations. On the flight to Bombay, he read a brochure he had picked up at the Indian Consulate. "Bombay," said the brochure," is a combination of the charms of San Francisco, the commerce of Chicago, and the cosmopolitan culture of New York." The consultant was very excited:

> When I got to Bombay airport and proceeded to Indian Airlines to catch a connecting flight to Aurangabad, I discovered that the airlines had promised eight seats to some government officials on their way to Delhi, and had given my seat away. So I had a day to spend in Bombay. I set out very early in the morning to see the sights and very soon saw a man who impressed me. He had obviously slept on the sidewalk the night before. He had with him two water containers. Right on the sidewalk he proceeded to wash his face, brush his teeth and gargle, which was an art in itself. All the schooling I had received about being a human being and everything I had expected of cities like San Francisco, New York, and Chicago collapsed around me. I stood there and looked at that man bundling up his belongings and standing up to go into the day, and I realized that that man symbolized the affirmation that life in any situation can be lived.

Nikos Kazantzakis' *Zorba, the Greek* is the tale of a man who loved the ups and downs of life. He had a scheme to build a trestled bridge from a mine down the cliffs to the coast so the minerals could be shipped out. When all the trestles were in place, and the railway installed, the great day came for the first test of the bridge. Down went the wagons loaded to the brim. Suddenly the vibrations began to disturb the structure, and it began to come apart, piece by piece, until the whole structure was lying among the rocks, demolished completely. Silence followed. It was the end of all his dreams. Suddenly Zorba decided to dance. He launched into the now famous Zorba dance to life and death. What a way to celebrate the destruction of a dream!

Affirmation is always possible in life, no matter what is happening. It represents a foundational faith in the goodness of life itself. However, affirmation is sometimes only possible after considerable processing of an event. And so, in the next chapter we will deal with self-conscious reflection as another foundational stance in life.

Exercise

Profound Truths become true for us only when we have grounded them in our own life experience. In the columns below, you will have an opportunity to apply the statements in the column headings to your own life.

LIFE IS GOOD	I AM RECEIVED	THE PAST IS APPROVED	ALL IS POSSIBLE

1. In the column, Life is Good, note those parts or aspects of life you struggle about naming "good".

2. In the column, I Am Received, write down those aspects of yourself—physical, psychological, emotional, mental, spiritual—that you have a hard time saying yes to.

3. In the column, The Past Is Approved, write down in a word or phrase those events in your past that you struggle over accepting forgiveness for.

4. In the column, All Is Possible, write down those hopes and dreams and decisions about your future that you can't accept as possible.

5. Write a sentence on what difference it would make in your life if you accept those parts or aspects of life in the first column as good.

_____

_____

_____

6. What difference would it make in your life if you could accept the fact that those things you wrote down in the second column are accepted.

_____

7. What difference would it make in your life if you were able to accept your whole past?

_____

8. What difference would it make if you accepted as fully possible all those things about your future that you can't accept as possible?

_____.

An Experiment You Can Try in Relation to Chapter 3:

CELEBRATING A STAFF BIRTHDAY: A good way to show real honor for co-workers is to reflect with them on their birthday. This can be done in ten minutes.

Opening

> Bring the cake in. Sing "Happy Birthday". Have the birthday person blow out the candles. Cut the cake and pass around.

Objective Questions

> OK, now we are going to talk with Robin.
> Robin, what have been the key events of your last year—at work, at home, or in your community?
> As a member of Robin's team, what scenes of Robin do we remember?
> What are some of Robin's real contributions?.

Reflective Questions

> What funny things do we remember related to Robin?
> What tasks do we remember her involved in?

Interpretive Questions

> Robin, what are you looking forward to in this coming year?

Decisional Questions

> What do we wish for Robin in this next year of her life?

Closing

> Robin, Happy Birthday! and all the best for this next year.

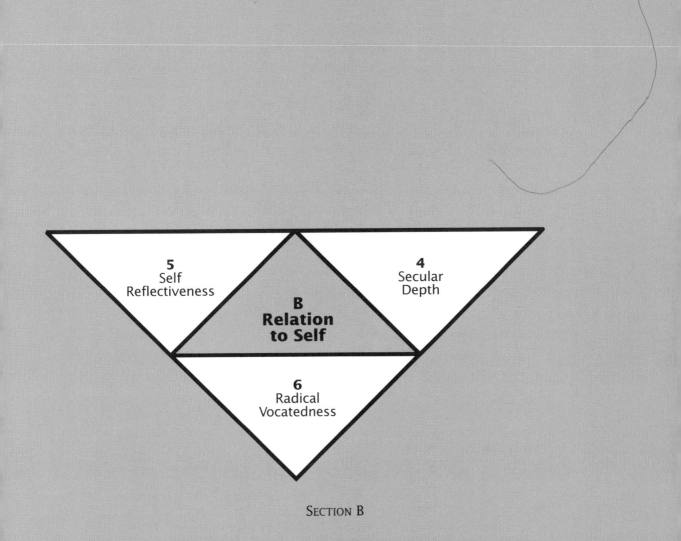

5
Self
Reflectiveness

4
Secular
Depth

B
Relation
to Self

6
Radical
Vocatedness

SECTION B

Relation to the Self

Self-conscious Reflection

Meaning in the Mundane

Profound Vocation

INTRODUCTION TO SECTION B

Without a way to relate authentically to the self each of us has and is, there is no way for a human being to live profoundly. Very busy people are finding that, without setting time aside for reflection or retreats they start losing their edge and running on automatic and, eventually, running on empty. People involved in social change or social work find that it's very easy to burn out: there are so many things to be done and people to be cared for, that it seems a luxury to spend time in caring for themselves. It seems as if they are abandoning what they so deeply care about. But in time, they learn to treasure the moments they set aside to find their centeragain, and discover that they go back to their work refreshed.

The first way we relate to the self is through *self-conscious reflection* that constantly dredges the meaning of the daily events in our lives. The second way is through seeing through the everyday events in our lives to the *meaning in the mundane* that is revealed. The third way is through going on the *journey of discovering our vocation.*

CHAPTER 4

Self-conscious Reflection

Experiencing Your Experience

Men go forth to wonder at the height of mountains,
the huge waves of the sea, the broad flow of the rivers,
the vast compass of the ocean, the courses of the stars,
and they pass by themselves without wondering.
AUGUSTINE:

The greatest danger, that of losing one's own self,
may pass off quietly, as if it were nothing.
Every other loss, that of an arm, a leg, five dollars,
is sure to be noticed.
SØREN KIERKEGAARD

LIFE INVITES REFLECTION

I remember the first time I became aware of reflecting. It was a dread-filled (and slightly fascinating) experience when I was seven years old. Our family had a small hotel on the bay where the Hastings River joined the Pacific Ocean. The view from our front verandah embraced the whole bay, the two breakwaters and the ocean beyond. At anchor on the far side of the bay was the immaculate, double-ended white pilot boat. Several times a week the pilot took *The Hastings* out across the bar between the two breakwaters, sounded the water depth, and proceeded out to the ocean to bring the timber ships into the port. My dad was good friends with the pilot. My father and I had a standing invitation to accompany him on Monday mornings. I looked forward to those days with unabated excitement. On one such morning my father fell off a ladder and sprained his ankle. No one thought to tell me. So as I stood on our verandah, I could see the pilot boat moving out between the breakwaters, and I observed that I wasn't on it. I immediately assumed that I had been left behind, so I kicked up a heck of a hullabaloo, until my sisters dragged me kicking and screaming to show me that my dad was not on the pilot boat. He lay in bed, with one leg propped up.

That was the day the pilot boat never returned. No one knew what had happened. The pilot boat had a cork bottom, so that if it capsized, it would automatically right itself. But all that was left, were the bits and pieces of wreckage on the northern beaches. My reflection went like this. If my dad hadn't fallen off the ladder and sprained his ankle this morning, we would both be drowned, since neither of us, nor the pilot, strange to say, could swim. That simple thought was buried in a great cloud of awe. Some mysterious synchronicity had preserved us from a watery grave. I was fortunate to be alive. There is nothing like a near-miss at death to concentrate the mind wonderfully and to evoke reflection. Life's journey is full of events, some major, some minor, but all significant when we allow time for reflection to dredge them for meaning.

My colleague Wayne Nelson gives an example of reflection:

I am out for a Sunday bike ride along the Lake Ontario beach in Toronto. As I peddle easily along, other recreational traffic grows thicker; it is the Sunday afternoon Beach rush hour. The roller bladers are out in force—a pair of skaters almost force me off the path. Families with little kids and grandmothers insist on talking in the middle of the pathway. Picnics spill onto the pathway. My progress becomes a series of starts and stops as I attempt to evade people. In some frustration, I try turning up a sidepath, and get blindsided by a roller blader passing on the right.

I grow hot under the collar: "Why can't people keep on their side of the path?" I growl to myself. A teenager on his bike is parked across the path, checking his tire, forcing me to a complete stop. "Excuse me!" I say, "Would you please get out of my way ?" He responds, "Hey, cool it, man, it's Sunday!" Under my breath, I exclaim, "Idiot!" By now, I am fuming. But his words somehow stick: yes, it's Sunday; day of rest—time to relax. Huh!

The sun shines high in the sky with a million diamond chips glinting off the lake. Yachts pull in closer to the beach. Youngsters are salivating over monstrous ice-cream cones. I say to myself, What's going on? How come these people are having so much fun? Yeah, it's Sunday. Why am I so angry about everything? And who said it was my personal bike path? The whole world is here, and I'm part of it all. All these people are being who they want to be. Hey, get with the program!"

Suddenly, I decide the kid is right. I need to cool it, relax. It is Sunday. It's a different beat. I need to get with it. I am too absorbed in my own sense of what's right. I can let things happen and go with the flow, at my own speed. I can enjoy the happy chaos of it all. I can live the actual life I have on my hands, instead of fighting it all the way

A REFLECTIVE PROCESS

What is happening in these stories is an in-depth reflection on the events of life. Certain events stick in our consciousness, like burrs and thistles that attach themselves to the socks of a bush walker. When they prickle, they demand attention. When we allow reflection, those happenings can become signposts in our life.

There is a reflective process (a philosopher might call it a phenomenological process) that is possible for digesting such events. It plays itself out in four stages.

Each stage is an intensification of the previous so that maximum intensification is reached by stage 4. This diagram attempts to get hold of the dynamic.

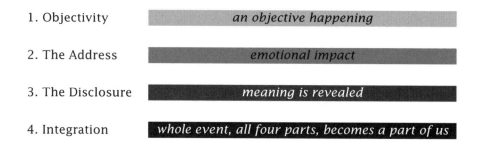

1. Objectivity	*an objective happening*
2. The Address	*emotional impact*
3. The Disclosure	*meaning is revealed*
4. Integration	*whole event, all four parts, becomes a part of us*

Stage 1 acknowledges the objectivity of the event as a happening in our life; it re-remembers the event and its components.

Stage 2 acknowledges that the event is an address on our lives; it recognizes the depth impact or the "Wham!" of the event with all the emotions of dread, fascination, shock, delight, disgust, wonder, puzzlement—whatever—that accompany it; owning up to how the event has resonated throughout our whole being; not trying to crack hardy about it, but naming those emotions and feelings as precisely as one can.

Stage 3 unwraps the event so that it discloses the meaning, learnings, insights, and implications for our life that are implicit in both the event and our internal response to it.

Stage 4 thoroughly integrates the event into our lives, so that it is flagged forever in our memory as a life-changing happening. Here we get said to ourselves that this event, which now includes all our reflections on the event, is our friend and advisor for life. This event is such that if we wrote it down on a card, we wouldn't be surprised if it appeared in letters of gold. This event now smacks of ultimacy—it is one of those events after which we say, "This is it! Life gets no more meaningful than this." So we continue to travel the journey of life with this event as companion.

Processing the events of our lives is life and death. One wonders what would have happened if Paul, after being hit by lightning on the road to Damascus, had just brushed it off, macho-style, and continued on his way. One wonders how the histories of India and South Africa might have gone, if the young lawyer, Mohandas Gandhi, after being thrown off the train at Pietermaritzburg for being "coloured", had just said, "Oh well, I guess that's that. Shows what happens when I stick my neck out."

Unless we process the events in our lives, we miss great opportunities;—learning and change just don't happen. Gandhi spent the night shivering away the hours in a corner, pondering the incident. In later years, he would say that his political mission in life began on that night in the waiting room at Pietermaritzburg.

REFLECTION AND LEARNING

When we don't stop to reflect, we are all our own biggest enemies. Only too willingly we get caught up in the daily rush: the rush through breakfast, the rush to work, the rush to catch up on yesterday's work, the rapid-fire communication at work, the overtime, the rush home. It is easy to get hooked on adrenaline. When we rush, somehow our life seems more significant. When we stop, we may feel too aware of our emptiness. We flop into bed at night, without reflection, without processing the day, and tomorrow, we do it all again. We sometimes descend into numb stupefaction through endless hours in front of the TV set, or the video game, or whatever we use as an escape from the burdens of consciousness.

Without reflection, it is possible to go through life making the same basic mistakes over and over again. Without reflection there is no real learning. Sable Island, 200 kilometres off the Nova Scotia coast, is a 200-mile sandbar, some above the water, some below. In the last 200 years, over 200 ships have run into it and been wrecked. There were all kinds of reasons: poor ship-to-shore communication, Atlantic storms, fog, the currents, poor records. Sable Island became a symbol in my mind of that point in our lives where we keep making the same basic mistakes and end up in shipwreck. Reflection is key to avoiding the same mistake over and over again.

The unreflective life is, at times, sanctified by the media. Not so long ago, there was a TV ad for a well-known four-wheel drive. The vehicle is depicted speeding down a mountainous road, maneuvering round a string of cyclists, navigating through log obstructions left by a tractor trailer that had gone off the road. The vehicle successfully threaded its way through an avalanche of rocks and averted further dangers by going off-road to finish up in the home driveway. After successfully avoiding all these dangers, what does the driver do? Go back and check on the driver of the tractor trailer? See whether the cyclists are OK? Hurry inside her house to call the police to inform them of the truck off the road and the falling rocks? None of the above. The driver looks in the mailbox and picks up the mail. The woman driver is depicted as alert, competent, on top of the situation, very pert, very cool. Not for her any dread attacks or sighs of relief. She is on to the next thing: checking the mail. The ad depicts a colossal failure to reflect and process recent experience, or to act on it responsibly.

This failure to learn from living is noticeable in history. Historian Barbara Tuchman, in her wonderfully sobering book, *The March of Folly*, examines the role of folly in government. "Why," she asks, "did the Trojan rulers drag the suspicious-looking wooden horse inside their walls, despite every reason to suspect it was a Greek trick. Why did successive ministries of George III insist on coercing rather than conciliating the American colonies, though repeatedly advised by many counsellors that the harm done must be greater than any possible gain. Why did Hitler invade Russia despite the disasters incurred by his predecessors? And why does American business insist on "growth" when it is demonstrably using up the three basics of life on our planet—land, water and unpolluted air?" Her litany of folly goes on and on. One aspect of this folly, the historian says, is the refusal to draw inference from negative signs....It includes the faculty of stopping short, as though by instinct, at any dangerous thought,...not grasping analogies, failing to perceive logical errors...and being bored and repelled by any train of thought which is capable of leading in a heretical direction."

Of course, there are reasons for being unwilling to reflect on what is happening. Reflection can reveal the need for change. Change is painful and exacting, and so we avoid reflecting about our lives or our societies. Stephen Crane describes these dynamics:

> I was in the darkness.
> I could not see my words
> Nor the wishes of my heart.

> Then suddenly there was a great light
> —Let me into the darkness again.

PAYING ATTENTION

How do we reflect? First, by paying attention to what is going on. If the driver of the four-by-four mentioned above were going to reflect, the moment she entered her driveway was the time to do it. An elementary act of reflection for her would be: what did I just witness? What is a human response? What do I need to do? This is simply paying attention to life, to what is going on. In the civilization depicted in Aldous Huxley's *Island*, minah birds continually evoke the attention of the inhabitants:

> Attention! Attention!
> Here and now, boys!
> Here and now!

Mindfulness is a function of wakefulness. The TV series *Columbo* portrayed a rumpled, weary detective with an old, beaten-up car, who looked as if he wouldn't solve a crime in a thousand years. But he had the extraordinary capacity to notice everything going on, without seeming to: the carnation being surreptitiously picked up by a prime suspect, an anomaly with the clock on the wall, a hand beginning to tremble, a cigarette ash in an odd place.

When I was a little boy, my father often got me working alongside him. He trained me to look ahead and anticipate the next tool he would need: a hammer, a pair of pliers, a screwdriver, a saw. After a while, the fun wore off that, and my mind would wander. All of a sudden, I would hear this sharp voice, "Stick a pin in yourself, Brian!" That meant, "Wake up, pay attention to what's going on. Stop daydreaming, and pass me the next tool."

Paying attention is also a matter of listening to what the other is saying, and listening with what someone has called "the third ear"—that depth listening which hears what lies below the surface. Paying attention involves noticing one's own bodily reactions to what is going on. Sometimes you may find your hands starting to tremble or get clammy in response to what someone has said, or to something on TV. It is important to note that. Sometimes when I am typing away and staring at the computer screen, my head starts to nod into a slight doze. Afterwards, if I look at what I have just written, there may be a message there. If what I wrote addressed my own life, then a little snooze may indicate that I don't want to deal with that part of my life, and so my awareness wants a little holiday. When that happens, I simply note it. After noting it a number of times I may see a pattern, and that pattern may be quite revelatory as to how I am relating to life. This kind of paying attention is called "noting".

STOPPING

To be mindful, to be able to reflect self-consciously, we must slow ourselves down in order to recenter ourselves There is a story about André Gide who was accustomed to travel very fast through the jungles of Africa. One morning the native guides sat in a circle and refused to leave the camp. When Gide urged them to get moving, they looked at him and said with firmness, "Don't hurry us—we are waiting for our souls to catch up with us." Many of us are far ahead of our souls. We keep going and going like the Energizer Bunny. But reflection requires a distancing—a standing back from what we have been doing, and consciously deciding to re-run the movie of our lives so we can see what is happening, how we have been responding to life, and how we might need to change. In other words, we have to *stop* to answer TS Eliot's question: "Where is the life we have lost in living?"

In an article in *The Toronto Star*, Elaine Carey tells of an interview with a successful businessman who had bought his BMW and motorbike, had travelled round the world, taken up hang-gliding, but found that it was never enough: He said, "By now, I thought I would have felt that I'd made it. Instead, I just keep saying, 'That's not it." The article goes on to tell how he had signed up for a five-day retreat in the Thousand Islands to help him put his house in order.

An article in *Time*, "Get Thee to a Monastery", tells how Catholic monasteries and convents are besieged with would-be retreatants booked months in advance. Some wake at 2:25 in the morning to follow the canonical hours throughout the day; others simply enjoy the silence of the monastery as an opportunity to pray, reflect, write in their journals, and deal with their inner problems. One retreatant said, "I come screaming in off the runway. This (the monastery experience) cools my jets." According to another, the experience of the daily office "gave him ballast and steerage".

Whether through the silence of monasteries or fly fishing, more and more people are realizing the importance of stopping—stopping the world of custom and convention and finding a different space in which they can look at their lives with fresh eyes. And so rock singer Alanis Morrissette goes to India for a year to experiment with meditation and soak up that Indian sense of transcendence. Poet and performer Leonard Cohen suddenly ups anchor and goes to California to spend time in a Zen monastery. Without such time alone with ourselves, it is difficult for us to experience our own experience, to get in touch with the actual lives we are living, and see what our lives need.

There is a story about a consultant doing some work with some staffers from Microsoft. At lunchtime, he found himself in the same elevator as Bill Gates, who was aware of his work. Bill asked him out of the blue, "Well, Larry, do you have a word for me?" Larry, who spends 60 days a year out of a busy consulting schedule in retreat, simply said to him, "Stop!" and got off the elevator. Mr. Gates' reaction is not recorded.

Maya Angelou makes the comment that we often think that our affairs, great or small, must be tended continuously and in detail or our world will disintegrate and we will lose our places in the universe. She talks about "the day away" she gives herself through which she unwraps the bonds that hold her in harness. She informs housemates, family and close friends that she will not be available for 24 hours, and disengages the telephone. "Every person," she says, "needs to take a day away, a day in which one consciously separates the past from the future. Jobs, lovers, family, employers and friends can exist one day without any one of us." "Stopping", or "a day away" may take the form of a weekend retreat, or a day of solitary reflection. It could also mean taking a sabbatical. More and more people realize that keeping on keeping on like the Energizer Bunny only results in the law of diminishing returns. We work more and more and produce less and less of real value. Burnt-out humans are generally not a greatly creative civilizational influence.

Establishing the solitariness necessary for reflection may simply be a matter of setting up a zone of silence. Dag Hammarskjöld, when he was secretary-general of the United Nations, set up a meditation room without any particular religious affiliation, so that members of the UN assembly could go there at any time and reflect. My wife, Jeanette, has set up a reflective zone in our living room, which consists of a chair facing the opposite way to the others, a sidetable, and a tape recorder. When she is in that chair in the evening, we know she is not to be disturbed. Reflection seems to go well when it is related to a certain space and a particular time.

DOING ONE'S OWN THINKING

There are times of crisis and great complexity when life calls us to think our life through, to keep pushing till clarity comes, even if it means staying up all night working with the issue. In our time, we need the capacity for a single-minded focus in our reflection that allows clarity or resolution to come. Otherwise we may be bothered by issues that keep coming back to plague us. There is no substitute for thinking life through for ourselves. In *The Symposium*, Plato tells this story about the extraordinary concentration that Socrates was capable of:

> One morning he was thinking about something which he could not resolve. He would not give it up, but continued thinking from early dawn to noon—there he

stood, fixed in thought; and at noon attention was drawn to him, and the rumor ran through the wondering crowd that Socrates had been standing and thinking about something ever since the break of day. At last, in the evening after supper, some Ionians out of curiosity brought out their mats and slept in the open air that they might watch him and see whether he would stand all night. There he stood until the following morning, and with the return of light he offered up a prayer to the sun, and went his way.

IMAGES OF REFLECTION

Reflecting on experience is like interacting with a radar screen. When we view the screen at first it might be blank, but then suddenly there is a blip, and in another part of the screen another blip, and another. When we look back over our experience, we look for those blips on our radar screen: events, happenings, interactions that have a particular awareness attached to them. In a standard day at the office, we have just interacted with a customer. Suddenly, someone walks up and says, "Mildred, you gave that customer the brush-off. I don't think that kind of customer interaction is going to get us into the future." That's a blip on our radar screen, demanding reflection.

In World War II, navy ships used SONAR to detect the approach of enemy submarines. The technology scanned underwater with a series of electronic pulses that let off "pings" at timed intervals. When a submarine approached, the distance between the pings decreased until a steady ping-ping-ping-ping-ping was heard, and it was time to go into action with depth charges. Some days, one's life becomes a whole series of pings impinging on one's awareness. At the end of the day, when you feel frazzled, upset, confused, and wanting to sort some things out, start with the pings. Attempt to isolate the events or situations where your life was "pinged". To go into the next day, without reflecting on the day that was, is inviting trouble.

EXPERIENCING OUR EXPERIENCE

For reflection is how we care for our consciousness. Without reflection, consciousness congeals, then hardens, and we find ourselves acting more like robots than human beings. Reflection enables us to interact with the reality of our lives, rather than wish-dreams or illusions. It enables the healing of our wounds, the affirmation of our actual lives, and our constant movement into the future.

So, how do we experience our experience? For example, one day I am sitting in my office, tapping away in fine style at the keyboard. Suddenly, a colleague walks in and says without preamble, "I just want you to know that what you said about staff relations at the meeting yesterday irritated the hell out of me," and walks out of the room. My first response is "Wow! what was that? My second, "What did he say?" My next response is to say, "Well, people get irritated all the time." And I go back to the computer, as if nothing much has happened. At night, I wake up thinking about his words, and I can't get back to sleep. I realize I have not really allowed those words to get to me. I have not processed what happened. So I decide to get up and write in my journal what happened, including remembering yesterday's meeting and what I said. I think I know what it was I said about staff relations that offended my colleague so much, but I decide to chat with him about the event next day. After the chat, I reflect some more in my journal. I decide that what I said in the meeting was ill advised and not sufficiently thought through. I decide to tell my colleague the next day that I went off half-cocked.

By such means, we dialogue with the stuff of life, so that it yields its meaning. It is too easy to react to life's events or go through life as if we were in a trance. Every second of this life is ours to live. Reflection helps us stand present to every bit of it. We were not given emotions because they tingle us, or give us a charge. We were given emotions so that we could experience our experience. If I feel terrible, if I feel like a failure, it is really important for me to find out why I feel this way.

INTENTIONALITY IN REFLECTION

Many of the events in our lives are like oysters. If we dig deep enough, we find the pearl concealed there. Reflection is the constant effort to push through mundane experience to reveal the pearl of insight, the "aha", the depth implications. In this way, we keep on turning the water of mundanity into the rich wine of meaning, so that we make new meaning over and over every day. This requires some intentionality. It assumes that we regard this reflection as important enough to allot some time to practice it. There are many ways to do this.

For example, as I think back over my day I come across an event that really collided with the routine of my life. To reflect on this I have to acknowledge that this was a real interruption in my life. So I ask myself what happened and start taking notes. Four simple questions can help me here:

What happened?

I was at our family doctor's clinic, because I was coughing so much and feeling generally run down. She had already determined that my systolic blood pressure was at 220—almost a world record. The doctor was going through a standard list of questions. The next question hit me right in the solar plexus: "Do you smoke?" I answered "yes".

"Good lord," she said, "You've come to me to find out why you're coughing and don't feel well. You've got to quit smoking!"

How did it make me feel?

I felt mortified, shocked, embarrassed, and angry that someone was telling me how to live my life. How I loved that pipe! I couldn't believe that someone was telling me I had to stop. I remembered how for many a long year a "smoke" had served as welcome pause and punctuation to my life. Now it was being ripped away.

What's the meaning of this event in my life?

It seems that if I want to maintain my mission in life, I need to maintain myself in good health. Stopping smoking is a keystone in that program.

What is an appropriate response? What do I need to do?

1. I am going to quit, right now, cold turkey.
2. I'm going to talk to my wife, and to some friends who have quit.
3. I'm going to tell all my acquaintances that I have quit, so they can hold me accountable to my decision.

This is only five to ten minutes' work, if that. Many find writing down reflections to be more helpful than an endless loop of brooding. Writing yourself through the four stages of the process helps concentration, enables closure through making a decision about the event, and lets life flow on, without being locked into what happened the day before.

Seeing through to the dimension of meaning is only the first in a series of very long steps. We know that it is one thing to "have a great spiritual experience" and go off like a fire cracker. It is another thing to stay awake, responsible and caring, for the long haul. Waking up is the beginning, but the journey is long, complex, and full of tank traps, speed traps, quicksands, sirens, and ogres. As we shall see in chapter 6, those who start out on this journey of the spirit with great excitement and in grand style run into what has been called the Dark Night. Those who choose to be social entrepreneurs, community or civic leaders may begin with great displays of charisma, but charisma wears thin really fast in the face of contradictions. Mothering or fathering a family similarly is great in the beginning when the experience is new. One seems to be on the very verge of the ultimate, only to be plunged into a dark night, after weeks of getting up in the middle of the night to comfort a child with teething problems.

For this reason, it is important for us to supplement daily reflection with regular reading of those who have been pioneers in traversing the journey of the spirit and communicating their findings. My list includes people like Nikos Kazantzakis, Teresa of Avila, John of the Cross, Hermann Hesse, Rabindranath Tagore, Carlos Casteneda, Jean Houston, and Joseph Campbell. They have described in many different kinds of poetry the ups and downs of the spirit journey. It is important always to have a map of this journey at hand as a backdrop to one's daily reflection. Which brings us to two further aspects of reflection: group reflection with a team and listening to our interior council of advisors.

GROUP REFLECTION

It would be a mistake to think that only individuals can benefit from cultivating the habit of reflection. The fruits of our solitary reflection are enriched when shared with those of colleagues. A team operating at high pitch in the workplace needs periods of reflection when it can talk together not only about its work, but about the way individual members are reacting to their work, what they are learning from it, and their insights on doing it effectively.

When reflection is structured into a group's life, it enriches both solitary reflection and the life of the whole group. For the past few years, ICA Canada has devoted one day a month to "research" which gives us a chance to dialogue on many different things, and reflect on specific aspects of our task. All kinds of spin-offs happen through such reflection: articles, books, new programs, new approaches to our consulting work. We wonder how we managed before we had "research days".

The Art of Focused Conversation, also published by ICA Canada, offers dozens of dialogues that can be had in work groups, or casually: conversations about news, the trends of the times, celebrations of birthdays, reflections on particular events, on and on.

A news conversation can be held at any time, and can be guaranteed to put the ongoing work in a new context. Two or three times a year the onrush of history is sure to throw up "events of collective amazement"—like the probe on Mars, the Montreal ice storm, or a local community "miracle." A group conversation can share people's depth responses and plumb the meaning of such events for the future.

Group movie conversations can reflect on a film that whole families or groups of people going from work have seen together. Why not gather afterwards, and have a conversation on the movie? The effect may be surprising.

INTERIOR DIALOGUE

To reflect is to digest our experience of life, to digest it and to dredge the meaning from it. But to reflect is also to dialogue with the wisdom that others have gathered from their own experience. Each of us manages to make friends with a number of people—some alive, many of them dead—who act as interior mentors, guides, advisors, constantly talking to us. For example, many Americans and others still hear the voice of John F. Kennedy: " Ask not what your country can do for you. Ask what you can do for your country." I'm sure many people still dialogue with those words. Kennedy is one of my interior mentors. These are people who have had an impact on our lives, for whatever reason.

This interior council can be made up of quite a lot of oddball characters. There are all kinds of people in our head. Some of the key ones inside me are the authors I mentioned a few paragraphs back. Then there is the Buddha, Homer Simpson (of the TV show *The Simpsons*), Dietrich Bonhoeffer, Teresa of Avila, Terry Fox, D.H. Lawrence, E.E. Cummings, General George Patton, President Truman, aboriginal George Winninguj. A number of people have made a direct impact on me, and they take seats in my interior council. I can hear Sister Mary Elizabeth who taught me in high school; I can hear my English teacher in teachers' college, my geography teacher at university, my father, and quite a number of colleagues that I have worked closely with in ICA. The Tim Taylor character from *Home Improvement* may be hobnobbing with Augustine; Buddha may be sitting opposite our home teacher from eighth grade; Grandma Gallagher may be arguing with Frederich Nietzsche who is trying to get Socrates at the end of the table to agree with him. There may even be a rock in somebody's council. Sometimes we hear hear voices we don't even want on our council—influences that might made sense at one time in our life, but nor now.

Some entities we carry round inside us are sometimes quite mean to us. One of my old teachers, Sister Maria Joseph, will intrude in her Irish accent every now and then: "Still careless, Stanfield? Still adding 7 and 4 to make 12? Accuracy before speed, please Mr. Stanfield" Sometimes they are exceptionally encouraging, telling us we really can do what we are in doubt about. These people inside us never go home. They are there all the time, night and day. Of course, some voices seem to contradict each other, but that's only because the statements are really dialoguing with each other. These people never really get angry. They just say what they see, then leave you with it.

We may even find demonic people like Adolph Hitler sitting in our meditative councils. But what we hear coming from him is truth. For instance, I hear him saying, "If you do what I have done, you'll finish up taking poison in a bunker in bombed-out Berlin, with the Avenging Furies of the coalition armies all round you." The challenge for us is daring to be present to this tribe of people within. When we dare to be present to our interior community, we never have to depend on the affection of others. These interior colleagues crow like roosters when we put one foot off the track, and call us into question. As soon as, for example, I justify what I am doing because someone has told me to do it, I can hear Dietrich Bonhoeffer yelling at me, "If your justification for what you're doing lies outside yourself, you are not free. You're no better than Adolph Eichmann who sent millions of Jews to the gas chambers because he was told to do so."

They don't even demand that I agree with them. When I muse over something with the people on my meditative council, I find that many of them are quite different from me. When I take an issue to them, they dialogue with me, back and forth. There are other councilors who give us encouragement, when things are tough, or who nurture us on the journey.

Certain artforms may show up on our council, like the Iron Man icon on the cover of this book. I know many people who are constantly guided by some of the poems of D.H. Lawrence that have been quoted in this book.

So, to be a spiritual human being is to consciously assemble the community you are going to live your life in dialogue with. Some writers are ashamed to refer to anyone else's books or wisdom, as if that detracted from their own originality. In the light of the interior council, I wonder if it is ever possible to be truly original. Even when we come out with what seems like pure creativity, we have to wonder who we are really quoting unconsciously, or whose work we are building on.

Our dialogue with these people is rarely about morality. They rarely ask, "Did you do this or that immoral thing?" These great people within are generally little interested in *petit bourgeois* morality. Their concern is authenticity. When they question us, it's not about whether we came late or had too much to drink, or flirted with someone other than our spouse. It's always about our relationship to life: what we are doing with our care; how we are exercising our responsibility; whether we are remaining conscious.

Who our interior friends are really determines who we are and will become. The old adage, "Tell me who your friends are, and I'll tell you who you are" is as true of our internal friends as our external ones. The real value of this exercise is that it brings intention to our meditative council, so that when we are confronted with an issue, problem, or decision, we can listen to what they have to say. It is helpful if we have some background on each of the characters, so that we know what they stand for.

These interior characters generally fall into four different roles:
• give me permission to be who I am
• make demands on me and hold me accountable
• act as exemplars of authentic living to guide me in my journey.
• act as colleagues or collaborators, or fellow struggler, in my work.

The exercise at the end of this chapter can help us put some intention into our meditative council, and self-program the topography of our selfhood. This is a guided solitary workshop for you to do all at once or in sections over time.

Exercise on the Meditative Council

A. BRAINSTORMING THE COUNCIL MEMBERS

1. Who are five people from history, or the present day, who need to be on your meditative council for the future? (for example: Nelson Mandela, Eleanor Roosevelt, Martin Luther, Madame Curie)

2. What five colleagues with diverse points of view do you need on your council? You may have had strong encounters with them in the past.

3. What five writers do you need on your meditative council and in your library

4. What five characters from novels, movies, or plays need to live on your council? (e.g. Joan of Arc, Scrooge, Mountain Rivera)

5. What are five art forms that remind you of your mystery, depth, and greatness and need to be on your meditative council? (for example the tree in the backyard; the Grand Canyon, Beethoven's *Fifth*, Van Gogh's *Starry Night*, the polar bear)

	PEOPLE	COLLEAGUES	WRITERS	FICTIONAL CHARACTERS	ARTFORMS
1					
2					
3					
4					
5					

B. PRIORITIZING THE COUNCIL

In this part of the exercise you will rank the 25 names you have written down. By filtering them through some categories, you will decide your top four interior councilors.

As you decide who to put in your first, second and third rows, consider who are permission-givers, who make demands on you and keep you on your toes, who are good examples for you and who work side by side with you on the job. (Try to spread them across the categories.)

6. On the interior dialogue chart below write five of the items from your list in each box of the first row. (See the four types above.)

7. Choose three of the five and write in the box immediately below in the second row.

8. Write two of the three in the third row.

9. Write one of the two in the fourth row.

What you have done here is to make a decision on the four members of the council you will listen to most because of their importance to you, and the ones you will give secondary regard to, and so on. This isn't a hierarchical arrangement, but a description of relative influence. So for example, if I have Homer Simpson in the first row, I may hear him bellowing out. "Dope! Take the easy way out, and go and have beer!" I will listen to what he has to say, but I won't pay a whole lot of attention to it. But if I have Dietrich Bonhoeffer in the last row,

PEOPLE	COLLEAGUES	WRITERS	FICTIONAL CHARACTERS	ARTFORMS
1 2 3 4 5				
1 2 3				
1 2				
1				

and he's saying, "Observe, judge, weight up, decide and act, and then surrender the deed to history," I pay attention, because I have made him a prime councilor. It is as if the last four in the row become the inner council; they get the best seats, and are allowed to talk the longest.

C. INTENSIFICATION ACTIONS

The next step is to select the voices of those interior advisors that we want to grow stronger in the next part of our life and create tactics to enable them to become a more powerful voice among our interior mentors.

10. Choose four out of the entire chart who need to grow stronger within your meditative council over the next year.

1. _____

2. _____

3. _____

4. _____

11. Here we want to get very practical and brainstorm ways in which these advisors can be made more influential. (e.g. I might read an advisor's book, do some research, make an art-form to remind you.) So, go ahead and list ten actions that will ensure that they become a primary force on your meditative council over the next year.

TEN ACTIONS

1. _____

2. _____

3. _____

4. _____

5. _____

6. _____

7. _____

8. _____

9. _____

10. _____

D. REFLECTION ON THE EXERCISE

a. What did you discover about your meditative friends?

b. What criteria did you use in deciding whom or what you would put on the next level?

c. How do you expect to be challenged in helping the council grow with you?

CONCLUSION

Our meditative council is never assembled once and for all. As our awareness increases and our challenges change, we reconstitute it so it best serves our life at the moment.

Chapter 5

Meaning in the Mundane

Finding the Windows to Spirit Depth

> On the way to the play we stopped to look at the stars. And as usual, I felt in awe.
> And then I felt even deeper in awe at this capacity we have to be in awe about
> something.... I decided I would set time aside each day to do awe-robics.
> JANE WAGNER

> It's like that door you find one day, way at the back of your closet. And you go
> into the closet and turn the knob and open it. And outside there it is: the immense
> Caribbean. And you can't believe it. You've lived here for so long, and you never
> knew that all this was right here the whole time.
> LAURIE ANDERSON

In the last chapter we described the task of reflection as "experiencing our experience."
This chapter takes it further. Whatever meaning can be found in life is located in the
midst of the everyday happenings and ongoingness at home, on the job, in this world.
We experience *transparency* when meaning shines through the mundane happenings of
life.

This chapter starts by describing the happening of transparency that reveals deep meaning in our mundane experiences. The next part investigates the states of being that can happen to us in the middle of the transparency happening. The chapter ends with several people's descriptions of this happening in various kinds of poetry.

A. The Happening of Transparency

THE NATURE OF TRANSPARENCY

Transparency happens when you can see through the mundane to the depth insight that lies behind it. The word *transparency* is rich in meaning and associations. My thesaurus relates transparency to words like translucent, diaphanous, limpid, and even lucid. So transparency has something to do with letting the light shine through, or being able to see through the surface to the depth of things.

Transparency is something like what happens when you hold a match under a piece of paper, but not too close to it. First you experience the heat. Then the paper turns brown, and then it pops into flame until a hole appears, and we see through the paper to what lies beyond. Sometimes you can feel it before you can see it.

Transparency is an external happening, as well as the happening inside the happening. One day my father dies. That's quite an objective thing. A week later, or maybe two years later, something happens that implodes the happening, something that has to do with the very depths of my own interior existence. Some people can have their mother die, and it does next to nothing inside. (Some people may actually be relieved that mama has moved on to another state.) For others, the death just tears the bottom out of their very being.

It's not just extraordinary experiences where this happens. More and more people encounter what might be called *meaning in the mundane*. In the past, we encountered the awe or the mysterious at the edge of life, at the edge of knowing. Heaven or hell and other ultimate categories were located in some basement or second or third story of life that had nothing to do with daily living. Nobody believes this any more, and any attempts to revive such second-story thinking are doomed. Life turns transparent for people and they find the very essence of life where they are—in the kitchen, on the street corner, in a community meeting. Encountering a dead bird on the beach freights the dread and fascination with their own death. Celebrating a birthday recalls one more time a person's unique and unrepeatable life, and the mystery of having made it into the world at all. In our times, we have discovered, or re-remembered, what seems like an extraordinary secret: the depths of life are not only found on a mountain in the

Himalayas, in some kind of mystical practice, or in a denominational church. Today people are finding profound meaning in the very midst of life.

For example, on the Discovery Channel on TV, I watch a kayaker weave his way down a mountain stream, around rocks, down foaming currents, into whirlpools, down rapids and even waterfalls, until he reaches calm water. Suddenly I see right through his adventures on that river to my own experience of my journey through life. I see how I navigated some passages well, while in others, I tipped over or rammed into a rock. Life is indeed a great adventure filled with awesome challenges. I am grateful that life is this way. Suddenly, I'm back to watching the program. I just took a little trip into a transparent dimension of life. I realize that life is full of these strange times when the awe breaks through and life become transparent like a clear pond so that, for a moment, we see through to the very essence of life.

When I revisited my native Australia a few years ago, some friends took me to a nature preserve in South Australia. It had a variety of the best-known local fauna, including an emu. An emu, a large flightless bird, roughly the size of an ostrich, padded round the enclosure, it seemed to give me permission to approach, so I got really close. It was about my height, so before long we were eyeball to eyeball. I found myself peering into that emu's eye—it seemed like it was three inches across, and wild of aspect. The emu's eye seemed to be looking straight through me. I realized I was in awe so thick I'd have to dust it away afterwards. The emu seemed to be saying, "I know you through and through, old fellah." I had to break off the contact. It was eerie.

Afterwards, I got to thinking about how life is full of this kind of encounter, where a simple event starts brimming over with awe. Such events seem to occur more and more in the midst of ordinary life.

The diagram below shows elements of the transparent experience.

WHY IS THIS IMPORTANT?

Before we go any further, we should ask, "Why on earth should I be concerned about looking for meaning in the mundane?

 This is a book about leadership. Leaders get pushed in all kinds of ways. They experience many things: disappointment, rage, exultation, abandonment and betrayal, victory, extraordinary comradeship, and deep solitude. At times they encounter experiences they cannot explain. They may begin to feel that some expirences are good and others bad. Actually, each of these experiences is a window to spirit depth. We do not have to run from these strange wake-up calls.

Everyone, but especially a leader, needs this kind of interior depth. Without a deep

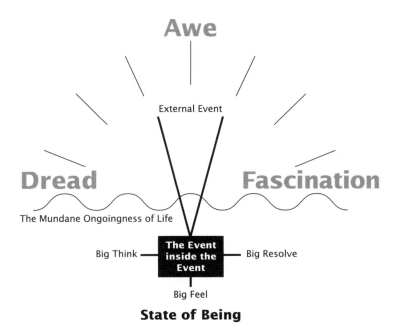

State of Being

understanding of what is happening to them, leaders tend to become martyrs. Without spirit, big and small projects tend to curl up and die. Leaders have to find the interior resources in any situation.

Finally, we all struggle with equating real life with the way things ought to be. At the launch of a project, there is often a feeling of great momentum, high vision, and much energy. As the project runs into difficulties, the leader finds that she is being tested. She may even be the subject of accusations by others or by herself. The leader needs the capacity to see through what is happening, accept it, and move on. Over and over again, we see that the key to real living is accepting things the way they are. When we do this, life opens up to us in a brand new way, and change becomes possible.

SECULAR MEANING, SECULAR DEPTHS

Now, the depth we are talking about is secular. There is nothing spiritual or holy about it. It is as ordinary, once we see it, as any mundane activity that we engage in. You don't have to belong to a particular religion to have the capacity for transparent experiences. I don't mean going to church, feeling particularly pious, and calling that profound. Feeling pious and reverent is not profound. It's simply pious. TV celebrity Roseanne Barr, who has starred in "Roseanne" through most of the 1990s and now, in 1999, has her own talk show, is probably the least pious person we have ever encountered. Yet, as she recollects her life in *My Life as a Woman*, she can come up with a statement like this:

> That's my mood tonight, when everything means something, everything is connected to everything else and nothing exists apart, even me. Every green thing is breathing, You can hear this hum—like when you're at the ocean almost—just a hum, everywhere. Maybe the sprinklers are on—the grass and stuff is getting watered and you can almost hear the drop of the water sliding over the grass. On nights like this while sitting all cozy on the floor and my legs cropped Buddhist fashion, drinking champagne out of these real pretty crystal goblets, I go, God, what an incredible life I've had and how lucky I am.

Roseanne talks here about an experience of profound meaning in the mundane. We don't have to look for it in some special world. Secular depth has to do with this kind of explosion of consciousness that happens in our day. It reveals the possibility of living a full human life by being aware of what is going in one's being.

Once a person starts getting the feel for this depth, it is possible to find it everywhere. One day I was walking, along with thousands of other people, through the popular Eaton Center mall in downtown Toronto. I was in particularly bad form. I had had a really hard week and felt not a little sorry for myself. Supposedly, I was looking for an umbrella to buy, but I was really trying to leave the week behind. Near the end of the concourse I sat down on a low bench. I could hear water behind me, but I was immersed in thought. Suddenly, someone beside me turned and said, "It's beautiful, isn't it?" I turned to look at the speaker, and said, "I beg your pardon?" "The fountain," he replied. I turned round to look at the fountain. Water was spurting towards ceiling under pressure from hundreds of spouts, and then falling with a crash. It was indeed beautiful. I stood up to avoid the crick developing in my neck. After a time of looking at it, I got the strangest feeling that the fountain was inside me: I could feel new life coursing up my body. I said to the man, "Yes, it is indeed, beautiful." And then I was driven to say, "And thank you." I walked away astonished at the power of that simple incident to breathe new life into me, and the strangeness in the midst of life that allows the most unlikely people to say the right thing at the right time. I found that I had just taken a little journey to the center of awareness. The question arises: How do I know this is an authentic experience of transparency? One test is the presence of awe in the event.

AWE

As we saw in Chapter 3, certain events carry within them a statement on our lives. We can try to evade that statement all we like, but it refuses to go away. The way we know it's real for us is the presence of awe. The experience of transparency throws us into the presence of awe. Awe is experienced as something external, like something filling up our interior space or the room. Awe is a sign of the presence of mystery in our midst. It is the forerunner and accompaniment of experiences of transparency. It has many faces. As Rudolf Otto points out in *The Idea of the Holy*, awe is always dread and fascination at the same time. It is the stirring of something uncanny, eerie or weird. It may take the form of shuddering; a sign that the mysterious may already be looming before the mind and touching the feelings. Or it may feel like a Queen's Birthday or Fourth of July fireworks display inside. There is an energy in it that is compelling and alive.

Awe is a definer of humanness. You have to be a human being to experience awe. No matter how many human properties apes or cats or dolphins may possess, the experience of awe is not one of them. Awe is as objective as bananas. When awe is encountered by a group, it is palpable, sometimes even frightening. Time seems to stand still. The pulse beats faster or slower. When a person experiences awe, it may be heavy (dread) or light (fascination). It may come with a tingle, or an odour, like roses or sulphur. It comes in all varieties, accompanied by a wide range of emotions, all the way from radical insecurity to ecstasy.

The 20th century has been full of collective experiences of awe: the wonder of airplane flight, the sinking of the *Titanic*, Hiroshima, the beep-beep-beep of the first spacecraft making its way across the night sky, the terrible angst of the Challenger disaster, the fall of the Iron Curtain, the wonder of the Internet's connectivity, the rise of globalization, and many more were all events dripping with awe, some full of dread, others replete with fascination.

The awe present in events of transparency is not some kind of individual pious, or even psychological, experience. Awe happens when we break through our experience to transparency.

Descriptions of transparency are ΩΩΩΩΩΩΩΩΩ in the language of *states of being*. When the awe of a transparent event impacts us, there is an accompanying *state of being*.

STATES OF BEING

A little philosophy here. By the time the 20th century rolled around, two main currents of Western philosophy had established themselves: empiricism, with its interest in objectivity, and rationalism with its idealistic view of objectivity. On the one hand empiricism made the world seem like an impersonal machine, unaffected by the way people live and think. And on the other, rational idealism tended to factor out the world, leaving only brooding, self-absorbed thought.

Thanks to the German Jewish philosopher Edmund Husserl, a third way of thought was introduced to the West: phenomenology. According to phenomenologists, the tendency to see awareness and reality as two separate things has led people to lose sight of their own experience. As a result they see reality from an artificial point of view in which their own lives and experiences are unimportant. Husserl and, later, Einstein and many others, deplored the way in which science since Descartes had imposed its attitude of objectivity on the world. The result is an "objective" reality with the human significance stripped away.

So, what is a state of being? Joseph Mathews spoke of it as "a big think", or awareness, "a big feel", and "a big resolve," all intertwined. For example, when my wife Jeanette and I had been married a few months, she began gently to raise the possibility of leaving Australia and taking an overseas assignment to another ICA location. I had never been out of Australia. The very idea of leaving it seemed utterly alien and fearful to me. One day, when we were lying on Maroubra Beach in Sydney after a surf, she broached the matter again in more direct terms. Her words had a real wallop, like a George Foreman punch to the solar plexus. I remember that I began to shiver (not because of the dip I had taken), then I turned away from her and pretended I hadn't heard the question. Actually, I was in a blue funk, terrified of what lay beyond Australia. Like Columbus' crew setting sail for the New World, I thought that once I left the shore, I would drop into a terrible abyss. That was the big feel. As we went home I continued to brood on the incident with dread. It was as if my wife, so gentle and unassuming, had turned into a blow torch for me. My big think was: the Mystery had lit a fire under my backside and I wasn't prepared for that, not lying on Maroubra Beach, soaking up the sun. The resolve was something like this: Stanfield, maybe you'd better start thinking about what it would take to dive off the high board into that abyss.

B. THE OTHER WORLD IN THE MIDST OF THIS WORLD

Some years ago, ICA staff did an extensive research project on states of being. They attempted to itemize and describe the different states of being one could experience. They came up with 64 states of being arranged in a series of charts called *The Other World in the Midst of This World*. The charts use the image of breaking through this ordinary world to the other world because of profoundly human experiences. This happens in the midst of our ordinary, mundane life, when life reaches out and grabs us, shakes us up, and drops us into the depths. We get into a conversation with a colleague, and, all of a sudden, the words our colleague is saying seem to drip with awe, and we realize we have just taken a quick trip to the "other world." We pick up a newspaper, and read of another car bomb in another Irish township, we see the photo of the dead and wounded, and life reaches out and grabs us again.

This other world exists only and always in the midst of this world. The other world comes into focus at the limits of our reason, but only and always in everyday things and events. It's the same old world, but with a glow. It's as if everything, everywhere, all the time reveals its meaning.

In the experience of the other world, a metamorphosis goes on in our interior being in which everything is changed, but nothing is different. The experience of the other world re-sensitizes us to the spirit deeps, to the experience of the awe, the foundational experience of all our affections.

This is a reality that every one of us can experience. We do, however, have a tendency to flee from these encounters with the deeps. But those of us who dare to stand present to our experiences and be aware of our own awareness can experience epiphany upon epiphany.

In our research, we found that the states of being in the other world fall under four different categories: states of being related to mystery, to consciousness, to care, and to tranquillity. Just as this world has in it land, rivers, mountains and seas, we saw in the other world, poetically speaking, the land of mystery, the river of consciousness, the freedom of every human being to live a creative life. We discover the mountain of care, as people wake up caring and ready to expend themselves for others. We discover the sea of tranquillity, the experience of unfathomable light, peace and joy in the midst of pain and woes. We no longer ask what life all about. We see four dimensions: mystery, consciousness, care, and fulfilment or tranquillity.

The charts in this chapter were assembled by ICA to create a map of the journey to the other world and provide a way to talk about it. We saw them as as set of images for articulating experience of people in the wonder and joy of two worlds. It is not seen as the final solution but as a step towards the participation of people like ourselves in the wonder and joy of two worlds, as a set of images for articulating experiences of the Other World in the Midst of This World. Perhaps I hear the post-modern reader saying, "Hey, why the big deal with all the schemas and charts? The stories are great on their own. We don't need all those chart categories!" While there is a postmodern incredulity towards the kind of meta-narrative of these Other World charts, there is also a deep longing for the kind of whole-system integrated knowledge that they hold.

Many times, I experience things in my life that I don't have a "handle" for. The charts help me to name those experiences without passing them off with a shrug. The poetry and metaphors used in the charts give us some language to mix in with our own poetry about our experiences with the other world. We can use these charts in a journal exercise where we combine their images and language with particular experiences they recall in our lives to produce our own poetic reflections.

Some states of being have more to do with the mystery in the midst of life: with confronting the infinite. They are experiences of wonder and humility related to being impacted, enveloped, recreated, and seduced by the mystery of life. Some have referred to the aggregation of these experiences as The Land of Mystery.

Some states of being are more related to the experience of constructing the self—inventing one's freedom of awareness, of inventiveness, of decision and obligation. They are related to the capacity of the self to transcend itself. These states are like being on a River of Consciousness.

Other states of being involve overwhelming care or responsibility in relating to the world—states of care as appreciation, compassion, responsibility, and motivity. These are the states of being experienced by the social pioneer, the community development worker, the doctor working at the medical edge trying to find a cure for AIDS, or the retired person teaching a child to read. We find them in our expenditure on behalf of others, the experience of care as a mountain, luring us irresistibly beyond ourselves. These states are on the mountain of care.

Finally there are states of being associated with difficulties, suffering and even death—certitude, problemlessness, contentment, and everlastingness. We find them when we feel confident in the midst of ambiguity, peace in the midst of stress, fulfilment in the midst of fragmentation, the eternal in the midst of finitude. These are the boundless states of being of the sea of tranquillity.

Life is full of such awe-filled, transparent experiences. We tend to forget about these moments, but when we remember one of them, it burns again for us.

Most of the important things in our past worth remembering are those times when the mundane blazed with insight and awe. Thinking of all the food one has eaten or all the fine times you have had does no good whatsoever; it just illuminates your misery in contrast. But remembering all of the moments of transparency you have are present to the mystery in the moment, it is as if all those moments in your past light up again.

HOW WE MIGHT USE THE CHARTS

How might we use these charts? There are several ways. One of the most simple is to photocopy the Other world charts, and use them for reflection.

Think back on your day and see if there is one event that is still reverbering in your being. Ask yourself whether it was more related to mystery, consciousness, care or tranquillity. Once you have narrowed it down, run your eyes down the columns of that till you find a state of being that seems to correspond. Now read the categories across the chart to check whether you have the right state of being. If you don't, keep looking till you have narrowed it down. If you can't find it, perhaps the state of being is on another chart.

Once you have done this a few times you get the hang of it. At the end of the day, you can pull out the charts, and run through them till you find the state of being and the language to describe it.

Suppose, at the office, within the space of one hour of your morning's work, you saw how to solve a critical problem that had been bothered you for weeks, a client called to confirm a substantial contract, and your wife phoned to let you know that your daughter had got a full scholarship to Harvard. At the last one, you let out a war whoop, then started to dance through the office, yelling, "Jumpin' Jehosaphats! I'm de man!" The rest of the office, startled, had made you stop and tell everything. At which point the boss called you into his office to tell you that you must be due for a substantial raise on the strength of the contract and your problem-solving capacities. In the evening, after you have come down to earth, you recall your day, and pull out your charts to see where that event showed up. You figure it might be the Land of Mystery, so you run down that chart. It is in trek III, somewhere between states of being 11 and 12, so you can use the language of both:

The Big Think: is something like: all is possible.

The Big Feel: forever surprised

The Big Resolve: life is endless celebration

You realize that you are having the time of your life.

The decision to stand present to the transparency of life as ordinary experiences open up to mystery, consciousness, care and tranqillity reveals that meaning is always there to be tapped. The charts give you a way to process the events of life so that the other world constantly bleeds through. Anyone who wants to make a difference in society with their life, will need to have access to the Other world; otherwise their care will burn them to a crisp. The charts allow us to get healing from what happens rather than be knocked over by it. They can help us understand in depth what is going on in our lives.

Finally, some events in life are so weird that it is natural to say, "I think I'm going out of my mind; no one ever told me about this." The Other World poetry gives us a way to say, "I'm not insane. This is a universal human experience; a lot of other people have gone through this."

One note of warning. Every religious tradition that points to a dimension of reality other than that immediately accessible to sense experience agrees on the danger of this kind of work. He who does not trust the Other World finds it dangerous turf. It can play tricks on one, even lay one low, especially the person who perceives the Other world but says no to entering it, or enters it half-heartedly. Some return from the experience as zombies—quite lucid about life, but hate-filled towards it. Thus, the Other World can turn out to be heaven or hell. The capacity to affirm our experience is as important in the Other world as it is in this world.

Before we go on, it might be helpful to state a few truths about transparency and states of being.

1. Such experiences are beyond the realm of good and evil. They are about states of being—the ontology of human experiences.

2. There is no sentiment in states of being. The experience of great moments of depth meaning does not liberate us from the tragedy of this world.

3. Similarly there is no hierarchy in states of being. No one state of being is better than any other, any way you look at it.

4. In the same way, states of being have no class structure. Everyone has access to them whenever they happen.

C. THE POETRY OF TRANSPARENCY

Poetry enables us to experience what the poet experienced when meaning bled through the mundane to the essence of life itself. It also gives us the opportunity to experience our own experience.

CONVENTIONAL POETRY

Gerard Manley Hopkins provides one sharply focused example of the poetry of transparency—poetry that is transparent to life's meaning. One of his poems begins with an autumn scene in which a grove of trees is losing its leaves and the onlooker, Margaret, expresses her sorrow over the fact. The poet asks her:

> Margaret, are you grieving
> Over Goldengrove unleaving?

The poet goes on to comment that, as she grows older, she will experience sights much sadder than that. Then he pushes through the event to the universal, or what is true for all people—sorrow's springs are the same: the death that we are all destined for.

It is the blight man was born for

It is Margaret you mourn for.

In looking at the dead leaves falling off the trees in Goldengrove, Margaret is really mourning her own death. Here, an ordinary event suddenly became an occasion that illumines life in great depth and intensity.

Some poetry helps us to experience what we are experiencing. Anyone who experiences weariness frequently in their life work will resonate with this poem of former UN Secretary-General Dag Hammarskjold in his *Markings*:

Tired

and lonely,

So tired

The heart aches,

Meltwater trickles

Down the rocks,

The fingers are numb,

The knees tremble.

It is now,

Now, that you must not give in.

Weep

If you can,

Weep,

But do not complain,

The way chose you—

And you must be thankful.

Such a poem prompts reflection. The poet seems to be climbing a mountain. We find ourselves asking, What mountain am I climbing? What makes me want to give in? What is it that makes me want to weep? What is "the way" that has chosen us? How can I decide to be thankful when I am bone-weary?

Another way to reflect on this poem is to view it as a secular psalm. These questions might be useful:

1. What is the state of being the poet is experiencing?

2. What happened to the poet the day before?

If we know anything of Hammarksjold's life, we might say, "Well, maybe he was at the United Nations Security Council, pleading with them to intervene in the Congo struggle, and he met with stony faces." If we don't know much of the poet's background, we could put ourselves in his place and create an answer from our own lives.

3. What was the poet's "aha" the next morning? What did he realize?

As we read the poet thoughtfully, we find that our own life experience is being interpreted for us with a new slant.

SONGS OF TRANSPARENCY

Songs can play the same role as poetry. We can reflect on the transparency that shines through great popular songs, even a simple old song like "Nevertheless":

> Maybe I'm right and maybe I'm wrong
> Maybe I'm weak and maybe I'm strong,
> But nevertheless I'm in love with you.

The key to reflecting on old classic love songs like this is that we set them next to own life situation. Maybe the "you" really is a lover; but maybe it's a project I have taken on, or the class of kids I teach, or a sculpture I'm working on.

Whatever our situation, when we ask questions like the following, the song's poetry can illuminate our situation. Or perhaps it is our our situation that illuminates the song's words.

1. What words or phrases became transparent for you?

2. What experiences from your past did you see when you looked through?

3. Where does this song speak to a situation in your own life at present?

4. What profound insight did the writer have when writing the song?

Many of the classic songs of Gershwin, Rogers and Hammerstein, and Cole Porter are amenable to this kind of reflection: "Night and Day". "Some Enchanted Evening", "I Could Have Danced All Night", "Smoke Gets in My Eyes", "I'll Be Seeing You" and many others all have this capacity for transparency.

Perhaps the reader is saying, "Well, that's all right to talk about the golden oldies, but what about rock and roll or contemporary music? Does it have this capacity for transparency?" This song by Los Angeles singer Ben Harper (lyrics by Maya Angelou) is in a radically different mode; the question is always: does it speak transparently to my situation? Can I ground the experience of the writer in my own life:

You may write me down in history
With your bitter twisted lies.
You may trod me down in the very earth
And still like the dust I'll rise.
Does my happiness upset you?
Why are you beset with gloom?
'Cause I laugh like I've got an oil well
Pumpin' in my living room
So you may shoot me with your words
You may cut me with your eyes
And I'll rise
I'll rise
I'll rise

The Other World

Area A • The Land of Mystery *humility god wonder*

	Objective pronouncement	Titles *you and me*	*myself and I*	Subjective declaration
Trek I **The awefull encounter** Impacted by mystery *the last up-againstness*	**1** death awaits every man	the time of my death	I am a condemned man	it just cannot be that way
	2 all is absurd	the eternal riddle	I am beyond reason	nothing makes sense
	3 finally no-thing	the last of the secrets	I am without ground	no place to stand
	4 and it's all a cloud of awe	lost in quicksand	I am in wonder	and everything is swirling
Trek II **The inescapable power** Enveloped by mystery *there is no escape*	**5** always in the midst	a foot in two worlds	I am both-and	it's all around me everywhere
	6 every moment	creeping with meaning	I am surrounded	no place to go
	7 no escape	the invisible force	I am caught in the middle	no way to win
	8 and everything's out in the open	the cosmic eye	I am stripped naked	and I'm absolutely vulnerable
Trek III **The transformed state** Recreated by mystery *all things are new*	**9** a strange power is borning	the giant stirs	I am really alive	everything is simply exploding
	10 everything is different	a stranger in paradise	I am transplanted	nothing is the same
	11 I am something else	my recent metamorphosis	I am not what I was	including me
	12 and life is endless celebration	everybody's banquet	I am perpetually new	and I'm having the time of my life
Trek IV **The inflnite passion** Seduced by mystery *the adoration of being*	**13** it's absolutely incredible	the spoof of life	I am unsettled	I can't believe it's true
	14 forever unknowable	the masked mystery	I am excluded	it's all beyond me
	15 eternally remote	the lonely one	I am abandoned	nothing seems secure
	16 and love has won the day	the perfect love	I am enraptured	and I'm just about to surrender

	Reflective *subject*	*concept*	**Affective** *a sense of*	*like being*	**Analogy** *it's like*
1	the creatureliness of man	radical contingency	terrifying numbness	mortally stunned	hearing the worms cough
2	the irrationality of life	absurd existence	benign madness	critically disorientated	riding a tilt-a-whirl
3	the absoluteness of nothing	ultimate reality	intense shock	irrevocably outcast	wandering in a thick fog
4	the objectivity of awe	primordial wonder	total paralysis	helplessly suspended	hanging over molten lead
5	the meaning of the eternal moment	incarnate living	double identity	fatally split	experiencing bi-location
6	the significance of omnipresence	ubiquitous otherness	constant pursuit	under surveillance	having nowhere else to run
7	the relevance of omnipotence	final limits	chronic weakness	perpetually conquered	racing in a field of tar
8	the import of omniscience	total exposure	deep guilt	permanently embarrassed	standing nude in Times Square
9	the unleashed vitality	vibrant powers	eerie strength	intensely enlivened	opening the floodgates
10	the transposed perspective	transformed existence	joyful anxiety	radically relocated	waking up on another planet
11	the actuality of possibility	second birth	trustful expectation	unconditionally recast	recovering from amnesia
12	the reality of change	dynamic selfhood	forever surprised	ceaselessly evolving	watching a pinwheel explode
13	the eternal apostasy	essential dubiety	irrational self-doubt	shatteringly ridiculed	feeling you've really been had
14	the revelation of enigma	cryptic disclosure	secret resentment	totally injured	being finally excommunicated
15	the unclosable gap	transcendent immanence	insatiable yearning	chronically homesick	knowing you'll never go home
16	the honor of the mystery	singular adoration	burning desire	hopelessly enamored	being reluctantly love-sick

The Other World

Area B • The River of Consciousness *freedom self awareness*

		Objective pronouncement	Titles *you and me*	*myself and I*	Subjective declaration
Trek V **The authentic relation** Freedom of awareness *I am my consciousness*	17	finally all is consciousness	me and my shadow	I am my awareness	I'm at the center
	18	transparently grounded	the last mystery	I am groundless	standing on nothing
	19	creating myself	the invented man	I am forming myself	building myself
	20	and there's a hole at the center	the unfinished symphony	I am never finished	and with no hope of any completion
Trek VI **The creative existence** Freedom of inventiveness *I am my originality*	21	a child of the fates	wheel of fortune	I am my temporality	this is the way I showed up
	22	yet no one to blame	without defense	I am my circumstance	there's no excuse
	23	we design our world	you've made your bed	I am my universe	I'm the architect
	24	and become the sign of life	the son of Adam	I am my species	and come do as I do
Trek VII **The moral ground** Freedom of decision *I am my conscience*	25	beyond good and evil	crossing the river	I am my stance	I determine good and evil
	26	we decide it all	all is permitted	I am my conscience	keep my own conscience
	27	wholly accepted	the beloved of being	I am well pleasing	am simply a delight
	28	and with a charge to keep	the king's business	I am commissioned	and I'm here on business
Trek VIII **The final accountability** Freedom of obligation *I am my answerability*	29	at last my native vale	long journey home	I am not a stranger	this world is not my home
	30	the gods take flight	the fallen angels	I am single-minded	all is relative
	31	the yoke is easy	the untouchable	I am unburdened	I just don't care
	32	and the mystery has its moment	the day the world ended	I am ordered answerable	and there's the ultimate court

	Reflective *subject*	*concept*	**Affective** *a sense of*	*like being*	**Analogy** *it's like*
17	the consciousness of consciousness	ultimate awareness	frozen lucidity	incessantly shocked	being hit by lightning
18	the relation to no-thing	eternal relation	incredible precariousness	irredeemably empty	standing on a mile of air
19	the being that creates itself	self transcendence	horrifying boundlessness	ceaselessly bewildered	meeting yourself coming back
20	the becoming within being	perpetual becoming	everlasting emptiness	unquenchably thirsting	discovering you can't stop the leak
21	the facticity of life	universal fate	unbelievable aloneness	suddenly adrift	being the stakes in a dice game
22	the given is my responsibility	relational situation	exclusive wakefulness	absolutely vulnerable	having no one to tell your troubles to
23	the world we create	contextual world-view	dreadful suffocation	unbearably entrusted	being asked to lift ten tons
24	the measure of a man	archetypal humanness	reckless impertinence	terrifyingly nonchalant	being elected the world's president
25	the ground of ethics	beyond morality	sudden reeling	scandalously intrigued	having broken thru a police barricade
26	the basis of judgement	intentional conscience	exquisite ambiguity	ludicrously unconstrained	being lost in a wilderness
27	the approval of being	cosmic sanctions	indefinable significance	exceptionally precious	finding your glass marble is a diamond
28	the one essential task	primal vocation	absurd election	destinally designated	being a Martian undercover agent
29	the eternal at-one-ment	original integrity	inexplicable rootedness	securely anchored	feeling you've been here before
30	a practical monotheism	worldly detachment	painful relief	surprisedly victorious	losing all your friends at once
31	the relativity of covenants	passionate disinterest	anxious deliverance	fearfully courageous	feeling your kite string break
32	the final judgement	destinal accountability	unconditioned submission	devastatingly obliged	having accelerator stick at 90 mph

The Other World

Area C • The Mountain of Care *service world agape*

	Objective pronouncement	Titles *you and me*	*myself and I*	Subjective declaration
Trek IX **The original gratitude** Agape is appreciation *I'm in love with life*	**33** a person just shows up	the human adventure	I am living a journey	I am given the chance to do a life
	34 on this planet	no universe next door	I am given a situation	in the only world there is
	35 with a lot of others	the family of being	I am one with totality	along with every creature
	36 and everything is unexplainable	nothing busting out all over	I am honoring the deeps	and each is a presence
Trek X **The universal concern** Agape is compassion *binding wounds of time*	**37** one day you just care	my brother's keeper	I am concerned	I now belong to all creation
	38 for the whole world	never look back	I am totally engaged	to serve it
	39 with all your heart	teardrops on the window	I am on the altar	with all my heart
	40 and then you get caught in doom	a far, far better thing	I am expendable	and to the cost of my life
Trek XI **The singular mission** Agape is responsibility for *everything is my brother*	**41** responsibility for all that is	I've got it all in my hands	I am the guardian	the world has become my ward
	42 what's no longer	in the beginning	I am savior of the past	plus all that's gone before
	43 what's not yet	tomorrow is forever	I am the future	plus all that's to come
	44 and there's no one to show the way	mister universe	I am history	and there isn't any pattern
Trek XII **The transparent power** Agape is motivity *the strength of ten*	**45** suddenly you see through all	the other wise man	I am clairvoyant	everything is suddenly clear
	46 develop a strange power	the pillar of iron	I am the rock	here I stand
	47 speak with authority	the healer	I am a charismatic	people are listening
	48 and begin to move mountains	the impossible deed	I am a miracle worker	and look at all that's happening

	Reflective subject	concept	Affective a sense of	like being	Analogy it's like
33	the incredibility of occurrence	individual fatefulness	breathless amazement	uniquely preferred	winning the super Nobel Prize
34	the arbitrariness of our universe	definitive predestination	hidden rancor	eternally immured	feeling a gun at your head
35	the oneness of all creation	temporal solidarity	unbounded rapport	awfully yoked	having a rock for an uncle
36	the mystery within each thing	sacramental universe	wondrous harmony	wholly engulfed	being perpetually astonished
37	the ground of human concern	primal sympathy	unabashed caring	freely bound	mistaking yourself for another
38	the explosion of fellow feeling	universal compassion	wide horizons	relentlessly driven	migrating to the moon
39	the consuming mission	sacrificial passion	continual sadness	emotionally drained	taking a one way trip
40	the identification with doom	soteriological existence	inevitable expenditure	poured out	swinging off the high dive
41	the care for the world	global guardianship	deep paralysis	forever encumbered	taking charge of history
42	the appropriation of the past	ancestral obligation	irrational inertia	burdened down	existing before dawn
43	the task of creation	futuric responsibility	heavy weakness	over rated	being ahead of all time
44	the burden of election	invented history	hilarious absurdity	devastatingly ridiculed	having the only set of keys
45	the gift of depth perception	diaphanous intuition	intellectual aching	beyond yourself	looking through a stone wall
46	the gift of depth motivity	interior discipline	incurable loneliness	eternally primed	imitating the Rock of Gibraltar
47	the gift of depth communication	impactful profundity	cautious confidence	unequalled adequacy	being forever on-stage
48	the gift of depth accomplishment	definitive effectivity	aweful danger	deadly accurate	commanding mountains to move

The Other World

Area D • The Sea of Tranquillity *fulfilment death happiness*

		Objective pronouncement	Titles *you and me*	*myself and I*	Subjective declaration
Trek XIII **The radical illumination** Certitude at the center	49	there's suddenly light both ways	the last dawn	I am in the light	I think I found Hesperides
light shines in shadows	50	you know everything	the fountainhead	I am learnedness	all is clear
	51	meaning is everywhere	the aweful truth	I am the Christ bearer	the logos too
	52	and you've become an avatar	one from depth	I am the way	and I'm the very keystone
Trek XIV **The unknowable peace** Problemlessness at the center	53	there is a strange victory	cynicism revisited	I am hoping against hope	I am now beyond expectation
security dwells in trials	54	no worldly cares	gone is the couch	I am de-burdened	burdens down
	55	no earthly foes	in search of enemies	I am enemy-less	nothing to hate
	56	and only integrity everyday	the great dragon	I am my own war	and it's just Satan and I
Tre k XV **The unspeakable joy** Contentment at the center	57	there is a different elan	the virgin spring	I am vibrant	I'm simply all a-tingle
rapture walks with woe	58	showers of blessing	let the sunshine in	I am gratitude	everything's a gift
	59	a strange gladness	my cup runneth over	I am effulgence	struck dumb by bliss
	60	and everything's worthwhile	happy death	I am my happiness	and what a time to die
Trek XVI **The endless life** Everlastingness at the center	61	for those who dare to die	the living dead	I am expired	I'm really very dead
death where is thy sting	62	there is another life	walking through walls	I am alive again	yet risen
	63	with those who passed	listen to the dead	I am community	with the saints
	64	and eternality is everywhere	grave, where is thy victory	I am more than conqueror	and on the way to forever

	Reflective		**Affective**		**Analogy**
	subject	*concept*	*a sense of*	*like being*	*it's like*
49	the all-embracing gestalt	seminal illumination	irrational convergence	unreservedly liberated	looking directly into the sun
50	the wisdom from nowhere	inclusive comprehension	shocking cognizance	absurdly assured	knowing the mind of God
51	the universal secret	contentless word	image explosion	sacredly empowered	discovering the mother lode
52	the embodied truth	personal epiphany	intriguing terror	preposterously nominated	being the last soul on a flying 747
53	the hope of no hope	creative futility	interior silence	perpetually released	running an endless marathon
54	the absence of cares	problemless living	detached trust	alertly relaxed	resting easy on a bed of nails
55	the freedom from hatred	transcended hostility	patient regard	cleanly restored	emerging from a stuffy sewer
56	the only human struggle	exclusive contradiction	sweet struggle	endlessly embattled	narrowing the war to one front
57	the animation of the deeps	vital spirits	throbbing exhilaration	tautly coiled	taking a cold shower
58	the acknowledge-ment of goods	spontaneous gratitude	teeming life	unavoidably plunged	receiving a bundle of gifts
59	the moments of rapture	blissful seizure	fitful dancing	electrifyingly alive	glowing after a mountain trek
60	the meaning of beatitude	final blessedness	enraptured stillness	harmoniously surrounded	playing in a great symphony
61	the dying to self	living death	physical detachment	gloriousiy condemned	waking up totally dead
62	the life of the dead one	resurrectional existence	objective power	irresistibly impelled	waltzing on the water
63	the fellowship of saints	everlasting community	supporting fraternity	agelessly wise	marching with all of history
64	the life beyond the grave	contingent eternality	existing forever	eternally present	reversing the time machine

Exercise

1. Brainstorm five significant events from your own life that hold different states of being. Put a star beside the event that has the state of being that is clearest to you:

_____

_____

_____

_____

_____

2. Describe the starred event briefly.

3. Write a sentence on what the Big Think was that came to you as a result of that event, or from reflecting on the event.

4. Write a sentence on the Big Feel of the event—you can use some of the language from the state of being description in the Other world chart, or make up your own description of how it felt, or both.

5. As a result of the event, your Big Think on the event, and the Big Feel that went with it, what kind of resolve just wells up within you, either then or now?

6. Write a *haiku* about any one of these experiences you have remembered. A haiku has three lines with five syllables in the first line, seven in the second, and five in the third. You can be as poetic and indirect as you like, but keep the poetry grounded in the event or state.

7. To start working with the states of being in the Other World charts, go back through each song or piece of poetry quoted in this chapter and relate it to a particular state of being. First, relate it to a topography: does it belong best in the Land of Mystery, the River of Consciousness, the Mountain of Care, or the Sea of Tranquillity? Then which trek does it relate to? Then which state of being does it reflect most closely?

CHAPTER 6

Profound Vocation

I Can Make a Difference

> This is the true joy in life, the being used for a purpose recognized by yourself as a mighty one;…being a force of nature instead of a selfish little clod of ailments and grievances complaining that the world will not devote itself to making you happy.
>
> GEORGE BERNARD SHAW

> It takes great passion and great energy to do anything creative….You have to care so much that you can't sleep, you can't eat, you can't talk to other people. It's just got to be right. You can't do it without that passion.
>
> AGNES DE MILLE

THE QUESTION OF THE HEADSTONE

Years ago, while teaching a course in Saskatoon. I stayed in an old hotel. On the day before the course started, I was poking round and found my way down to the basement. Lo and behold, there was a kind of carpenter's workshop where coffins were being made. No one was around. There was one coffin, sitting on trestles, with the lid lying slantwise across the top. Driven by some whimsy, I clambered up into the coffin, lay down, then pulled the top over me. I guess I wanted a surrogate experience of being entombed. I had no profound experience. Instead, lulled by the darkness and silence, I just fell asleep. I woke some time later, when a colleague came to call me to supper. I answered from inside the coffin. His fright got quite a few laughs at the dinner table.

Putting ourselves in our coffin or inside the urn of ashes makes for an interesting reflective exercise. In the case of the grave site, we can picture the headstone, see our name carved with the date of our birth and death. And the epitaph. What words would be inscribed in the stone to sum up the whole purpose of our life? "Husband of Sally, father of James? Or "I did a hole in one?" Or "I made ten million?" Or, "I gave my life to change the face of education in my community?" Most of us will find it's a real challenge to answer that question: what few words would summarize our vocation and life work?

Unfortunately, the word, *vocation*, for a long time was monopolized by the church to refer to the "calling" experienced by clergy, monks and nuns, and by the professions to refer to the work of architects, doctors, lawyers, or nurses, or to those in technical training in a vocational school. I remember a visit to our high school by a religious-order recruiter. After talking at length about the vocation of being in a religious order, he asked us to write on a slip of paper *yes*, if we had a vocation, *no* if we were definitely not interested, or *maybe* if we might have a vocation. I found out later that he interviewed all the yesses and maybes. I found myself on the horns of a dilemma. The headhunter was a big, big man, and I was a very small young man. I, not wishing to commit, yet not wanting to displease, wrote, maybe—a little word which set me on the path of 20 years' experience in a Roman Catholic religious order.

Vocation is an issue for all of us, not just those who commit to religious life or a profession. Each of us is a quantum of energy. If we look around today we see a lot of people without any focused way to expend their life energy. They seem to have little sense of their life work, or even their purpose in living. A lot of us equate these terms with our job, but life purpose refers to far more than the kind of job we have, although it is related to it.

Finding our vocation does not come easily for most of us. It is a matter of aligning three things:

- the needs of society

- our own interior needs related to our inclinations, our gifts, and our sense of potential

- our life purpose.

Knowing our vocation is just the beginning. For vocation is a life journey with different phases. Three parts in this vocational journey can be identified:

1. the recognition of our vocation

2. vocational crisis and surviving betrayal

3. persistence—keeping on keeping on.

And quite often the vocation itself changes.

LOCKED-UP ENERGY

Poet David Whyte describes the energy in each one of us waiting to be expended:

> Always this energy smoulders inside;
> when it remains unlit
> the body fills with dense smoke.

James Hillman and Michael Ventura in *We've Had a Hundred Years of Psychotherapy and the World Is Getting Worse* point to one area of locked-up energy. They assert that psychotherapy has exaggerated self-searching and neglected what the world wants from the self. Therapy has turned good citizens into "patients" and locked their civic engagement into ongoing therapy. According to the two authors, we have to work on cures that are beyond my cure, not just parents, childhood, or relationship problems. The dysfunction in the society is affecting us. "You can't sign a peace treaty with society through therapy."

A second place where energy is locked up, at least in Western culture, is in seniors. Society imposes a role on people as they reach a certain chronological age. "At this age," in the words of social scientist Alex Comfort, "they retire, or in plain words, are rendered unemployed, useless and in some cases impoverished.... It is a demeaning idleness, not being called on any longer to contribute, and hence being put down as a spent person of no public account, instructed to run away and play until death comes out to call us to bed." We know how to fritter away years of experience and much acquired wisdom on the golf course, or just sitting at home, doing nothing in particular—the kind of disengagement T.S. Eliot describes in "The Love Song of J. Alfred Prufrock:"

> I grow old . . .I grow old . . .
> I shall wear the bottoms of my trousers rolled.
> Shall I part my hair behind? Do I dare to eat a peach?

Alex Comfort calls for "a second trajectory" for retirees—a new way to re-engage, but in a way more suited to their years; in other words, to find the vocation for the rest of their lives. The elder's role is a great role—the historical statesman, the wise woman; the symbol of transcendent wisdom. The elder encourages those around to reflection. Even in the 70s and 80s of one's life it's possible to dream new dreams for society—witness grey-haired Nelson Mandela leading South Africa into a new multi-racial destiny; Michelangelo undertaking his greatest work, St. Peters in Rome, at 79; Golda Meir playing a leadership role in Israel in her seventies; Frank Lloyd Wright completing his masterpiece, the Guggenheim Museum, at 91. At any age, there is room for new beginnings and fresh ventures useful to society.

Vocational energy is also locked up in the family. People marry partners they feel they can be happy with. Some seek partners who will, hopefully, preserve them from much of the pain of the world, help them build a cocoon to protect them from unhappiness and despair. The home can become another bottomless pit into which they try to pump the whole Sears catalogue as well as Martha Stewart's products, only to realize that their fine purchases all end in garage sales. There is little time for community, except getting the kids to school, and maybe going to PTA meetings. Life is jobs plus home. There is little sense of common purpose that might keep them going when all the rest caves in. So, instead of growing together, marriages flame as each partner blames the other for failing to support them psychologically. A common life purpose can keep a family moving forward.

Another place where energy and creativity get locked up is in our everyday work. Our economic structures deny the usable energy of the unemployed, so millions of people feel terrible about being unemployed. At the same time, employed people are often woefully unhappy about their work, yet it can be incredibly difficult to leave even unsatisfying jobs in order to find something that matches their interest and passion. The fact is that most people labor through their life without ever fulfilling their life purpose. What would it take to challenge the pattern of unfulfilled living, and give people the possibility of finding fulfilment by doing their life's work?

LIFE PURPOSE

Judy Harvie has spent a lifetime helping people through vocational transitions like this. She writes:

> Endings bring with them confusion and interrupted identity. New beginnings require letting go, allowing wide open dreaming of new paths and images.... In order to move through this period of perceived chaos, we need to develop skills which will help us meet our physical, emotional and social needs. Coping skills

include physical exercise, massage, visioning, relaxation, meditation and keeping a journal; as well as forming a social support network of family, friends, and sometimes therapists. Using these skills and support we can acknowledge, accept and defuse our negative emotions, allowing us to move on safely to the redefinition of who we are. Instead of thinking we are what we do, we need to learn to think about who we are and how we express ourselves in our talents, interests and values.

Sometimes, this can be just a matter of switching the story about the work engaged in. Psychologist Roberto Assagioli tells a story about interviewing three stonecutters building a cathedral in the 14th century.

When the first stonecutter is asked what he is doing, the man replies with bitterness that he is cutting stones into blocks, a foot by a foot by three quarters of a foot. With frustration, he describes a life in which he has done this over and over, and will continue to do it until he dies. The second stonecutter is also cutting stones into blocks, a foot by a foot by three-quarters of a foot, but he replies in a somewhat different way. With warmth, he tells the interviewer that he is earning a living for his beloved family; through this work, his children have clothes and food to grow strong, he and his wife have a home which they have filled with love. But the response of the third stonecutter is radically different. In a joyous voice, he tells us of the privilege of participating in the building of this great cathedral, so strong that it will stand as a holy lighthouse for a thousand years.

In *Working*, the inimitable Studs Terkel invites ordinary people to talk about their work. One of his interviews was with a stonecutter who talked about his work like this:

> It's a pretty good day laying stone or brick. Not tiring. Anything you like to do isn't tiresome. It's hard work: stone is heavy. At the same time you get interested in what you're doing and you fight the clock the other way. You're not Martha' for quittin'…. Stone's my life. I daydream all the time, most times it's on stone…. All my dreams, it seems like it's got to have a piece of rock mixed in it…. I can't imagine a job where you go home and maybe go by a year later and you don't know what you've done. There's not a house in this county that I haven't built that I don't look at every time I go by. If there's one stone in there crooked, I know where it's at and I'll never forget it.

"Life purpose" points beyond jobs to something that people decide to commit their lives to. Once you clarify this basic purpose, then you have multiple options for significant work. For example, you may say, "My life is about promoting a healthy lifestyle: I am now selling insurance both to support my 'real' aim and as a vehicle through which to meet people and to encourage healthy practices. I also belong to a health club and volunteer time with a local clinic."

In addition, some people feel called to demonstrate authentic living in a particular way and to act as signposts to others on the journey of life. To be sure, every vocation can have this sacred purpose.

THE CHALLENGE OF VOCATION

In the movie, *The Circus of Dr Lao*, the widow, Mrs. Howard T. Cassan, came to the circus in her flimsy brown dress and her low shoes and went direct to the fortuneteller's tent. Inside the seer, Apollonius, told her she might be expecting too much from the interview. Undaunted, she replied that she wants to know when oil will be discovered on her acres in New Mexico. The seer answered that it will never be discovered. She went on to ask what kind of man will come into her life. The seer responded that she has had all the men she is going to have, and remarked that he saw the remainder of her days as quiet, boring collections of hours. "You will not travel anywhere. You will think no new thoughts. You will experience no new passions. Older you will become but not wiser.... And for all the good or evil, creation or destruction, that your living might have accomplished, you might just as well never have lived at all. I cannot see the purpose in such a life."

We need a new ethic to encourage people to channel their creativity away from themselves and back onto the concrete tasks that need doing in these times—rebuilding local community, engaging youth and elders engaged, improving the quality of life, curbing innocent suffering, enabling local partnerships and international cooperation to deal with social problems, and caring for mother earth. Rabbi Heschel reminds us, "Over and above the din of desires there is an objective challenge to overcome inequity, injustice, helplessness, suffering, oppression. Over and above personal problems, there is a question that follows me wherever I turn. What is expected of me? What is demanded of me?" In other words, vocation.

The real question is the basic aim of our work. Towards what are we moving? A soldier in the Saudi desert said that he wasn't willing to die for cheap gasoline. More and more business managers are saying that they aren't willing to live the workaholic life for a percentage of the market share. A vocational path based on successive promotions is losing its attraction as corporations flatten their hierarchies.

TWO ASPECTS OF AUTHENTIC VOCATION

In any authentic vocational decision, there are two considerations: the needs of society and the needs of the self.

First, the needs of society. We are dealing here with whatever deals with social problems, heals society's fractures, and transforms society into a better place to live. Without consideration of the needs of the globe, vocation can become another form of self-actualization, without any reference to the needs of the six billion other people. Who is going to take responsibility for the future generations to ensure they have enough economic, political and cultural resources to make it. First Nations people in North America speak of living one's life on behalf of the next seven generations. Dietrich Bonhoeffer put the ethical question this way: "How are the coming generations to live? My generation had very few ideas of how the rest of the world lived and got by, or not.

This first came home to me when I was teaching school in the 1950s. One night, I went with a group of teachers (and 5,000 other people) to hear English socialist Douglas Hyde speak in Sydney Town Hall. He was an absolutely electrifying speaker. For two hours he spoke of the conditions of "the third world". At the time, "third world" was a brand new term for all those nations whose living conditions were considerably below those of the West. Mr. Hyde gave us the 3-D tour: the poverty, the dehumanizing conditions, hunger, cowdung floors, injustice, the villages, slums, all in 3D. You could have heard an ear-ring drop. People sat transfixed. It was as if someone had pulled back the curtain and revealed everything they didn't want to know about the world they lived in. In those days, of course, no one was saying, "Think globally, act locally." Afterwards, the group of us went out for a drink. We said nothing, absolutely nothing. It was difficult even to look one another in the eye. None of us went off to work in the villages of India or Nicaragua, at least not then. But that talk blew out the context of my vocation immeasurably.

Exposure to different context-shifting events can help form, expand or firm up vocation. Many parents have found that travel can be an eye opener for their young people grappling with this question, especially if the travel takes them beyond the usual tourist circuit and involves them in contact with other cultures. Finding out how the other half live is usually a real eye-opener, and can expand the options and the context for vocation. Development volunteers, or Peace Corps workers experience this. I know some medical students, for example, who visited Central American villages during university holidays. Now, as doctors, they find time to go back each year to use their medical skills to improve life in the villages. This has become part of their vocation.

James Hillman described another vocational consideration in his book, *The Soul's Code*. He called it the acorn theory. Each life has its own innate constellation of gifts, talents and ways of being. When Joseph Campbell told TV viewers how important it was to "follow their bliss" he was alluding to this dimension of vocation.

The attempt to respond authentically to our acorn's drive for realization inevitably comes up against the ban of society: "You can't do this; it's impossible. Nobody needs this. What you need to do is to take over your father's business." At this point, many have seen a kind of impertinence take over. We show up terrified by our own power. We are afraid to say it out loud or be fully aware of it. We articulate it to ourselves in the mirror. There is this sudden realization that all our life we have been living like a dwarf. With this knowledge, the giant breaks loose inside, and we decide to be the giant we are and break through all obstacles. What becomes apparent is that we and we alone are responsible for creating our life and our future, that no one else can do it for us. The 13th century nature-lover Francis of Assisi abandoned his rich father's house, his inheritance and all his possessions, and stood naked in the town square as a sign of the radical detachment he would give his life to. Francis went on to found one of the most radical religious orders of the Middle Ages.

It is sad to meet people who have been deprived of their destiny. A barber in Dartmouth, Nova Scotia, told his life story while he cut my hair. He said after he had been cut hair for twelve years, he suddenly got a crazy urge to be a paramedic in the Northwest Territories. He did the training, and spent several years dealing with emergency health and accident situations in the Territories. The difference between barbering and being a paramedic was night and day. He got an enormous charge out of flying into impossible places, ministering to people on the spot, rescuing them from hair-raising situations, and getting them to hospital. He realized this was what he was born for. He was good at it, and he loved it. Then he fell in love and wanted to marry. The woman said, "If you're going to marry me, it's back to barbering with you. I can't tolerate being married to a high-risk job," so he went back to barbering. It seemed he had got a wife and lost a vocation.

Vocation brings two strands together: the needs of our society and the needs of our own inner being. How they come together can be somewhat of a mystery, or more intentional. Maybe in our social analysis, we conclude that our calling is to care for the earth's environment. After ten years of this work, we suddenly come to a screeching halt. We find that we have an absolute passion for the biology of wetlands, and so we must go back to university to study biology. One thing leads to another and we finish up with a doctorate in wetland biology on our way to becoming a leading global advocate of wetland preservation at UNESCO.

Vocation is often an unfolding process where one step taken leads to another and another with possibilities revealed at each step. A young woman is possessed by the urge to travel. She tries every means. She attaches herself to well-off people as a personal aide; she gets courier opportunities; she joins a merchant ship crew for a working cruise through the Pacific islands; on the way she keeps a journal of all her travel experiences. She has a wonderful sense of the magic of place. One day she shows her journal to a reporter who works for a major paper, who says she has a real flair as a travel writer. She ends up writing on travel for a well-known paper. People are captured by how she can draw them into the mystery of different places, and at the same time be very practical. She urges her readers to step out beyond the standard tourist enclaves to experience the larger country.

This confluence of what I want and what the world needs is not an easy thing to achieve. For some of us, it is easy to be intoxicated by the idea of realizing our innate capacities to the exclusion of the needs of the world. For others the vocational decision is dominated by the needs of the world, so that vocation becomes a species of martyrdom, disrelated from one's own sense of personal potential. And it is easy to just opt for a job and forget about vocation. No wonder that Kazantzakis described the struggle with vocation as "a claw clasping our heads." This struggle never leaves us. If one's vocation is to heal bodies as a physician, every day that doctor has to decide whether she's going to the hospital or health center or not. Every day she has to decide whether she's going to give every patient her best, or slip into robot mode and shovel patients in and out. Every day she has to watch what's going on inside her: is something shifting in her vocation? And what does she bring specifically to her work that no one else does?

So now we have three rudders by which to steer our life energies into the future: the needs of the world, the needs of our inner being, and the sacred purpose of our life.

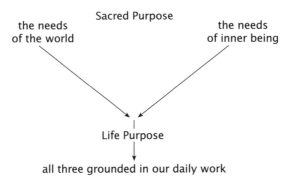

What might that look like? Suppose I decide to become a teacher. I know that kids are not being educated well, and I want to make a difference in that (needs of the world). I like kids, and my limited teaching experiences were very rewarding. I really look forward to the prospect of being a teacher (needs of the inner self). But beyond that, I want to do more than pass on knowledge. I want to break open kids' sense of their own potential as human beings (life purpose). Maybe it works like this: the needs of the world act like an external summons. The needs of the inner self create curiosity and energy, the sacred purpose provides depth motivation, and the work of the teacher in certain places provides the playing field.

THE STANCE OF THE VOCATED ONE

In *The Encyclopedia of World Problems,* Tony Judge lists 21,000 discrete global problems that need solutions if the world is to achieve its potential. A cynic looks at this mountain of problems, and says, "It's impossible to make a difference. Whatever you do is just spitting in the wind." In spite of the cynics, individuals everywhere insist on making a difference.

Vocational clarity brings with it a life mission, a life work, that takes our whole life. It has the feel of Martin Luther King's "I have a dream..." There is the satisfaction of seeing your work and action as significant doing—doing that makes a difference. It carries the feel of "This is what I'm here to do; everything in my life so far prepared me for this." US President Jimmy Carter put it this way: "I have one life and one chance to make it count for something...I'm free to choose what that something is, and the something I've chosen is my faith. My faith demands that I do whatever I can wherever I can, whenever I can, for as long as I can with whatever I have to try to make a difference." Through Habitat for Humanity, Mr. Carter spends his life getting houses built for people less well off.

Many aware, caring people find the prospect of dying without having made a difference in the world intolerable. In *The Possible Human,* Jean Houston quotes a 78-year old retired nurse bounding up the stairs to open a conference in Helsinki:

> So many people are losing heart, not me! I have lived through four wars, have seen unbelievable suffering and misery, and you know what? I am full of hope for the human race. We are tied to each other in ways not possible before. We must now begin to live and grow together to become what we can be. I have dedicated the rest of my life to helping make this possible. I have no money and few have ever heard of me outside Finland, but no matter. The time is ripe, ripe, ripe and I know that what I do will make a difference.

Once our vocation comes together for us, other elements of our life line up behind it. Søren Kierkegaard used a phrase to describe the single-mindedness of the vocated person: "Oh, for the glorious tranquillity of willing one thing, with all my heart and soul and mind." Perhaps that phrase, "willing one thing," best describes the stance of the vocated one.

THE VOCATIONAL JOURNEY

The vocational question is never finally answered. Life keeps unfolding. What we thought was a lifelong vocation may turn out to be a temporary occupation which life opens up to a larger picture. We may think our vocation is to be a teacher, and later we find that, yes, teaching is part of it, but our vocation is exploding children's sense of potential, and a little later exploding everybody's sense of potential. Teaching simply becomes the vehicle for our real vocation. The important thing is to do our vocation wholeheartedly even though it continues to develop.

Our vocation gives us a way to bring together our passion to create and our obligation to serve the needs of the world. In Jean Anouilh's *Antigone*, King Creon says to Antigone:

> It is easy to say no. To say yes, you have to sweat and roll up your sleeves and plunge both hands into life up to the elbows. It is easy to say no, even if saying no means death. All you have to do is to sit still and wait. Wait to go on living, wait to be killed. That is the coward's part. No is one of your man-made words. Can you imagine a world in which trees say no to the sap? In which beasts say no to hunger and propagation?

It seems that the happiest people in the world are those who have said that yes, have surrendered themselves to the call of their vocation, and then give themselves to it day in and day out.

However, pursuit of vocational clarity is a lifelong journey. In his analysis of the vocational journey my mentor and colleague, John Epps, says there are three major stages: recognition, crisis and persistence.

A. RECOGNITION OF VOCATION

Recognition has to do with choosing our vocation. It seems that the great heroes were "called" and "commissioned." Stories about leaders from Moses to Gandhi, to Mother Teresa describe situations in which the central figure was yanked into a new orbit by forces over which the subject had no control. Moses had his burning bush, Gandhi, his experience of being thrown off the train in South Africa.

A colleague tells of his journey into vocation as a young person:

> My image of dealing with the vocation is that you're facing a climb upwards, and there's a crevasse; the only passage upward is a cleft in the rocks, like a chimney you have to shinny up. It gets wider toward the top, so it gets a little trickier as it

goes. That first came into my consciousness when I was a senior in college. I was headed for being a research chemist. That was my occupational choice; and it wasn't a new decision. I had been taking every science course I could find ever since about the eighth grade. I was interested in science; I was good at it. I had several stories about the importance of being a research chemist—I started university shortly after Sputnik went up.

Then along about my senior year several things began to happen all at once. The girl I was dating was a year behind me in school and so that relationship was in jeopardy. I had to decide what I was going to do after I graduated. I put out a lot of applications to graduate schools. I finally got a chance to do some research, but it was awful being in this laboratory for eight hours a day. All I could see was all day long in the laboratory tomorrow and the next day and into the sunset, and I wanted no part of it. I didn't dare tell anybody that, because everyone knew that that was going to be my occupation. The other thing that happened seemed insignificant to me at the time. Somebody gave me a copy of *The Last Temptation of Christ*, by Nikos Kazantzakis.

It dawned on me that I could not decide about next year, save I decided my whole life's occupation. And I could not decide what to do save I anticipated the whole future. Any decision had that kind of import to it. I began to discover the business about not deciding is deciding. You know, we don't have a static situation; we're always on a boat going down the river, and we either paddle upstream or we paddle downstream. If we don't paddle, we go downstream. And not to decide is to go along with the current trends. I experienced it like giving birth. It was laborious, I know that. And it was long; it was nine months long; struggling to try to give form to a decision that would honor what I knew was already there in the situation.

The vocational question often gets raised by an event that interrupts the normal routines of life and triggers questions. Another colleague tells of such an event:

For me it happened when my husband died suddenly. We had been married forty years. When he was gone I had to face the question of what I could do with the rest of my life. What did I want to do? What did I need to do? Did I really want to go on living in the English village where we had lived for twelve years. Did I want to go on running the village fetes, pouring tea for socials, giving talks to the Women's Institutes? Could this conceivably fill my life? No, it couldn't—no doubt about it. I felt I had to do something different. I must go away somewhere where nobody knew us as "us" but would get to know me as me. But what could an untrained widow of sixty do to fill her life? I went straight into a profound despair.

In some fashion we get selected. It may be through falling into despair or through unavoidable attraction. Whether through attraction or compulsion, the selection is never welcome. A life purpose closes other options, some of which are very desirable. Our first response is always *resistance*. It's never what we sought for ourselves.

Yet it will not go away. Whatever excuses we give or however unprepared we seem to be, the purpose draws us like a magnet until finally we surrender our alternatives and take it on. And what a trip it turns out to be—something new around every corner, ample freedom and responsibility, plenty of room to use whatever talents and resources we bring, and most important, a deep sense of satisfaction. We seem to have come home, to have found our niche, to have reached the goal of our vocational pursuits. It seems to be "as good as it gets."

And just as we are settling in and beginning to reap the benefits of the situation, it all falls apart. We experience betrayal.

B. Crisis: Surviving Betrayal

This crisis and betrayal is linked to experiences which could be called the Dark Night and the Long March.

No amount of lucid analysis or even cynical anticipation prepares us for the betrayal that takes the significance out of our enterprise. It can be as minor as a toothache or a less than glowing performance appraisal from a supervisor, or it can be major as losing our job or discovering an unknown medical problem.

Whatever the external event, its impact is devastating. Suddenly life's meaning is gone. We see the triviality of our accomplishments, the thoughtlessness of our colleagues, the pettiness of our cares, and the futility of it all. Most of all, we are alone. Anyone who has ever tried to get anything done in the world goes through what was called in the last chapter "the dark night of the soul." At a certain point what was incredibly clear to us becomes so opaque that we feel blind. What motivated us begins to collapse. We can't seem to make decisions any more. Our passion seems to dry up, and we find ourselves just going through the motions. We experience ourselves as humiliated, weak, full of resentment—and suffering.

At this point, we can easily abandon the whole vocational project, and become a beachcomber, or take some sensual plunge in San Juan. But it is important to affirm this aspect of the vocational journey, because it is a path to the future and a new opportunity to deepen. Once we affirm this sense of betrayal, we can enter "secondary vocation".

Robert Shropshire describes this kind of event:

> I had been working in inner city and third-world development projects for several years. My next assignment was India. When I arrived at the Bombay airline terminal I encountered a family of beggars. The little girl of the family cried continuously. Part of her upper lip was pink from crying and she sniffled all the time. She would run up and ask you for baksheesh. If you didn't come up with any baksheesh, her next move was to fall on her knees. I was not naive so I didn't really break up in the face of that, on the surface anyway. We got out of the airport and were headed towards Bombay. Along the way I noticed a lot of big culverts—those big sewer drainage pipes about five feet in diameter. They had rags hanging over the ends. I asked the colleague who met me, "What are those?" And he said, "People live in those, and when they do not pay their rent they are evicted." Evicted from a sewer pipe? I guess they throw your one pot out into the street. But, can you imagine? Evicted from a sewer pipe! After that experience, I found myself charged up with motivation. I was raring to go. I almost tore off the car door trying to get started with my work, because I was going to end all this. And so, I travelled around the sub-continent teaching courses to adults, and trying to fire them up with a vision of community transformation. After three years, when I felt as if I had poured out my life, I got a telegram that said I was being transferred. On the way to the airport, there were still people living in those sewer pipes and the same little girl was at the airport, a little older now. I could see that India could use up my life a hundred thousand times and never even feel it. And I found myself saying there is nothing in the world that will ever motivate me again.

At that point, we either throw our vocation overboard, or we develop a kind of secondary vocation: a vocation that is beyond spontaneity, beyond enthusiasm, beyond our romantic sense of vocation. We realize that doing what we do means that we get all used up. We surrender to being used up. This is something that happens to us all.

Described in modern literature as "mid-life crisis," this experience of crisis and betrayal is portrayed by popular psychology as something to overcome. Doctors prescribe everything from exercise and diet to counseling and medication. Most of us could benefit immeasurably from these things. But when one has been betrayed, they are irrelevant.

The only path through this experience involves the classic stages of grief: denial, anger, bargaining, and accommodation. It helps to identify the value we held that has proven untrustworthy, and to let ourselves lament. But we need to avoid placing blame. After all, it is no one's fault that we were living in illusions of security and significance;

we all do. And life continues to confront us with reality. So we lament, but we do it discreetly. No one can help us, and most comments made by friends only confirm our pain. Art can be a medium of release—music, painting, literature, movies, even TV. They all offer expressions by people sensitive to the "down side" of life and participating in them can be cathartic for us.

How can we make it through this experience of the dark night? We survive by knowing that this experience is no mistake—it is being in tune with the human condition, and wholly right. Furthermore, were we to select some other cause or vocation to follow, it too would reach a stage of crisis. Life is just not made the way we want it.

There is an aspect of secondary vocation that is relevant to those of us who have been up to their armpits in social engagement, whether in the civil rights movement, village development work, working in the inner city, or some such. After some years, the self talk easily devolves into something like this: "Well, I've paid my dues to the world; I was on the front lines in the civil rights marches in the 60s, I worked at local community reformulation in the 70s, I've raised money for inner-city youth in the 80s until I got sick to death of writing proposals; I served my time. It's time for me to take it easy. Or, "I sign all the right petitions, contribute to good causes and vote for the least bad choice in every election; isn't that enough, for God's sake? What do you want? Blood?"

There are times when circumstances push us to cash out for a while, look where we've come from, consider where to move next. Taking a sabbatical can be the right thing to do. Sabbaticals give us a fresh perspective, recharge our batteries, give us a new chance to develop our life work. But, once the energies are recharged and the direction is clear, it is time to put the old body on the line again. The siren call of entropy never goes away, and neither does the call of vocation.

C. Persistence: Keeping On Keeping On

It is difficult for us to continue with business as usual when our sense of meaning has gone. The Stoic Greeks are said to have excelled in it, but stoicism is a defiant selfishness with heart for nothing but its own emptiness. Our aim should be to invest our unworthy work with all the passion, energy, creativity and enthusiasm that we can muster—even when we know it is trifling in the cosmic scheme of things.

When we feel the utter and complete worthlessness of what we are about, so that never again can we be devastated by betrayal, *then we can absolutely forget it.* We don't need to let anyone know that we know it. It becomes a deep secret that we guard with our life. And we can treat the work and our workmates and team members as though they were the most outstanding realities in the universe.

What makes this possible? While we struggle with life's meaninglessness, it suddenly becomes clear that if nothing is significant, then everything is significant. The paradox of being transforms our existence. It works like this: once we see our life and work in this context of heightened significance, then it is trivial along with everything else. But this very context pervades everything that is, gives it meaning, and we find joy in it. In this third phase, our life is about perceiving and disclosing significance in the details of life and work.

And we begin to notice that people seem to benefit from our efforts. Not that it matters, for they too are fallible; but there seems to be a level of effectiveness not previously noticed in our work, whatever our job. Perhaps it's because of our attention to minute detail.

The three-part vocational journey of recognition, crisis, and persistence happens over and over during a lifetime. It's as though the three form a spiral on which we move as we live and work.

This is what it means to have a life purpose or vocation: to expend our energy in pursuit of the unattainable and, in the process, to disclose the value that lies in life. This is why we look to some people for how to live with authenticity.

As long as we stay aware of the journey itself and our place on it, then we assume a certain passionate nonchalance about the particulars of our work. Whatever it may be, it is both unfulfilling and deeply meaningful. It is worth doing well and passionately but it is not the source of our significance. We begin to relish the paradoxes of life. Growth in the journey continues to open us to a new set of learnings on which we build the next stage.

Personal Workshop on Vocation

This workshop can help clarify our vocation, or help us through a transition. Choose a time and a space where you can work without interruption.

I. Make three lists:

    I. the natural gifts you have

    2. the general competencies you have

    3. the specific skills you have developed.

NATURAL GIFTS	GENERAL COMPETENCIES	SPECIFIC SKILLS

II. In the chart below, list at least 12 things you care deeply about in relation to the world, society, other people, the past, the present, and the future—or anything else. Use the columns, or anything else, to help you think of as long a list as you can. The first line are a few examples.

WORLD	SOCIETY	OTHERS	PAST	PRESENT	FUTURE
Yugoslavia	Health care	youth AIDS	certain public monuments	failure of education	How to care for local community

III. What are ten ways your gifts and talents could be used to make a difference to the future of any or all of these cares?

1	6
2	7
3	8
4	9
5	10

IV. Write a long paragraph that states the unique contribution you intend to make to our time and place.

V. Take a break and come back later to answer these questions:

1. What did this session feel like? _____

_____

2. What happened to you? _____

_____

3. Where was it most useful? _____

_____

4. What are your next steps for taking this further? _____

_____

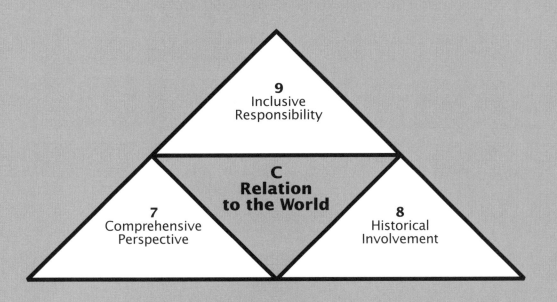

Relation to the World

Introduction to Section C

While the last section focused on the depths to be found in the self, this section speaks about our relationship to the world. The chapters examine the stances of comprehensiveness, historical involvement, and inclusive responsibility.

The way in which we relate to the world is as much a test of our authenticity as our relation to our selfhood. Profound experience can easily turn into a kind of self-centerdness, unless we can ground ourselves in what is happening in the world. The world is what stands between our journey of self-awareness and mysticism. It calls us to stand comprehensively present to the world's wonder and suffering. It summons us to stand present to all of history, our own history, yes, but also the history of the world, as we pay attention to the demands of the future. At times, the world calls us to responsibility; it beckons us to clamber onto the stage of history and demand change. Without this constant engagement with what is going on in the world, we would all limit our potential impact.

CHAPTER 7

The Comprehensive Perspective

Resisting the Urge to Reduce

That which you ignore
Will rise up and strike you.
JENNY HOLZER

It is a pity when discussion of the big picture is relegated to cocktail party conversation. That is crazy. We have to learn, not only to have specialists but also people whose specialty is to spot the strong interactions and the entanglements of the different dimensions, and then take a crude look at the whole.
THOMAS L. FRIEDMAN

REDUCTIONISM

Thomas Friedmann's quote underlines one of the dominant trends in our times: the multiplication of specialists and the paucity of generalists and, with that, the increasing inability to grasp things within a larger context, an overarching big picture. When we can't see the forest for the trees we experience a failure in our comprehensive vision; we are unable to grasp the big picture. Of course, the big picture is the forest, as well as all the trees together and each of the trees held in a unity with the others.

On a visit to the Ontario Science Center years ago, I saw a documentary film about relating to the whole, *The Power of Ten*. It shows a snapshot of a family having a picnic in a golf course, then it expands the space of the picture by a power of ten and shows the whole golf course; then it blows up that picture by a power of ten, so that you see Miami, then the Florida peninsula, then eastern North America, then the whole continent, then the globe, then the planetary system, then the Milky Way, then a big band of dark space, then star upon star of outer space. Then it takes you backwards till the camera is focused on the outflung hand of one of the picnickers, and it takes you through the same process further through the cells of the human body, right down to the atomic level, where the atomic components are arranging themselves like solar systems. The movie is mind-boggling. You see yourself as a creature connected to the whole universe, and as a universe within yourself.

In the planning processes of large organizations. Joseph Jaworski in *Synchronicity* describes the comprehensive scenario-planning process of Royal Dutch Shell. Instead of relying on forecasts, the Shell Group plans for the future through the use of decision scenarios. Scenario planning, for Shell, is not about making plans, but is the process management-teams use to change their mental models of the business environment and the world. The team of scenario planners includes experts in economics, sociopolitics, energy, the environment and technology. These experts conduct ongoing conversations with fifty or so top managers in the Shell Group and with a network of remarkable, leading-edge thinkers from around the world in many disciplines: politics, science, education, business, economics, technology, religion, and the arts. Every three years or so, they synthesize this information into two or more scenarios—stories of how the business might evolve over the coming years and decades. This comprehensive approach to strategic management has, in part, led the Shell Group to be regarded by many business leaders as one of the best managed companies in the world.

There are times when the overwhelming reality of life in the early 21st century makes us want to dig our heads in the sand like the ostrich, or confine our attentions to what we feel we can manage, like "Me, my wife, and my pet parakeet." But life challenges us to stand present to all of life as it is happening to us. Comprehensiveness means that our map of reality, or our context, takes in everything we can: there is nothing left out. If we are responsible for a family, we have a picture of all aspects of the family in our head: its nurture, diet, budget, chores, education, relation to the community, its purpose in the world, family gatherings, vacations…the whole enchilada.

WHY BE COMPREHENSIVE?

1. *The systemic nature of reality demands a comprehensive approach.* Most of us are familiar with the need to keep many plates spinning at once in an organization or family. Specialists and generalists need each other.

2. *The comprehensive picture provides perspective on the details.* In the Clinton scandal in the US, once Congress focused on Clinton's sexual improprieties, government processes easily slipped into farce and began to compete with the entertainment industry; national problems of women's health, welfare and safety were neglected. Clinton, the president, was leader enough not to allow the problems of Clinton, the husband, to interfere with running the country and its foreign policy for long.

3. *Comprehensive, whole-system designs can care for everyone.* When, for example, there is no integrated health system that assesses needs and directs finances to serve the needs, hospitals finish up trying to save their own shirts.

4. *Comprehensive integrated pictures of life's processes enable personal responsibility.* Continuing with the health care example, without our involvement in and responsibility for our own health care, our national health care and local insurance companies would be swamped with medical and hospital bills. Our health would also likely be worse.

5. *Models that are not comprehensive create chaos.* If, for example, a family does not plan for health care, the first big medical emergency will swamp the family's cash flow projections, creating financial problems.

WHOLE-SYSTEM MODELS

In the last twenty years we have seen whole-system models built on care for the environment and on health care. Such comprehensive models can also be created for other aspects of life. Most of us are now pretty clear that there is a lot more to health care than just seeing the doctor. We are all getting used to the mantra of balanced diet; exercise; adequate rest; relaxation; deep breathing and so on. Our idea of health has been blown out to the comprehensive. As a social concern, we now understand health as a whole system whose components include such things as clean air, purified water, fish, meat and farm products free of harmful chemicals (which in turn calls for a revolution in agriculture), and so on. This is because much of the work in health now is not just preventing illness, but promoting healthiness and wellness. Big-picture factors that promote health such as rewarding work, opportunities for relaxation, feeling one is making a contribution, are all health-promoting factors, or determinants of health.

BEING COMPREHENSIVE

What is involved in being comprehensive?

1. Being comprehensive means that we are prepared to deal with the totality of life: all parts, all points of view, the whole world, all of history, all peoples, the whole scope of humanness, all the dimensions of society. The political correctness trend that flourished through the 1980s and 90s irritated people, myself included, who deplore the McCarthyist tone of its most rabid proponents. Yet one of the functions served by the PC phenomenon was a heightening of sensitivity to the multidiversity present in the world today, and an honoring of it. It took me a while to understand why the inhabitants of any part of India were suddenly being referred to as East Indians—in contradistinction to West Indians and American Indians (and the Cleveland Indians).

2. Thinking comprehensively demands homework from us. If, for example, we are a community worker, a thorough-going analysis of a community's problems will be needed at some stage. When ICA was involved in the 5th City community reformulation project in Chicago, staff and community leaders went door to door asking about the problems in the community. More than 5000 problems were collected and organized into economic, political and cultural issues. When Tony Judge, President of the International Association of Associations produced his *Encyclopedia of World Problem*s, it contained no less than 21,000 problems. That is being comprehensive, even though daunting.

3. To be comprehensive is to be inclusive: it sees to the inclusion of all aspects, even the parts you don't know or like. A community meeting needs to have all sides and aspects of the community represented: both sides of the tracks, all cultures, rich, middle-class and poor. This is not political correctness—it is plain political savvy and sound sense. Gandhi had to take a representative of the lowest caste in India, a Harijan, into the Indian legislature, and stand with him to remind the Congress that they needed to pay heed to all the castes, not just the higher ones.

In any community project, it is important to find ways to enlist the cooperation of both friends and enemies: perhaps those more conservative elements in the community who like to keep things the way they are. Otherwise the project may be doomed. In one community in India where ICA worked, the upper caste (the Brahmans) would not eat with the lower caste people. The Harijans decided to organize a community feast. They told the Brahmans that there was no way development could go forward in that community unless they could have inclusive gatherings. And so one day, the Brahmans sat down with the Harijans and took a common meal together. They began to find other ways to work together to improve their village.

4. Comprehensiveness insists on a synthesis that pulls things together into wide-screen pictures, instead of always pulling things apart. So many meetings and research projects lack ways to pull data together so that it can be acted on. Excellent methods are available for gestalting and synthesizing data from a multiplicity of sources into one readily graspable picture. Peter Senge, for example, has educated us on whole-system thinking in which we constantly grasp for awareness of all the parts in a system and their interrelationships. In *The Fifth Discipline*, he shows over and over again how a lack of feedback between the parts of a system can bring down the whole system.

5. To be responsible at this moment in history, everyone needs models of reality. We know that any model we create will be relative: it will not be final or absolute. Our models need to be internally consistent, and hold traditional wisdom, not focused on the fads of the time. If we don't like the comprehensive models of other people, the onus on us is to build our own. Creating your own comprehensive context allows you to reflect on what is happening rather than butting into someone else's context. Comprehensive mental models enable engagement from the broadest context. They shift our story of what is important and help us to take a proactive stance. A person operating out of a comprehensive context is dangerous to have around because of embarrassing questions or assessments:

"This plan seems to have left out anything on our corporate culture. This company will go downhill if it ignores our values and the staff's goals."

"How is this new policy going to affect Beth Mills on the shop floor? How will she respond to this?"

"The marketing plan has nothing to say about how we are going to handle the West Coast. Don't we intend to sell to the West Coast?"

"I notice that the CEO and the Board have all voted pay raises for themselves. What's the plan for the executives and the rest of the staff?

"I notice that our monthly staff awards never seem to go to any of our Jamaican staff. Are they all as incompetent as that?"

These are the kinds of questions (especially the last two) that can make people wince, but they are indispensable. Those who ask such bold questions are often referred to as "whistle blowers". There should be a role in every organization called "The Whistle Blower representing the Comprehensive." Some one or ones have to be assigned to play this role, even though it is often a thankless one. Otherwise strategy suffers, plans are reduced, and policies slip into the dehumanizing. "What's left out?" or "Who is omitted?" are questions that check for comprehensiveness and inclusiveness.

BENEFITS OF COMPREHENSIVENESS

Having comprehensive pictures of reality changes how we take in current affairs or the news. When reading the daily paper, we might ask a different set of questions. Rather than questions like, What's in fashion? What's happening to our favorite celebrity? Or, how are pork bellies doing today? we ask, "What's happening in the three places I have decided to watch: the Russian Federation, former Yugoslavia, and Central Africa? What is developing there? What are the new issues? How are they being dealt with? (How would I deal with them?) Or, what's going on about the three issues I feel I have a stake in: privatizing water, bank mergers, and the new local developments near Gerrard and Main Streets? When reading the news, a comprehensive screen helps us select what to read. We can refuse to get sucked in by the latest political scandal that has the press and TV salivating, because it's giving everyone a holiday from delivering "all the news that's fit to print" and allowing them to hunker down over politicians making a spectacle of themselves. One of the reasons for the reputation of *The New York Times* or *The Christian Science Monitor* is their capacity for reporting from a comprehensive take on what is news.

When we operate out of the comprehensive, we can ask useful questions: what is telling the media that issue X should be red-hot news? Why is so much TV coverage being given to what is to me insignificant "fast-breaking" news? Why is so much news about X, Y and Z being ignored? And we can question the particular spin put on things, so that we are not sucked into someone's reduced context. Who says any kind of tension is bad for you? Who says Prozac is the best thing since sliced bread? Depression (despair) can force us to rethink our lives and be the launching pad for our personal transformation. Unless we have a comprehensive context that covers all of life, we become a sucker for every theory or every new product that comes along.

Different people find different aspects of life unpalatable, even shameful. Some people do not like to be confronted by poverty, powerlessness, victimization, unjust treatment. Some who visit Acapulco or Miami make sure they do not venture beyond the tourist enclave. They are not prepared to stand before the poverty of the village or the slum, or the poor and powerless. To decide to stand before all of life and to take it all into account is no small thing.

Finally, inclusiveness is a dimension of comprehensiveness. Inclusiveness is the style of honoring all human beings, and taking everyone seriously. This is particularly important in meetings, when it is easy to write off what certain people say and, in the process, not hear their perspective. ICA Canada consultant Jo Nelson facilitates groups all over North America, from San Francisco to Yellowknife, from Baffin Island to Chicago. She has boiled down her experience of facilitating hundreds of groups into five points that she rehearses before encountering a new group:

- Everyone has wisdom.

- We need everyone's wisdom for the wisest result.

- There are no wrong answers. (There is wisdom in every response.)

- The whole is greater than the sum of the parts.

- Everyone hears others and is heard.

By its very nature, comprehensiveness is a challenge for everyone. I guess we all have our wish list in this arena. Here are a few "what-ifs" I'd like to see happen in relation to comprehensiveness.

What if doctors' prescriptions considered *all* aspects of the human being's health and wellness, instead of those in the standard medical paradigm? One might be asked about one's diet, exercise, whether one meditated or reflected daily, or how one handled stress. A prescription might not be always a drug. It might include: more reflection, writing in your daily journal, yoga, or social experiences or context-expanding trips or experiences. We don't want to have our lifestyle prescribed, but some recommendations can help in areas we need to develop.

What if lawmakers and politicians, instead of taking their priorities from the polls and the lobbyists, decided to choose topics for debate out of a comprehensive screen. They could use the social process as a comprehensive grid for approaching all the issues of the country: economic, political and cultural.

Dealing with the comprehensive is a primary stance when dealing with the world. It covers planning, implementation, one's relationships, who gets included in what, what how we stand before in life, how we create our context, how we do strategic planning, how we educate, how we govern, how we sustain health and humanness, and how we give each other our due.

COMPREHENSIVE MODELS

This section shares some examples of comprehensive models so that we can see the difference they can make in the way we view the world. The four models presented here cover:

1. a model of comprehensive curriculum in education

2. a geo-social analysis (grid) of the world

3. a triangular model showing how the processes of society relate to each other

4. a model of the journey of an organization

Another example of a comprehensive model is the map of 64 states of being in the charts on the Other World (*see Chapter 5*).

It is important to note that those who constructed these models viewed them not as reality, but as a necessary overlay on reality to enlarge our perception of reality.

EXAMPLE 1: *A Comprehensive Education Model*

I have been personally appalled at the education available in our times. It seems to me that most of it tends to cultivate not a love for the larger picture or context, but the habit of reductionism and fragmentation. All of us are familiar with the tendency to reduce the boundaries of our work to what we can comfortably handle. This is reductionism, as is the refusal to be exposed to larger pictures of life than those we have. Many people give up any quest for a comprehensive ethic and opt for situational ethics, where every encounter conveniently has its own ethical principles. They feel that no overarching set of values can be applied to any situation. Universities, especially those responsible for post-graduate studies, seem to push students into ever narrower fields of investigation, rather than interpreting relationships within big picture reality.

We are all familiar with how school systems apply the model of the Industrial Revolution, dividing time up into segments (45 minutes for history, 45 for geography), creating memory made up of a group of episodes unrelated to each other. Subjects tend to be compartmentalized, without any thematic relation to each other.

In my experience primary and secondary education seemed incapable of passing on a big picture, or even a continuous picture, of any subject. Hhistory and geography were the worst. Perhaps, it was easier to notice in history and geography. One year, we would study the great navigators and explorers; the next year it seemed to be the wars associated with the British Empire in the 17th and 18th centuries: Wolfe and Montcalm and Duplessis and the Surajah Dowlah and the Black Hole of Calcutta and all that. The next year it was ancient history: a bit of Egypt, Mesopotamia, and the Rosetta stone.

We are becoming more and more convinced that education really needs to deal with all of life since, when we come into adulthood, it is not just those parts of our lives touched on in the school curriculum that we have to deal with. All of life, in its manifolcomplexity comes flooding in on us: budgets, finances, political involvement, learning, skills, relationships, raising kids, work, house maintenance, ethics, the meaning of life in the particular, dealing with questions of religion and spirit. What school didn't prepare us for we have to learn ultra-fast. In areas where we are not capable of this, we crash.

In ICA we were obsessed with creating a useful curriculum that included all of life that could be taught at any age. We wanted it to cover skills, knowledge, and life meaning. Eventually we came up with the model below, represented by interlocking and interrelated triangles.

We wanted the curriculum model to work over against the major contradictions of contemporary education which we saw as:

- reductionism, randomness, and fads in curriculum designs (so we used the same model at all levels, from preschool to adult education

- utter separation of the disciplines from life questions (so we included both methodology and final meanings

- the divorce of the sciences from the humanities (so we paired one of the sciences with one of the humanities to produce courses in psychology and art, science and philosophy, sociology and history• the increasing rarification of education in high schools and higher education (so we ensured that everything taught was grounded in the lives of the learners.

We were after a curriculum with a common basis that could be augmented and increasingly complexified to meet the needs of anyone from two to 100. The curriculum was always aimed at the particular developmental level. This curriculum allowed a two-year old to experience basic images from the natural sciences, psychology and sociology, history, art, and philosophy, and what life is all about (final meanings); primary school students would do the same subjects, but at a more complex level, as would high-school students. In other words, at every level, education would deal with the whole of life.

The methods curriculum ensured that the curriculum was practical. These methods were based on knowing, doing and being:

- *intellectual methods* (reflection, study, making a presentation, and curriculum building);

- *social methods* (workshopping, planning, gridding the globe and neighborhood, problem analysis, planning, and social trends analysis)

- *motivational methods* (reflective and motivational tools.)

ICA tried out these life triangles and the idea of the spiral curriculum in two settings. One was the Fifth City Preschool now 35 years old and repeatedly honored for its pioneering role; the other was the Global Academy—an eight-week intensive residential school for adults comprising the full spectrum of society all the way from street kids to pillars of society. An inspection of comprehensive curriculum books on the Internet today reveals that comprehensive curriculum is regarded as something for only "gifted students".)

Both the Academy and the Preschool dealt with the life questions, Who am I? What do I do? and How do I be? In the preschool, the kids learned about the limits, possibilities and decisions to be made in life. In the Academy, adults examined these issues in greater depth. So preschoolers learned that they lived in the universe; that each of them was a unique, unrepeatable human being ("the greatest"), and that each of them could bend history. They expressed these in rituals.

One day an inspector was hovering round the 5th City Preschool and began talking to a three-year-old. He just happened through his questions to trip the ritual responses. "Who are you? asked the inspector. "I'm the greatest!" said the preschooler on cue. "Well,

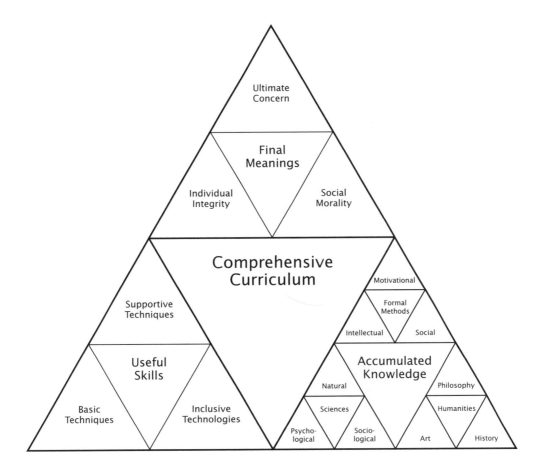

where do you live? " I live in the universe!" "And where are you going now? "I'm going to bend history!" The inspector went on his way, not sure what he had run into.

The point here is not so much what ICA did some years ago, although it is good to know that it can be done. The point is that, if education is to be redone in a way that meets the needs of society today, the comprehensive curriculum is one significant place to start.

EXAMPLE 2: *Geo-Social Reality*

When I was eight years old, my mother brought an atlas home after a trip to Sydney. I spent hours tracing the maps and writing in the names, until the book fell apart, and it was time to get another. I began to realize that map-makers had been struggling for a long time for adequate ways to create a flat image of the world. On the Mercator Projection, Canada and Russia and Greenland seem huge. The oval Mollweide Projection showed all the continents in their right relative areas, but really squished them out of shape. Later I became familiar with the Phillips Projection which achieved the seemingly impossible goal of showing correct relative areas in a rectangular map.

Cartographers struggled with the categories of area and shape in portraying the relationship between people and geography. I first encountered the struggle in the ICA when I was introduced to the global grid, a highly stylized way to represent the globe.

Part of the research that went into this model of the world shown below was deciding how many continents the world really has, not the artificial continents: Asia, Europe, Australia, etc. depicted on Mercator Projection—but the full panoply of spaces where there is a relation between a space and a people. From this angle, nine geo-social continents stood out, arranged in three different cross-sections of the world.

The stylized model below shows the parts of the globe comprehensively and in dynamical relation to each other. The fundamental set of relations between parts of the globe was assumed to be tri-polar, rather than bi-polar. The globe was imaginally divided into three Spheres, East, West and South; each of the three spheres was then divided into three geo-social continents, arranged to reveal the essential roles and tensions of the continents. We observe that the basic tension is between East and West, with Sphere South mediating the tension. We are aware that in Sphere West, the primary tension has been between North America and Russia, mediated by the continent of Europe. In Sphere East, notice that the basic tension is between South Asia (India, Pakistan, etc.) and China, mediated by the continent of Southeast Asia and Pacifica (Australia and the Pacific Island groups). This one has erupted in wars from time to time. In Sphere South, the basic tension is between Latin America and sub-Saharan Africa mediated by the continent of North-Africa and the Middle-East.

Tri-Polar Continental Dynamics

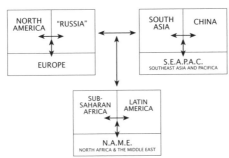

When this abstract model is placed over the actual geography of the globe, we get a stylized picture of the geo-social continents called the global grid:

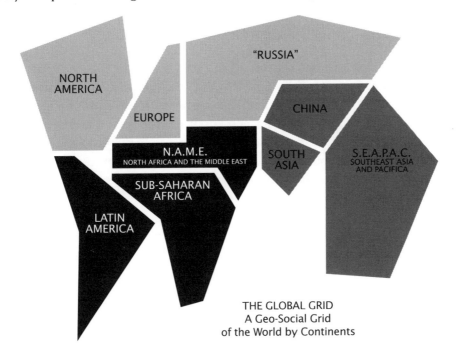

THE GLOBAL GRID
A Geo-Social Grid
of the World by Continents

When I was first introduced to this way of depicting the world, I noticed that the geo-social grid has a number of features that make it an interesting tool for looking at the world:

1. The list of continents is different from the usual listing. It breaks up the huge Asian continent into its main components and gives them the status of continents. So China with its 1.25 billion people is rightfully a continent as is South Asia (India, Pakistan, BanglaDesh, Nepal, Bhutan, Sikkim) with its one billion people. Southeast Asia

and the Pacific Islands are treated as a continent, as is the area encompassing North Africa and the Middle East, a geography largely dominated by desert and the religion and culture of Islam. Russia and the area of Africa below the Sahara are also treated as continents. So the grid relies not only on the shape and geography of large land masses but also on the social and cultural content of the geography.

2. The grid simplifies and stylizes the shapes of the continents to make them easier to remember. As few lines as possible are used to draw each continent.

3. Since the grid attempts to show people in relation to geographical space, large oceans are omitted to allow continents to be shoved up against each other.

Models like these give us different eyes and ears to understand what is happening behind the daily news. Anyone with this picture was not unduly surprised, for example, by the series of START treaties between Russia and the US in the 1970s since, geo-socially, the US and Russia belong in the same sphere. Similarly, it made sense when the Berlin Wall fell and the Iron Curtain collapsed in 1989, since Russia and Europe belong in the same sphere.

Although there are tensions between all of them, the major tension for all these geo-social continents of the West will always be with the East—hence, the Korean War, Vietnam, tensions with China over Taiwan, and the Western trade missions to China. The West now recognizes that both China and Russia need to be acknowledged as part of the world community through symbols such as "most favoured nation status" or space partnerships. Sphere South has continued to hold the tension between East and West with its requests for development, its demands for participation in world trade treaties and lending institutions such as the World Bank.

Latin America keeps demanding participation in NAFTA, just as nations from North Africa and the Middle East, like Turkey, push for involvement in the European Economic Community. Western factories continue to migrate following the advantage of cheap labor and liberal environmental policies in the South and East.

This global grid can be further broken down into areas and regions by dividing continents into six areas and areas into six regions, and so on down to the local level. The local community can also be gridded as a community familiarization exercise. These grids give people a way to keep a complex set of geographical and cultural relationships in mind when listening to the news or considering local issues.

EXAMPLE 3. *Sociology: The Social Process Model*

We can do the same kind of wide-angled comprehensive analysis and model building on the dimensions of society: economic, political and cultural. Without the processing, pro-

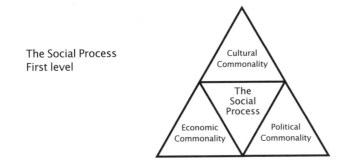

The Social Process
First level

duction and distribution of resources (the economic process) there is no life for the political process to legislate on behalf of, to protect, and, care for. Without the political dimension, it's "every man for himself," and too bad for those of us left out. Without the cultural dimension, the other two processes have no wisdom, no family or community systems, no art or symbols to create meaning.

ICA created these triangles in 1971,in the midst of a major research effort to discern the major issues in society and to map out an appropriate response. I had only just joined the ICA staff at the time When I first heard about this research effort, I was very skeptical. The first step was a massive literature review by ICA staff around the world. Every one of ICA's offices around the globe was allotted a number of sentinel books in many disciplines (sociology, history, culture etc.) to study for the key insights. In this way a one-year study of 1000 pivotal books covering all aspects of the workings of society was completed. The data from all the books was used to create a triangular model of

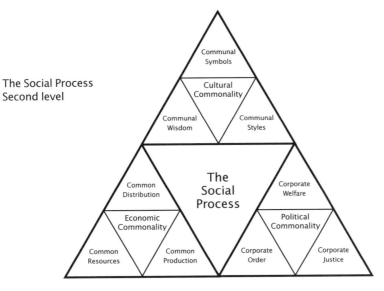

The Social Process
Second level

the Social Process down to six levels. I remember teams of people sitting on the floor and working to fit scores of these triangles together in a rationally consistent pattern. Then I became quite excited about it. I saw that what we were building was probably the most complete and comprehensive model of the processes of society ever created. A thousand people spent a month using the social process triangles to develop a practical vision, obstacles, proposals and tactics for working on social change.

Normally, when we think about society, our picture probably includes the economic dimension, something called "politics", and maybe health and education services. But society holds many more aspects. The triangles are an attempt to hold all the major processes of society and show their relation to each other in a rationally consistent manner.

The figure above shows second-level processes. Each dimension is divided into three aspects.

The third-level triangles (below) show how the second-level processes are each further broken down into three processes.

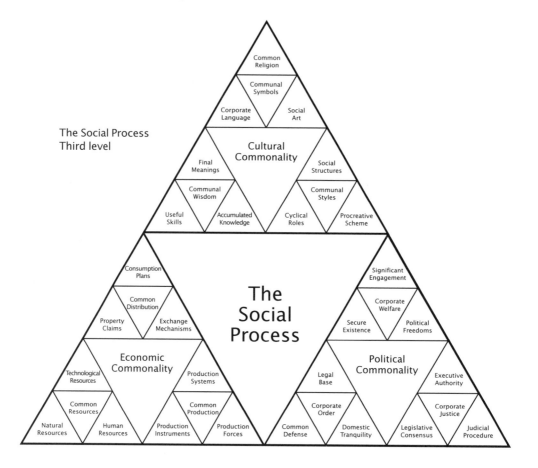

The fourth level has 81 triangles and the fifth 243, holding the stuff of the social process. The ideal (rarely found) is a balanced tension between the economic, the political and the cultural. When this happens, society is in a healthy state. When these three processes of society are not held in balance, society gets sick. When we are deprived of the means of adequate livelihood, political chaos and rioting can result. When we are deprived of participation in the political process, our livelihood is likely to suffer while masters grow rich on the resources denied us. When our culture is taken away from us, we easily become political and economic victims or find our lives devoid of meaning.

These triangles have been found to be invaluable in analysing trends, plotting social issues, looking at history, or even reading the morning newspaper. They remind us that there is more to life than any one focus—money, politics, or the arts. (A full description and all the levels of these triangles can be found in *The Social Process Triangles*, by Jon and Maureen Jenkins.)

EXAMPLE 4: *The Journey of the Organization*

Another comprehensive model that many have found useful is a map of the journey of an organization. Recently people who study and consult with organizations have been working hard to understand not only the value scales of different groups, but also their life journeys as they evolve in structure, leadership, participation, values and skills.

Some organizations assume that if profits are good, the organization is on the ascendant. Maybe not. Other groups assume that if the workers are performing and making no trouble, then things go well. Others again look at the structure of the organization and how it encourages ownership and creativity.

Silver-bullet strategies, such as re-engineering or total quality management, inevitably fail to fulfill their promise of all-round transformation. More and more, orgnizations are beginning to realize that they have to change their whole network in many dimensions—a process that has been called "whole-system transformation." A first step in this wholistic change is transforming the organization's current worldview. Then it must create the consensus to choose a new and desired worldview. When the image shifts, the priority values shift. It is not simply the focus, structure and leadership of the organization that change, but the core values, skills and operating styles.

To develop a new worldview, an organization needs a vision. It needs an image not just of greater size or profitability, but of higher maturity and fulfilment. It also needs a way to see where it is stuck at present, and an overview of the whole journey of possible development.

How might organizations get a picture both of where they are and of what is possible using a whole-system approach to development? ICA Canada developed the model below, using categories from the work of the late Willis Harman, of Harrison Owen, and especially of Brian P. Hall, who has spent 30 years researching human values and organizational development. The complete development model has seven phases, but for the sake of accessibility is presented here in four.

In today's world, it's so easy for commentators on world affairs to rely on one explanation, one cause. There are those who think everything can be explained in terms of political power. Others believe that it's all a matter of technology, that the Internet and the Web will determine the future direction of history. Still others look at the world through environmental eyeglasses and what must be done to save ecosystems, while

The Journey of an Organization
from *Edges*, 1997

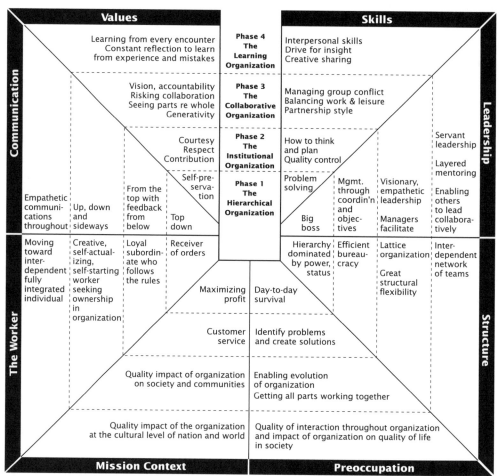

ignoring the need for development. Other analysts look at the world and see the clash of cultures as the key to international affairs.

One of the benefits of having a model like the social process triangles is that it constantly reminds you of the big picture of society and the many lenses it can be viewed through: economic, political, cultural, education, style, symbol. It deters us from the sad fate of tunnel vision. Thomas Friedman says in this connection in *The Lexus and the Olive Tree: Understanding Globalization* that a lot of people are going to have to go back to school. He believes that re-education is of great importance for journalists and strategists who have to "learn to think like globalists." Educators and journalists focus on highly specialized areas of expertise. They ignore the fact that in today's world the borders between local, domestic, international, political and technological affairs are all collapsing.

New generations of leaders and politicians will need to be trained to think comprehensively. It is no longer adequate, says Friedman, merely to take in parts of the picture, or pigeonhole priorities so they can be pursued separately and simultaneously without any idea of how one is going to support or undercut the other. Today, however, generals are in short supply, due to the ever-narrowing specialization in academia. The fact that greater value is placed on functioning at depth within a narrow or single field than broadly across several means that it will be more and more difficult to produce national and local leaders who can operate an eagle eye over a broad field, without being buffaloed by complexity.

A comprehensive context also includes the relationship to time and history, as we shall see in the next chapter. An authentic relationship to the world hinges on the cultivation of a large mental space and a long mental time frame. Living in a large space and a big time makes it possible to develop a strong ethical stance.

Exercise

1. Everyone has biases. These biases often prevent us from seeing or accepting the whole picture. In relation to each of the following entities, what are the biases or "blind eyes" that impede you from seeing the whole picture

CATEGORIES	BIASES	HOW BIAS CUTS OFF THE WHOLE PICTURE	ACTIONS YOU COULD TAKE TO COUNTER THESE BIASES
1. Choosing a car	"classy style"	blinds us to greenhouse effect	Read up on the environmental aspects of autos re emissions, fuel types & consumption
2. Family spending	for example, "kids first"	nobility bias that inhibits parents' need to care for themselves & society	develop a comprehensive budgeting that ensures money for all aspects
3. "The real news"			
4. The different types of people in your workplace			
5. Places in the world			
6. The cultures of the world			

2. List what you consider to be the ten most important news events of the last ten years. Opposite each event, note the geo-social continent on which 1t occurred.

_____

_____

_____

_____

_____

_____

_____

_____

_____

_____

3. What are the five most important social issues of our time? Consult the social process triangle on page 150. Opposite each issue, note whether it is economic, political or cultural.

_____

_____

_____

_____

_____

CHAPTER 8

Historical Involvement

Climbing Onto the Stage of History

Honor the past
But welcome the future
And dance your life away at this wedding.

E.E. CUMMINGS

Leap on the stage
to give a human meaning
to the superhuman struggle

NIKOS KAZANTZAKIS

IMAGES OF HISTORY

It is a pity when we think of history as a subject only taught in school. Part of being human is to see oneself intricately linked to the historical process—past, present and future. For history does not come rolling in for us on a scroll. We create it by our involvement and actions. History is something up close and personal to all of us. It is our very lives, our past events, our present situation and our future destiny. We also

156

reflect the history of our family, our area, our nation, our civilization, and the entire globe.

Most of our images about history need changing. In school, history seems as if it all has to do with the past. But we hear of people who are making history by their deeds in the present, for example, the Americans and Russians involved in building a space station. Then we hear of native North American tribes, who make their decisions on behalf of the next seven generations, so that the future is their context for every decision. So we come to understand that history also has to do with the present and the future.

With all the emphasis on the history of the past, we come to think that history has already been made. Not so. Each of us can affect history by what we do with our lives. Everyone is a historian. I participate in history: I am my history. History is the time of our lives. We live in history.

We also tend to think of history as a long straight line. But obviously the straight line can be bent. The history of British India looked permanent enough that it seemed to stretch forever into the sunset, until that little man Gandhi came along. Then the British left, and India was on a new path quite discontinuous from its past. The direction of history was changed. When enough people see that the way history is moving is not beneficial, they can create another vision of history moving differently. When enough human energy gets behind that vision, history budges, bends, and creates a new way.

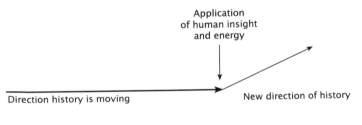

THE PRESENT

HISTORY AS INFINITY LOOP

So, it seems that history is made up of more than our past. The past is the source of our personal and social memory and wisdom. It is also the source of much of our pain. The future is the place of our intentions, hopes, fears and expectations. The challenge of living fully in our present always involves our gathering the yield of the past and choosing the meaning of the future. The future defines the present by a question, an issue, or a problem that affects a life decision. The future challenges the past, and judges the undertakings of the present.

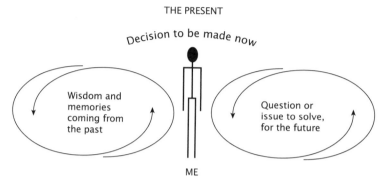

History as Infinity Loop

Every important decision joins together the dynamics of past, present and future in the life of an individual or organization. For example, if your current car has seen better days and you go out to buy a new car, you may find your memories of your dad's and grandfather's cars have given you a certain admiration of big cars—you recall with nostalgia the big Chevy Impala of the 50s with the swooping tail fins. Maybe a big car would be nice. But then out of the future comes the question, "Is such a big gas guzzler with its emissions and its consumption of fossil fuels what the future of planet Earth needs?" You remember the greenhouse effect. You remember a talk you heard by Ralph Nader about cars and the green house effect. You think of other values like safety. Do you really need a vehicle with a good steel frame or rollbar that will give the kids a better chance in an accident? And then, out of the future comes a bigger question: with each car contributing to chaos in the globe's climate and weather systems, is it moral to get another car at all?

This infinity loop—where the past, present and future raise a stream of questions, dialogue and decisions—happens moment by moment in our lives. The future has raised a real question; the question has looped through your present situation into past memories about cars and wisdom about the earth's situation, then back into the present with the question of values, then back into the future with the question of what kind of car. As you stand in the present, you are right in the middle of the historical process. Voices whisper to you—your dad, your kids, Ralph Nader, the world's climate. You decide you are not going to buy a car at all. For a year, you will use for transportation a combination of bicycles, taxis and public conveyance.

So, whenever we make any significant decision we stand in this infinity loop of past-present-future, and by making a decision based on wisdom from the past, we are partic-ipating in history, willy nilly. These days, with our understanding of how life is related to life, we are clearer about the possible impacts of our decision-making. We know that our

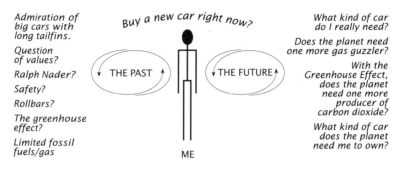

THE PRESENT

Crisis of decision: Decide no...

intentional decisions about the kind of food we buy, the jobs we take, the way we talk to others, make an impact on history.

DEFINING EVENTS CREATE OUR HISTORY

Neither our lives nor history are one, undeviating straight line. Events break into history and move our world into a new historical time. A near-fatal accident that leaves us in a wheelchair for a long time divides our life into two eras: the period before the accident (no wheelchair) and the period after it (wheelchair). On a larger stage, such events may define a whole age. The dropping of the atom bomb introduced the nuclear age in 1945, just as the beep-beep-beep of Yuri Gagarin's spacecraft in the night sky inaugurated the space age in 1957. The media like to call these defining events.

At some point in the 20th century, perhaps through Teilhard de Chardin's *The Phenomenon of Man*, humans realized that "they are now at the tiller of evolution"— evolution will go whichever way we steer it. That is one of the defining insights of our time. Those who understand this are contemporary people. Tampering with the natural creation is considered unnatural and dangerous by good people, such as those demonstrating against genetically modified food.

In 49 BC, Caesar crossed the Rubicon out of Gaul into Italy against the orders of the Roman senate. The Rubicon was a small river which marked the boundary between Italy and Cisalpine Gaul. The moment he crossed that river, he knew things would never be the same. It marked the opening of the civil war against Pompey, and led to Caesar's dictatorship of Rome many years later. "Crossing the Rubicon" has entered popular parlance as a metaphor for a decision or action, after which things are never the same.

We can all look back in our lives to decisions we made where we crossed our own Rubicon. Leaving home, a marriage, or a job, can be very much like crossing the Rubicon for us. In this kind of event , we find ourselves in a whiplash of time.

Such an event is made up of some external impetus, some internal insight and an epoch-making decision. We experience it as both harrowing and life-giving. At the moment of such a pivotal decision, time comes to an end, and starts up again on the other side of it, but it feels like a different kind of time. These events end one phase of our life and launch another.

Our life is going along pretty predictably until things start happening that, per-haps, call it into question. At this point, the line of our life is subject to a kind of fibrilla-tion. Things get a bit bumpy. Then, when we make the big turnaround, our life is still pretty bumpy because we're trying to get used to living this new kind of life. And then life evens out again, as we attempt to adapt ourselves to the new environment. Until the next turnaround.

Here, we are not just talking about events in the lives of history's saints. All of us lately have heard of people who have cashed out of their rat-race professional lives, and enrolled in Volunteers Abroad or engaged in risky rescue work in extreme conditions. Quebec performer Leonard Cohen enters a Zen monastery to do Zazen for a time. The wildly popular rock singer Alanis Morrissette suddenly goes to India for a year to learn meditation. There is a sudden realization that to enter a new phase of their work, they have to stop and regroup internally. Without these sudden kinds of events and deci-sions, lives get too narrow, too stale, too set.

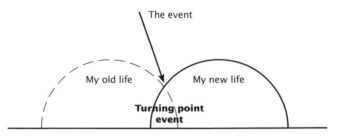

Moment of decision

THE PHASES OF OUR LIVES

Various cultures have wrestled with ways to give meaning to history, especially and the time of our own lives. What does it mean to be young, mature, older, or elder? India has an understanding that each of us has four lifetimes. Rabindranath Tagore defined them as:

- *brahmacharya*, the period of discipline in education

- *garhasthya*, the world's work

- *vanaprasthya*, the retreat for the loosening of bonds

- *pravrajya*, the expectant awaiting of freedom across death.

Most of us, too, can plan to live through four phases of life. First, there is youth from birth to twenty, a time of growing up, of learning how to reflect, of learning life and a trade or profession. The second phase is from twenty to forty—a time of building, of stretching one's wings and shoving our life energy out into society. Thirty is only halfway through our second lifetime. The third phase is forty to sixty, a time of shouldering increasing responsibility, being a leader in some way. When people today are celebrating their fortieth birthday, they see a whole new life ahead where they can pull their values into focus, and enjoy a new-found maturity of outlook. The same thing happens at 60. This is the beginning of the fourth phase, a more reflective phase, less on center stage, but when some find a brand new trajectory of interest and engagement in life. From 60 to 80, we become the guide, the old sage who demonstrates and teaches the way, who gives the truths and allows younger people to grow.

With so many more people living longer, (the fastest growing population in North America is between 80 and 85) perhaps there is also a fifth phase from 80 to 100, another lifetime to be endowed with meaning. With these life phases, each of us can be the historians of our own lives, and create our own history.

HONORING THE PAST

We generally understand that we need to celebrate on birthdays or anniversaries, at Christmas and Thanksgiving. Some families and organizations are in the habit of conducting a historical review at the end of the year or quarter, where they name the significant events that happened during that time, and name the periods where events cluster. This naming can absolve the frustrations of the past and give permission to move into the future with fresh energy and commitment.

Honoring the past also means taking into account the work of those who went before. Daniel Boorstin's trilogy, *The Discoverers*, *The Creators*, and *The Seekers*, does an extraordinary job of holding up and celebrating those who discovered the reality of our world, recreated our consciousness through their achievements in the arts, and sought meaning and purpose in our existence. We are always building on the shoulders of the past. Part of living is acknowledging the contributions of others to the work we are doing. So, the writer of a report acknowledges the work of those who gathered the data and pulled it together. The writer of a book acknowledges all the sources that are being used, if the author is honest. A group doing research does not start off from scratch, as if they are researching an issue with no past. They search the files, the library and the Internet so that their work builds on relevant findings. And they recognize this prior work in their report.

It is refreshing to know that we don't have to compete with the past, or pretend that we post-moderns are the only ones with wisdom, or that our problems far exceed in complexity any of the past, so that the past has nothing to say to us. We can build on the wisdom of our ancestors, realizing with the author of *Ecclesiastes* that "there is nothing new under the sun."

However, our roots are really in the future, while we honor the past. It is the future that calls, beckons, and summons us to imagine it, so that we are not overwhelmed by the issues it brings.

HONORING AND LETTING GO OF THE PAST

At the same time we live in the now. When no decisions are pending, we feel free to be our being fully in the present. In that great old play, *Our Town*, Emily gets caught up in the sense of being privileged just to be alive in the present moment. She exclaims,

> Oh, earth, you're too wonderful for anybody to realize you!
> Do any human beings ever realize life while they live it?
> Every, every minute?"

In the present, our future and our past are ours. People who are never aware of "now" lose the possibility of resting in the present. They are held by the guilts and mistakes of the past and cannot separate from them, or they escape toward the future, planning, dreaming, unable to rest in the present. An old story of two monks always holds for me how difficult it is to live in the present moment:

> Two monks journeying home came to the banks of a fast-flowing river, where they met a young woman unable to cross the current alone. One of the monks picked her up in his arms, set her safely on her feet on the other side, and the two monks continued on their travels. The monk who had crossed the river alone could finally restrain himself no longer and began to rebuke his brother, "Do you not know it is against our rules to touch a young woman? You have broken the holy vows." The other monk answered, "Brother, I left that young woman on the banks of the river. Are you still carrying her?"

Michael Ignatieff writes in *The Warrior's Honor* about places like Yugoslavia and

Rwanda where healing and forgiveness are very slow. He comments that one of the difficulties experienced is that "the past continues to torment because it is not past." These places are not living in serial time but in simultaneous time, in which the past and present form a continuous agglutinated mass of fantasies, distortions, myths, and lies. Reporters in the Balkan War of the 1990s often found that, when they were told atrocity stories, they were uncertain whether these events had occurred the day before, or in 1941, or 1841 or 1441. For the tellers of the tales, yesterday and today were the same. Crimes can never be fixed in the past; they remain locked in the eternal present, crying out for vengeance. Ignatieff says that one of the things that needs to happen in the Balkans is to relearn how to forget. Forgive? Yes, always. But there are times when a whole people living in an eternal present of the wrongs done to them needs to forget. The Serbstill remember Roman injustices done to them 1500 years ago as if it were yesterday. Ignatieff continues:

> All nations depend on forgetting; on forging myths of unity and identity that allow a society to forget its founding crimes, its hidden injuries and divisions, its unhealed wounds. Paul Tillich, in *The Eternal Now*, corroborates that: "If too much is preserved, and too little forgotten, the way is barred: the past with its infantile forces and memories, overpowers the future. Life can not continue without throwing the past into the past, liberating the present from its burden. Without this power, life would be without a future; it would be enslaved by the past.

Perhaps one of the most important roles in the world today belongs to people who are assigned or try to be special envoys, mediators, or negotiators. When they stick themselves in the breach of history in Northern Ireland, Palestine/Israel, Kosovo, or wherever, they insist with their lives that the future be born, the past be forgiven and put away, and old wrongs be properly healed and buried.

This is just as true in our own lives. Unless people find ways to distance themselves from certain events in the past when they were wronged, abused, or put down, those memories become like lead weights as people try to swim the waters of life, even when they are not conscious. In the light of affirmation, it is possible to re-vision one's life historically in the manner of Hugh McLennan when he declares in *The Watch That Ends the Night*:

> That which is darkness, also is light.
> This, which is no, also is yes.
> This, which is hatred, also is love.
> This, which is fear, also is courage.
> This, which is defeat, also is victory.

But, without taking anything away from the need to forget, it seems that the real question has to be, "What does the future require that we recall or remember from the past?" And obviously, that is going to change as our grasp of what the future requires changes.

So we are called to honor the past, live in the present that is given, but have our roots always in the future—always whirling through that dynamic infinity loop—what it means to live in history.

HUMAN BEINGS CHANGE HISTORY

But history is a lot more than "things happening to us." Our personal history, like history at large, is both active and passive. History happens to us, and we happen to history. As a character in the movie *Primary Colors* declares, "History's what we're about; what else is there?" History is a human invention: it does not come floating in on a scroll. It is constantly being created and made by the willed decisions of human beings. In answer to the question, "Does the world allow for my will?", historical human beings have always said, "Yes." The future is built by human decision and can at any moment be altered by human decision. There is a story about the samurai Nobunaga that illustrates this:

> Nobunaga, a great Japanese warrior, decided to attack the enemy, even though he had only one tenth the number of men that the opposition commanded. He knew that he would win, but his soldiers were in doubt. On the way he stopped at a Shinto shrine and told his men: "After I visit the shrine, I will toss a coin. If heads comes, we will win. If tails, we will lose. Destiny holds us in her hand." Nobunaga entered the shrine and offered a silent prayer. He came forth and tossed a coin. Heads appeared. His soldiers were so eager to fight that they won the battle easily. "No one can change the hand of destiny," his attendant told him after the battle. "Indeed not," said Nobunaga, showing a coin which had been doubled, with heads facing either way.

At any one moment we face the product of all the decisions we have ever made. If we could organize all these decisions into patterns, we might find what we stand for as individuals. But history has always been made by the power of human decision, by "iron" men and women, who stand and declare with their lives, "History is going to go this way!" "Who says so?" "I say so!"

CLAMBERING ONTO THE STAGE OF HISTORY

We have noticed in our lives how the old and the new struggle. All history is this struggle between that which is no longer and that which is not yet. It is the tension between the ever emerging new and the old that is ever passing. In every age, we can see these opposing forces—those defending the cherished values of past tradition, and those directed toward the future that is becoming. So, history is more than a book; it is also a stage where humans are invited to leap up and create forward-looking movement in the civilizing process, to do something that changes history, or creates the new. In recent history we have seen one movement after another climb onto the stage of history and demand change, whether they stood for the emancipation of slaves, the integration of "coloured people" in North America and South Africa, better conditions for workers, women's rights, a protected environment, or a more comprehensive education.

At particular points, individuals decide to say "no" to what they see as inhuman or unjust, and start the ball rolling towards a more human and just future.

My mother sat me down one day as a child to tell me a story about my father:

> Your father was president of the Sydney Rotary Club and a delegate to the International Rotary Conference in Tokyo. This was in 1928. He invited me to go with him on the Cunard liner. Three days out from Sydney, a Grand Ball was held, and all the ship's passengers were invited. There were many Australian and British people on board, as well as people from Japan and from all over Asia. As the band struck up and the first dance started, Bob Stanfield noticed something strange: all the Asian people were dancing on one side of the ballroom, and all the whities on the other. As he looked further, he noticed a ribbon down the middle dividing the hall in two. He turned to me and said, "Grace, do you see the absolute bullshit going on here? Give me your scissors!" (Being a seamstress from way back, I always carried scissors in my purse.) I knew what he was going to do, so I said, "Now, Bob, don't do anything impetuous." "Impetuous!" he replied, "I'm going to stop this nonsense right now." I guess he figured that if the Rotarians stood for fairness, promoting good will and better friendships, this arrangement was not going to do it. So he strode over to the ribbon, waited till enough eyes were fastened on him, cut the ribbon in grand style, took the scissors back, and then crossed the line and asked a Japanese woman to dance. People got the idea, others also crossed the line, and the ballroom was integrated there and then. That happened years before you were born.

While visiting the Black History Museum in Dartmouth, Nova Scotia recently, I learned about Viola Desmond (1914-1965). In late 1946 this successful Halifax business woman was making a business trip to Sydney, Nova Scotia, when her car broke down in New Glasgow. Forced to stay the night while her car was getting fixed, she decided to catch the evening movie in the Roselands Theatre. No one had told her about the unwritten law concerning the good seats and bad seats. So she sat downstairs in the white section, rather than upstairs in the black section. When the manager told her to go to the balcony, she refused. She offered to pay the extra ten cents for sitting downstairs, but the police dragged her off to the police station. In the process her clothes were torn and Viola was bruised. She was accused of defrauding the Nova Scotia government of an amusement tax in the amount of one cent. For this she was fined and imprisoned. As a result of her imprisonment, a defense fund was organized, and the equivalent of the NAACP formed. Her imprisonment brought the Jim Crow laws to everyone's attention.

A CONSTANT TASK

Civilization is constantly being pulled down, like humanness itself, and is always being rebuilt by the decisions of ordinary people using whatever tools they have, as in this story that comes from the *Adelaide Fountain Newsletter.*

> It was Sarajevo in 1992, a time of civil war. Demagogues lit bonfires of hatred between citizens who belonged to different religions and ethnic groups. Everyone became an enemy of someone else. Many were maimed. Many were killed. Those who did not die lived like animals in the ruins of the city.
>
> Except one middle-aged man, Vedran Smailovic, a cellist with the Sarajevo Opera Orchestra. Every day, dressed in formal black evening clothes, he came to a street corner in front of a bakery where mortar fire had recently killed 22 people waiting for bread. Sitting in a fire-charred chair in the middle of the street and braving sniper and artillery fire day after day for 22 days, he played the profoundly moving "Adagio in G minor" attributed to Albinoni. Actually the piece of music owes little to the Baroque composer as it was constructed by musicologist Remo Giazotto from a manuscript fragment found in the ruins of Dresden after the Second World War.
>
> The original fragment survived the fire bombing. Perhaps that is why Vedran played this music in the scarred street in Sarajevo. His music was stronger than hate, gis courage stronger than fear. And in time other musicians were captured by his spirit, and they took their places in the street beside him. Anyone who could play an instrument or sing found a place at a street intersection somewhere in the city and made music. In time the fighting stopped.
>
> The place where Vedran played has become an informal shrine, a place of honor for Croats, Serbs, Muslims and Christians alike. They place flowers where he played, commemorating the hope that must never die—that someday, somehow, the best of humanity shall overcome the worst.

An artist in Seattle read this story in *The New York Times* and she organized 22 cellists to play in 22 public places in Seattle for 22 days. On the final day all of them played together in one place in front of a store window displaying burned out bread pans, 22 loaves of bread, and 22 roses.

People came. Newspaper reporters and television cameras were there. The story and pictures were fed into the news networks of the world, and also passed back to Smailovic so that he might know that his music had been heard. Now others have begun to play in different cities.

History and civilization depend on people who never say die. Kazantzakis called the long line of those who have given their lives to building civilization "the Crimson Line". Wherever they show up, they weave, spin and build on behalf of the humanizing civilization of the future.

Kazantzakis heard all those from the past who have weaved and fought on behalf of the civilizing process crying out to us: "Finish our work! Finish our work!" Someone in ICA put Kazantzakis' words to the music of the country song, "I Walk the Line" by Johnny Cash:

> We are one body with the human race,
> All who are, will be, and ever have been,
> "You must not die," the dead cry out within,
> "Finish our work! Finish our work!"
> We choose to hear the cries from history
> Of pioneers in responsibility,
> Who struggled for a world they did not see,
> "Finish our work! Finish our work!"

So how do we sum up in a nutshell this stance of historical involvement?

- It holds the perspective that we all participate in the past, present and future every time we make a significant decision.

- Our own personal history is created by our individual decisions as well as by those sentinel events of our time that create turnarounds in our lives. In the light of these events we write our own history and live out our own great story.

- We honor the past and seek its wisdom, but we always find our life in the present moment. To this end we distance ourselves from the past, letting go of its grip so we can welcome the future and respond to its issues.

- In this way, we are free to climb onto the stage of history and make an impact, helping to change the direction of history.

- Everyone's actions decide our future. If we decide nothing, or do nothing, that still makes an impact, even if is a negative one. The insight is held in Edmund Burke's oft-quoted statement, "All that is needed for the triumph of evil is that good people do nothing."

Of course, we know that most of those who bring about change with their very beings are forgotten. Lawrence of Arabia blazed briefly onto the stage of history in World War I and worked wonders. After the war he played a brief role in the peace treaty. Once off the historical stage, he was quickly forgotten by his compatriots. Some few who clambered onto history's stage will be remembered and recorded by history; most will fade away unsung and unheralded by future historians. But the future will be different because of them.

Exercise: Creating a Personal Lifeline

CONTEXT

Every human being has a history of life-changing events where, on the one side of the event, life was one way, and, on the other side of the event, life was somehow quite different. In this exercise we will create a picture of our personal history listing these events and arranging them along the line of our lives.

PROCEDURES

Part A: Listing the Events of My Life

1. We want to create a list of the key events in our life. For each item below, write a key event from your life and the year it happened (guessing, if you have to):

Kinds of Events	*Year*

- an angry argument: _____
- the death of a beloved relative: _____
- making a whopper of a mistake: _____
- a major success in your life: _____
- an accident to yourself:_____
- a great book or movie that happened to you personally:_____
- the time you experienced an "awakenment": _____
- an act of god like a hurricane, earthquake or flood that you experienced _____
- a strange encounter: _____
- some event that made you see through: _____
- a family drama: _____

List any other key events that don't fit above:

_____

_____

_____

_____

2. Now put a star beside the five big events in your life.

OVERALL TITLE FOR MY LIFE					
TITLE				TITLE	
TITLE	TITLE	TITLE	TITLE	TITLE	TITLE

✳			✳	✳		✳		✳		✳	
1935			1950	1955	1960		1970		1980		1990		2000

0	5	10	15	20	25	30	35	40	45	50	55	60	65
birth	broke leg		aunt dies	married	database		wilderness		argument with wife	Major crisis		breakthrough in vocation	
			first job	disaster!			experience mystery						
			graduation										
				Gandhi Movie	Emily born			retreat					

Part B: Drawing the Lifeline

3. On a sheet of paper, turned lengthwise, draw a line about one-third of the way down your page.

4. Now divide your age by five to get the number of spaces to divide your line into. (If you are forty-two years old, you will have nine five-year spaces. If you are sixty-four, you will have thirteen.) Now divide your line into that number of spaces, and mark the years of your life 5, 10, 15 etc.

5. Write all the events underneath your lifeline (as shownin the example).

Part C: Creating the sections of the chart

6. Make a star for each of the five key events on the lifeline where they occurred and mark them on the top of the line with a big star and a brief annotation.

7. Most or all of these were turning points. Draw lines up from the baseline at each of those points so that your chart now has six divisions.

8. Consider how each of those major events changed your understanding of yourself.

Part D.

9. In the light of that, give a factual or poetic title to those six parts of your life that captures its unique character.

10. Add another row above the sections and group the sections into two main parts. Give both parts a title that describes it.

11. In the top row of the chart give your whole life up to now a title that pulls together the other titles.

Part E. Reflect

What happened to you as you did this exercise?

_____

_____

What did you struggle with most?

_____

What came clear to you in the process?

_____

_____

Who would you recommend this exercise to?

_____

CONCLUSION

As we sketch out this lifeline, or chart of our life, we are creating what can be the skeleton of our personal story. We can use this skeleton to recover and deepen our own story. According to Jean Houston, a deeper story sustains and shapes our emotional attitudes, provides us with life purposes, and energizes our everyday acts. It offers us both meaning and momentum. Everything coheres when a deeper story is present." Readers may be interested in her book, *The Search for the Beloved*, for methods for deepening their personal story.

CHAPTER 9

Inclusive Responsibility

Shouldering the Load

In responsibility both obedience and freedom are realized.
DIETRICH BONHOEFFER

It often seems easier to complain about the ways things are
than to take responsibility for initiating change.
FRANCES VAUGHAN

MORAL METAPHORS

I am walking down Danforth Avenue in Toronto, minding my own business, when a very thin man, somewhat dishevelled, asks me for spare change. "Wow!" I exclaim to myself, "this is the third beggar today." I used to meet beggars daily when I lived in Bombay, but I've never gotten used to the experience. And everyday, I seem to face more demands from other people's needs. What should I do? I could just do what I am asked—in this case, give the thin man money. I could tell him to get a job, or give him a little lecture on self-reliance. I could suggest somewhere to go for help. The simplest thing is to ignore

172

him and walk on. I have tried all these responses. I have asked other people what they do, and they all answered according to their own values. At one time, perhaps, we agreed on what should be done. Not any more.

NEW MORAL METAPHORS

Today we are all carving out new moral systems. We see clearly that moral principles are human inventions, and as such, are relative. Today it's not just a matter of deciding right from wrong. Often as not, we have to decide between right and right, and wrong and wrong. In our times, as Camus said, we are clear that the cry for clean hands that might come from making the exactly "right" decisions is the cry of a damned soul. There are no clean hands. For many people who appreciate their own degree of moral probity this is painful. The fact is that our time uses a different metaphor and a different set of principles. In many situations we have to deal with, there are no rules. We have only our critical intelligence to determine what is really needed. Today, we ask not what is right, but what is responsible. Not what is good or bad, but what is befitting or appropriate. Not whether it is honest or pure, but whether it is necessary and responsible.

Some time ago, I received a difficult assignment. A colleague's drinking problem had taken a turn for the worse. I was asked to see that he booked into a treatment clinic, then visit him every day, and ensure that he was taking his prescribed pill. Then I was to accompany him to a series of Alcoholics Anonymous meetings, and when he returned home, continue to visit in order to check on the pill-taking. He was an older man, much senior to me both in years and experience. I was deeply embarrassed at having, in my mind, to treat my elder as a kid; he, for his part, was offended by having this watchdog check up on him. I felt like a heel. I could feel all my liberal tendencies rising up in sympathy for him. I didn't want to ask him the hard questions, I just wanted to be his buddy—a nice, kind, regular guy. When he left the clinic I would visit his home. Finally, I went to see my boss, and said, "Do you know what kind of pain this assignment has given me so far?" He said, "Look, I know it's hard; you want to be his friend, right? But you have to decide whether you're going to be a nice guy, or whether you are going to do what's necessary to get that man sober and back to doing what he does best." So, for another month I kept up the visits and each day asked the question, "Well, Jack, have you taken your pill?" If he hadn't, I would demand that he take it on the spot, then submit to his resentment. If anyone had asked my why I went through with all this, totally contrary to all my natural leanings, all I could have said was, "It was necessary." I felt no virtue in it. It seemed to me that I was being an interfering bastard. But I knew that someone had to be the bear in that situation for the sake of Jack's future, his family's future and the tremendous talent he had. The old ethical metaphors of "being nice" and "empathizing" and "being a good friend" didn't help me here.

When we ask what is necessary, rather than what is right or wrong, we up the ethical ante. When we ask what history requires of me or what society or humanness needs, we enter a different ethical space. Similarly with these questions: "Do I need to pick up my child now, or will a little more time help him find some independence?" "Will a glass of Scotch help or hinder me in what I am trying to accomplish?" "Does history require complete honesty or a little white lie?" These questions illuminate a wide canvas of context for the ethic of responsibility.

THE ETHIC OF RESPONSIBILITY

The ethic of responsibility means making decisions from a context that is history-long and world-wide. In this context Socrates, for example, decided it was necessary to be a philosophical wrecking ball over against the double standards of the philosophers of his day. Dietrich Bonhoeffer, living in Germany under National Socialism decided, with others, that all of history required that Hitler be murdered. Nelson Mandela, at one stage in his life, decided that armed insurrection was responsible, the only thing that would pose a real threat to South Africa's apartheid system. Now, relatives of terminally ill patients are deciding that what is responsible is to hasten their death. None of these acts are sanctioned by old moralities. Bonhoeffer and Mandela's conspiracies were illegal, and immoral, but, judged by the verdict of history, necessary.

I am guided in this section by the writings of Dietrich Bonhoeffer in his book, *Ethics.* Born in 1906, he played a significant role in the ecumenical movement in Germany during the inter-war years, and from 1935 was in charge of an unofficial, later illegal, theological seminary. After his church activity was forbidden by the Nazis, he left for the United States in 1939. He went through a harrowing process of deciding whether to stay in the safety of the United States or to return and face the music. He decided to return to Germany just before the outbreak of the Second World War because he felt the need to be with his own people.

Bonhoeffer was invited to join Germany's official counter-espionage service as a secret agent, where a conspiracy against Hitler was being developed. As a member of the counter-espionage he visited ecumenical leaders in Geneva and Sweden, where he appealed for British support for those plotting against Hitler.

Bonhoeffer was executed in the closing days of the Second World War, when the guns of the Allied advance could be heard in the distance. He died at the hands of one of Hitler's special commandos in the concentration camp of Flossenburg, in Bavaria.

Bonhoeffer's greatest theological influence came after his death, with the posthumous publication of his *Ethics,* and the letters and papers he composed while in prison.

I think Bonhoeffer knew so much about decision-making because of the difficult decisions he had to face in his own life in Hitler's Germany: whether to register for military service? He didn't. How far can a Christian minister use violence? It was he who asked for Hitler's head. Whether to leave Germany? He did, teaching for a year in the United States. Having left Germany, whether to return? Having returned, whether to cross the line and conspire against Hitler? He did. Could he be party to an assassination? He was. I find that I can put great trust in a writer who has wrestled deeply and died on behalf of the convictions he wrote about.

Bonhoeffer helped me understand something for the first time, namely, that responsibility holds obligations and rights, obedience and freedom in the same universe. In a highly charged situation, he showed us not only how to make decisions out of the big picture, but to do so in freedom and ambiguity, while taking the consequences of our deed. I saw that freedom and obligation always exist in tension with each other, a tension which, Bonhoeffer reminds us, is held by the concept of responsibility. In the diagram below, imagine a rubber band holding together obligation and freedom. The tighter we stretch that rubber band, the greater the possibility of authentic responsibility.

So it is clear that we are not going to get anywhere with the concept of responsibility until we clarify obligation and freedom, one at a time. Such a sequential approach has its dangers. It's important to remember that unlimited obligation is always in dialogue with unlimited freedom, so we can navigate this next section.

OBLIGATION

As human beings, we have obligations. Other people and organizations make claims on our life, whether it's the government demanding taxes, the crying child wanting food or comfort, the beggar in the street wanting money, or our supervisor assigning tasks. In each case, we are expected—obliged—to respond. Our obligations are always greater than we want to admit. It is fairly easy to recognize our obligations to partner, children and work, but we have a harder time saying yes to our larger obligations. Which raises the question of just how much obligation we have?

We know, as employees, that we are obligated to our job; otherwise, we are likely to be fired. But are our fellow employees any of our business? Bonhoeffer says they are. Our own conscience says they are. We know that the boss has an obligation to the whole operation, but what about us? We are obviously obligated to do the work we are paid to do. But what about our relationship to our boss as another human being? Is this stretching it too much? Bonhoeffer says there are times when we need to take responsibility even for the boss. What about our fellow workers? What does it mean to take responsibility for them every day? We are also responsible for the organization becoming what it needs to be. Then, what about the community where we live? Are we obligated to that? We know we are. What about region or our country? We know we are. What about Brazil? Bosnia? Rwanda? The oceans? The answer is yes—our neighbor is all over the place. Relatives make demands on us. E-mail opens up relationships, but also asks for favors and places demands. The question is always, "How much obligation dare we bite off?" Bonhoeffer says we cannot be free *or* responsible unless we are 100 per cent obligated.

As soon as we hear those two words, our stress levels start climbing. As I look at my desk at home, there are funding requests from three different health organizations (give to one, and the rest get you in their databases). I have an e-mail asking for money to let a young lad go to Vietnam as a volunteer. Another e-mail is inviting me to a conference. A facilitator in Bosnia is asking me to send them a construct. My aged mother-in-law wants me to take her to the doctor. An old person on the 18th floor wants me to help her move out of her apartment. The cat needs to go to the vet for annual shots. Every night on the news, I watch the refugees pouring out of Kosovo, the daylights being bombed out of Belgrade, and I struggle to make sense of it. At work, I have a five-thousand word article due on Friday. This is how the comprehensive context of obligation comes to me personally. It is not an abstraction. The point here is not the challenge of responding to all these obligations, but simply the fact that we show up obligated in many different contexts. We can acknowledge that as the way life is, or hide from it.

Individual obligations often come to us as more than we can possibly handle. I remember the first time this happened to me. This was after our family had retired from the hotel, and we were living out along the river. We had a jetty and an open 18-foot launch that I got pretty good at handling. A local businessman was starting the first airline service between our town and Sydney, using World War II Sunderland flying boats. These planes would land on a straight stretch of the river and, by arrangement, use our property and wharf as a terminal. On the appointed day, the Sunderland made a perfect landing in the middle of the river and dropped anchor in mid- stream. Somehow, the passengers and their luggage had to get to shore, but apparently that part of the arrangement was not very clear. So my dad said to me: "Brian, you'd better go out in the launch and pick up the luggage." I felt like saying, "This could be out of my league." But I steered the launch out to the flying boat. My two twin sisters came with me, consumed with anticipation, because there was to be a swimsuit fashion show on the wings of the flying boat for promotion of the airline. I made eye contact with the navigator. He looked at me, all four foot six inches of me and said a little skeptically, "You are the luggage boat? Blow me down! Well, here comes the luggage."

We loaded the boat with as much as it would take, and at that point I got scared. A wind came up and a chop developed on the river. We had about three inches to the top of the gunwale. And then, amazingly, four people got in. Now water started slopping over the gunwale. Suddenly I realized that I was responsible for the boat, the luggage, the passengers, and probably the future of that air line. The boat could sink in the next few minutes, and the luggage and passengers would be floating down the river. Well, I put the motor slowly into gear and edged out into the stream really slowly and got the chop at my rear, and made my way bit by bit toward the jetty. My two sisters, fascinated by the fashion show, had no concept of the danger, or what I was going through. I got all the way back to the jetty and moored the boat and got everything off without swamping the boat or losing the luggage or drowning the passengers or ruining the airline. For a while, in that situation, I was Atlas bearing the weight of the world and the future of that airline service. On that day, I learned what it means to act without the support of anyone.

We tend to shy away from obligations, but then what dawns on us one day is that there is no limit to obligation and responsibility. Obligation is everywhere. It's easy to say to sundry examples of global need, "That's none of my business." It's all of my business. There literally is no limit to responsibility. It's just there, totally, entirely, it's all one ball of wax and any attempt to divide it up fails.

With so many obligations, is there any time left for what we personally want to decide?" Enter the wonder of human freedom.

FREEDOM

As human beings, we show up obligated. But, as human beings, we also show up free. (Do I hear a sigh of relief?) We have freedom of decision: we can freely make decisions on our own. We are not bound by the past. We don't have to do something a certain way because we did it that way last time, or because "it has always been done that way." We are not bound by other people's expectations of us. When of age, we can make decisions on our own without asking others' permission. We can dare to risk boldly. We can dare to act. When we are requested to do something, we are free to ask "why?" When old laws no longer serve, we are free to make up new laws.

The ethic of freedom gives us 100 per cent permission to be our unique, unrepeatable selves, making our own decisions, not allowing ourselves to be limited by the images others have of us; free to create our own lives as we want them to be, free to use our time, our resources as we decide.

Freedom is always something to be realized, grasped and used. Without it, we are left to try to fit ourselves into the box of morality. Once freedom is realized, there is no box. Freedom means that we create our own morality. I can play any role needed. In Camus's terms, I can play the role of the lover. Like Don Juan, who loved every woman he came across, I can decide to love any situation I am in to the hilt. If I'm a teacher, I decide to love those kids to the limit through my excellent teaching. Or I move into a situation, decide to love it, and with a few words transform the mood of that situation. Or I can decide to be the actor who can play any role needed: a clown, if humour is needed; a leader, if it's a chaotic situation; or a priest, if there are wounds to be healed.

The experience of freedom is like a heady drug—it's exhilarating, dangerous, full of risks. It's the feeling of diving off the high board, or having the accelerator stick at 80 m.p.h. The only question for us is, "Is that the way life is?"—we test our experience of life to decide what is authentic. Another way to say it is that we live life over the abyss. In the Canadian National Tower in Toronto, over 1, 000 feet up, there is a section of the flooring made of transparent six-inch glass. While the signs say that walking on the glass is quite safe, that it is strong enough to support six elephants, it is always interesting to see people's reactions. When I walk out and stand on the glass, I can see the ground below a long way down, but I am symbolically out over nothing. The last time I was there I noticed that some people, in spite of all assurances, refused to step on that glass flooring. The kids, for their part, were dancing all over it. You could see two quite different responses to the idea of being out over the abyss.

Many people refuse the wide-open spaces of freedom, preferring to live on what Hermann Hesse called "the trusty railway track", because it's sure and certain and safe. We get a glimpse of the tragic dimension of this railway track in Margaret Lawrence's *The Stone Angel*. The main character Hagar is near the end of her life, reflecting on it.

> I lie here and try to recall something truly free I've done in ninety years.
> I can think of only two acts that might be so, both recent.
> One was a joke.... The other was a lie.

THE TENSION BETWEEN OBLIGATION AND FREEDOM

There is tension between obligation and freedom: that is just part of the structure of life—the way life is for all of us. We don't like tension: we prefer things to be black or white, cut and dried, straightforward. This tension between obligation and freedom is difficult. Decisions are fraught with ambiguity. On the one hand we want to keep our freedom, and on the other to honor our obligation. How in practical terms can we achieve both? We look for something that keeps the tension, but also serves as some kind of guide.

After these paragraphs on obligation and freedom, you might assume that, when we make a decision, we automatically have to decide between obligation and freedom. Now, the next two sentences need to be written in letters six inches tall. *The alternatives are not between whether we are going to be free or obligated. The challenge in every decision we make is to be one hundred per cent obligated and one-hundred per cent free at the same time.*

Bonhoeffer described, tellingly for me, what happens when we break the tension between obligation and freedom. He said that, if we make freedom independent of obligation, we follow the ethic of the irresponsible genius. That is, we float our way through life moved, not by the vision of what is necessary, but by an unending sequence of spontaneous inspirations without any context.

At university, I ran into a delightful guy, full of great jokes and endless ideas of what to do. One week, he said he was learning Greek, the next week he joined the local dig sponsored by the archeology department. He told me he was going to volunteer in Bhutan. The next week he was madly in love with an archeology undergrad, and vowing he was going to take up pottery. And so it went on, the weird, wild and variegated life of an irresponsible genius.

If, on the other hand, we make obligation independent of freedom, we follow the Kantian ethic of duty: we do what we are told not because it is historically necessary, but, like Adolph Eichmann, because someone has told us to. When Adolph Eichmann was brought to trial, and asked why he killed so many million Jews, he said, "I was only obeying orders." When we abandon freedom because it is too demanding and decide to simply do whatever we are told, we become a slave.

In an article in *INC.* Magazine, Bill Bartmann, founder of Hawkeye Pipe Services describes how he saw his company go under. It owed creditors more than $1 million. In this situation, most people file for bankruptcy protection or reach a liquidation agreement with creditors, who usually get a fraction of what they are owed. But Bartmann decided to take the difficult and responsible decision: to pay back his debts regardless of how long it would take." It just seemed inherently wrong to try to escape by using a law as an escape hatch or excuse. "It took him two and a half years from the time he shut down, but Bartmann paid everyone back in full. He said, "Business people understand the reward side very easily. I don't think they understand the reciprocal side is that they should be obligated to pay the piper, if indeed there are any assets with which to do that." The question is, "Do they have a responsibility beyond the legal requirements?" The answer must be: decidedly yes. Existentially, the debt is still there, even if the law says it's been dealt with. As the responsible one, we can no more hide behind the law from one's obligations, than we can hide behind anything else. Of course, part of the pain for those who decide to pay debts all the way is that they can point to people living in five-million-dollar houses and with $100,000 cars who took the easy and legal way out and offered their debtors 30 per cent or nothing. Doing what is legal is not necessarily the same as doing what is responsible.

Bonhoeffer goes on to say that both the person of duty and the irresponsible genius carry their justification for their deeds within themselves. So if I am a person of duty and someone asks me why I took the dog for a walk on this particular morning, I'll say, "Because it's my assignment this week, and I always do my assignment." Ask the irresponsible genius the same question, and the answer is likely to be: "Because I felt like it, and I always do what I feel like."

But the responsible one dares to act under obligation and in freedom. In responsibility, both obedience and freedom are made real. Responsible action is subject to obligation and yet it is creative. When a truly responsible person is asked why she took the dog for a walk, she will say something like, "It was necessary. Something had to be done. The dog was running round and round in circles, and threatening to scratch the sofa to shreds." The responsible one does not carry her justification within herself but within the context that made the deed necessary. Well, who says it was necessary? She says it was necessary.

What might a free responsible decision look like? We make a lot of such decisions in the constant attempt to balance the obligations in our lives. Suppose my family meal prep assignment chart has me down to do dinner prep on Monday night, and about 4 p.m. on Monday my boss asks me to stay back after work to finish a report. Here are two obligations clashing with each other. The boss is waiting for my reply. Do I automatically give in to the boss? That would be abandoning freedom. How do we hold the prior obligation and make a free decision out of what we sense is necessary? Some quick tactical thinking could solve it. "Mr. Blackburn, I can't fill your request this evening, as I have a prior engagement. But I know someone who could do it for you. How about that?" He's a real stickler, and says, "Hey, this is what you get paid for." If we find that no one else at home can do the cooking tonight, we see that, either way, we are going to land in trouble. If I assume that I *have* to do the extra assignment because the boss asked me to, and I always do what the boss asks, then I am no longer free; I'm just another slave to duty. Ditto for what my spouse says. So how do I responsibly handle this?. I make a free decision. Maybe, if this kind of thing happens too often, I just go home to fix dinner. Maybe I do the work on the document, and catch a cab home hoping there will still be time for me to prepare a late dinner. Holding the tension between obligation and freedom is never easy.

THE PROCESS OF DECISION-MAKING

At times the ambiguity and perplexity can be excruciating. We have to look at all aspects of the situation and the relevant values. We need to consider the people involved and the purpose of the undertaking. We have to consider all this, weigh up various options, decide and act. Some of us are good at considering, but that's where the process stops. Some are skilled at weighing the pros and cons, but their decision gets lost in the fog of ambiguity. Some can decide quickly but not act, some are good at acting without any evaluation.

At the same time, we need to examine our motives, as well as the prospects of success in the undertaking. Our neighbor always comes as an intrusion into our lives like the baby crying in the middle of the night. We decide what to do in the midst of innumerable perspectives, or as Bonhoeffer says, "in the twilight of good and evil." And sometimes we have to decide not only between right and right, but between wrong and wrong.

Bonhoeffer says that, as free people, nothing can answer for or exonerate us. No law can justify the responsible deed. As persons of responsibility we decide alone without any appeal to authority or attempt at self-justification. We simply surrender the deed, and let history decide whether it was "right or wrong."

An example of this process is when a family decides, following a living will, to take a terminally ill relative off life support. They have to get as much information as possible from the doctors on the patient's prospects. They have to examine their own motives and values and intent. There is as yet no law which will justify their decision. They have to choose between keeping the patient alive and prolonging her suffering, which has been considered the moral thing to do, or cutting off that life. They also know that they are the only ones who can decide, without any attempt at self-justification, but with the simple understanding that this deed was necessary.

In Elliott Leyton's book on the work of Doctors without Borders, two doctors and an Italian nurse reflect on contradictions in their work. They are really talking about the ambiguity of deciding priorities in emergency situations:

> We come here with our European notion of how to avoid cholera, typhoid, dysentery, and we say, "The water you drink carries things that make you sick and kill you and your children, so you must boil your water before drinking it." But if they are to boil the water, then they must spend much more time gathering wood to make the fires— and this is critical time that every member of the family must normally devote to growing their meager crops on their tiny plots. So now they have clean water, but not enough food to eat; now they will die not of cholera, but of starvation.

TAKING THE CONSEQUENCES

One of the most unpalatable aspects of making free, responsible decisions is taking the consequences. For our responsibility does not stop with the deed we have done. There will probably be repercussions or consequences. They go with the territory. We just can't say afterwards, "Hey, I did a responsible deed. That was hard enough. You can't saddle me with the consequences. I did the best I knew how." That's not how it works.

In the movie *Lifeboat,* survivors of a sinking ship occupy a lifeboat. Some sit in the lifeboat, while others are in the water, hanging on to the sides. The ship's mate decides to take responsibility for the situation. The lifeboat is about to sink, because too many people are on board. He commands some of the younger ones to get out and hang on to the side. Those on board rebel against what they consider to be his high-handedness. The mate takes a gun out from the boat's rear compartment and says that anyone who does not obey his orders will be shot. He is clear that the boat is close to sinking, and that the attempt to save one or two more may result in the death of everyone. So he decides to save the ones in the boat. In the process he shoots a couple of people to maintain order. Thanks to the mate's efforts, the lifeboat stays afloat and everyone on board is picked up and makes it to land. A number of those who were saved immediately go to the police and have the first mate charged with murder. He is tried, and on the witness of several passengers, sentenced to life imprisonment. Perhaps there was another way to ensure the survival of the passengers but it, too, would have had consequences, some intended, others not. This is an extreme example of taking the consequences of one's deed.

RESPONSIBILITY DAY BY DAY

Fortunately not all situations of responsibility involve such dramatic responses as in *Lifeboat.* With our systemic understanding of the way life is related to life, the scope of ordinary decisions that involve responsibility has expanded exponentially. Our awareness of the need to care for the environment has further expanded the context of ordinary decisions. And so we routinely consider what is ecologically responsible when we decide about shopping, waste removal, investments or transportation.

So, when buying a packet of frozen green peas, we may look at the label, and ask, "Is that the company that turfed Indians off their land in Central America in favor of creating massive farms for producing vegetables for the frozen-food industry? Don't they use genetically modified seeds?" Or, if we are buying tennis shoes, "Is this the firm that uses sweated child labor in Indonesia?"

Very often these days, decisions have to be made in situations of incredible complexity. We avoid responsibility when we try to deal with the complexity by taking refuge in one source of information only, and cutting ourselves off from other sources. We have to dare to ask questions, to verify information, and listen to contradictory points of view. In other words, we have to build up our own picture of a situation, and do our own homework. To automatically submit to the dominant view is to surrender responsibility.

Environmentalists always need to be mindful of the whole context and the principle of comprehensiveness. In the spotted owl controversy in the US Pacific Northwest a few years ago, it was a common assumption that the environmentalists held the high moral ground because they wanted the spotted owl protected at all costs as an endangered species. Unfortunately, their approach would result in the loss of many jobs in the lumber and related industries, and several small townships would become ghost towns. A contextual, comprehensive ethic would assume that both the spotted owl and the people who would be out of a job, and the communities which would be disbanded all had rights to be considered as part of a solution.

We know teachers and principals who want to make efficiency and order the prime values that determine day-by-day decisions concerning the classroom rather than creativity, learning, cooperation and plain fun. When the profit motive becomes the only value in business, it is at the expense of workers, safety conditions, a supportive work environment.

A letter from a colleague working for Amoco describes some of the responsibility issues that arise there. They must be true for many workplaces.

> The major task here is to distinguish between responsibility and accountability, Responsibility has the narrower definition. For instance, we can delegate responsibility, but not accountability. If we as a manager, delegate the responsibility and the project fails, for whatever reason, it is the manager that gets asked the questions of accountability, rather than those who had the responsibility. This treats people like children. Giving line workers responsibility without accountability is

tokenism of the worst kind. It dishonors people. It is paramount that workers be given the support they need to be successful.

In our dealings with other human beings, this ethic asks: "What does the other need? Where I might want sympathy for myself, that might not be what the other needs. He may need a good kick in the pants, so to speak. Or affirmation. Or an illusion pointed out. Or the opportunity for reflection. What the other person needs is a very different question from what would I like.

LISTENING TO YOUR HEART

The decision-making approach of Bonhoeffer is quite rational, perhaps over-rational, the reader might say. The analytical side of making a decision does not mean the right decision is guaranteed, any more than making an impetuous decision.

However, there are times in life when rationality gives way to a leap in the dark. We have considered the situation till we are blue in the face. We realize something else is needed. Before I got married, I weighed the matter up hill and down dale. The subject of my thoughts was buxom, fair, had a similar purpose in life, but something in me would not let me take it past the advance and retreat process. One night, I was sitting at my desk with mind at idle, just doodling. The next moment, I was seized by a terrible clarity. I picked up my pen and wrote: "On the fourth of July I will marry Jeanette Marks." The fourth of July was a symbolic day for us. It was my birthday, and as she was American, it was her national day.

There were some problems. We had not dated yet. It was already June. I had not asked Jeanette, or anybody else. At the time, I thought I was out of my mind. I could not understand how I could do such a thing. All I knew is, that at the moment I had complete clarity.

I am not suggesting this as a model way to approach marriage. But sometimes, acting on a strong intuition is exactly what's needed. Well, we did get married and are planning to celebrate our 30th anniversary on the 4th of July. When your heart starts to bellow like a young calf, it is good to listen to it.

Exercise

There are times when all of us land in a real pickle, when life gets so unbearably complex that making even a simple decision seems difficult. It is as if we are caught in such a net of over-lapping obligations, values, and assignments that paralysis sets in and we tend to say, "Oh, the heck with it all!" Paralysis often occurs through a combination of putting off tasks to be done and decisions to be made. Self-disgust sets in and we become our own worst enemy. Sometimes, some simple, objective structural methods can help unblock the paralysis.

Here is an exercise you can do in that situation, or in your present situation that may help clarify the next thing to tackle.

1. Make a list of all the things, assignments and chores that are weighing you down.

2. Rank them. 10 for the most important, 1 for the least important.

3. Create a timeline for the next two weeks and slot the most important tasks (say, those that got a ranking of seven or more) into a time when they can be done.

	MONDAY	TUESDAY	WEDNESDAY	THURSDAY	FRIDAY	SATURDAY	SUNDAY
A.M.	report	proposal				take John to baseball	work on patio
P.M.			call babysitter				
EVENING	taxes	help John with reading	shop for partner's birthday gift	attend community meeting	relax		

DECISIONS

4. Make a list of the decisions you have been postponing.

5. Mark the decisions that need to be made this week (***), next week, (**) and some time in the future (*). (Remember you are not doing a strategic plan; you are trying to free yourself up from paralysis.

6. Create a 4" X 6" table below with next week's decisions in the left column and your answers to the next three questions in the three columns to the right.

DECISIONS	INFORMATION	CONVERSATIONS	VALUES
1.			
2.			
3.			
4.			
5.			

7. What information do you need so you can make the decisions slotted for this week?

8. Who do you need to have conversations with?

9. What are the values you want to hold for each decision?

10. On your timeline above, mark the day and time when you intend to make the most important decisions (***).

CONCLUSION

The way we get out of our complexity jams is by objectifying what is to be done and what decisions need to be made, and putting on paper how and when we are going to deal with them. Then, do it.

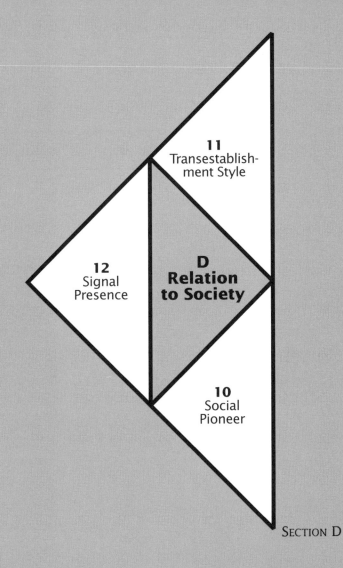

11
Transestablish-
ment Style

12
Signal
Presence

D
**Relation
to Society**

10
Social
Pioneer

SECTION D

Relation
to Society

Social Pioneering

Transestablishment Style

Signal Presence

Introduction to Section D

This section is about pioneering social change. In one sense, this last section simply describes ways to care for society—how to bring about social change, how to create new structures to sustain society, how to nurture the life quality in ourselves and others.

Social pioneering is quite a different approach from many around today. It is not about liberal do-goodism; it distances itself from the band-aid approach; it does not start by blaming the government. It approaches social transformation out of a comprehensive analysis of social trends and issues, rather than the espousal of single-issue causes. It attempts to move society forward without confrontation or agitation, but through engaging people out of a consensual understanding about what is necessary. Social pioneering takes no sides except creating effective alternatives, and letting those who want to hang on to the past do so. In the midst of doing their work, social pioneers don't forget the quality of humanness that beckons to others and lures them on to greater heights and more intense experiences of being human.

CHAPTER 10

The Social Pioneer

A Wedgeblade Inserted

> Never doubt that a small group of thoughtful, committed citizens can change the
> world. Indeed, it's the only thing that ever has.
> MARGARET MEAD

> At every moment of crisis an array of humans risk their lives in the front ranks as
> standard-bearers of history to fight and take upon themselves the whole responsi-
> bility of the battle.
> NIKOS KAZANTZAKIS

LIVING ON BEHALF OF THE FUTURE

This chapter is about "social pioneers" who decide to live on behalf of the future and
make a difference with their lives. Everyone cares. But there are some people who
choose to act on their concerns in order to address some social malaise.

Most of us are aware of the social collapse surfacing around us. We read of injustices in the newspaper, observe them in our workplace, or know people who are falling

outside of the care structures of society. We notice the homeless trying to sleep outside in mid-winter. We see our environment getting more and more polluted. We ask, "Should we be doing something about this?" But the moment passes. We are too busy or we simply do not know what to do. Some people excuse themselves by saying, "The social and physical world is so far gone, that wanton neglect is OK. So we had better hurry to get what we can for ourselves, while we can."

Others feel overwhelmed by the world's problems and by the frazzledness of their own lives. They are likely to say, "Social pioneer! My God, it's all I can do to get my child off to school in the morning and myself to work. At the end of the day I'm exhausted! Social pioneer—you've got to be kidding! I couldn't even begin to tackle more than is on my plate."

Others experience their care as an open wound. On the one hand we have the daily experience of feeling the suffering of the world through the atrocities and extreme need reported in the news. On the other hand, we experience not being able to do enough to respond to a world that desperately needs our care. We deplore those who, though they have considerable skills and resources, do little or nothing.

Still other people are involved up to their necks in building a new society and binding the wounds of time. The most unlikely people show up caring.

THE SOCIAL PIONEERS

In every corporation, organization, association, school, prison, legal institution or government, there are people who care and people who do not care. Here and there, maybe, we find those who see where the forward flow of energy is getting blocked and take responsibility for affirming that life force on behalf of everyone else.

So, if we were to spend some time in a particular government office, we would probably find two or three people who keep looking for ways to change the system so as to better serve the sick and elderly constituents. In a primary school, we might come across two teachers who have started an English-as-a-second-language course for parents who are newcomers to the country. In a large corporation, a handful of managers may meet regularly over lunch to look at a more environmentally friendly form of waste disposal. In a local community, we might find people meeting to start up a local barter program to help the poor and the jobless stay on their feet. In a large factory, we might come across a handful of workers meeting to figure out how to deal with a safety problem that has arisen when certain machinery is in use.

The common factor in all these situations is a core of people trying to find a new way of doing things to deal with specific social problems. I happen to believe that in every part of society and in every organization, there are people who are sensitive to what is needed, and dare to respond on behalf of the whole society or the organization. The response generally takes the form of taking a risk to meet a need that cares for the whole, but in the particular situation.

Take, for example, the case of Indian environmentalist and physicist Vandana Shiva in India. She tried to stop her country from signing the General Agreement on Trade and Tariffs (GATT) in 1995 because it would, among other things, give free rein to big corporations to take out private patents on the genetic heritage of rural India. She was unsuccessful. Since the signing of GATT, many patents, including ones for basmati rice and the neem tree—a sacred tree of great spiritual and healing properties referred to in India as "the tree of life"—have been filed by overseas companies who try to force anyone using these "products" to pay them seed royalties. Unable to get her government to stop the practice, Vandana trained a group of young lawyers to go out into the Indian countryside and help the peasant and rural farmers go into their fields and farms, woodlands, mountains and wild spaces, and gather every living plant species they can find. They then catalogue the seeds in a community seed register where they are forever held for the community and are, therefore, forever off-limits to patenting by private corporations. Transnationals are scrambling as they cannot keep up with the grassroots movement now sweeping not only India, but Africa and Latin America as well. I believe that the determination of local people is always the world's greatest hope. But it always takes that sensitive and responsive element to start the ball rolling.

THE MISSION

When we decide to be social pioneers, we take on our own mission. We don't just have a mission. Like the astronauts heading for the moon, we are the mission.

Since the beginning of time, people have banded together to take on various missions to transform the present and build the future. From the Neolithic people signalling the new at Stonehenge, to the Chinese literati travelling the countryside to bring new insight to the peasants, to the early Christian cells communicating their good news, to the monasteries and guilds of Medieval Europe who created care structures for journeyers and tradespeople—there have always been people who saw their vocation as illuminating life in the present, building new social structures for the future, or demonstrating a radically new life style in contrast to current reductionisms. Hermann Hesse referred to this dynamic in history as "the League". Paul Ray has referred to them as "cultural creatives—the standard-bearers of integral culture in our time." Kenneth Boulding has referred to them as "the invisible college":

There is in the world today an invisible college of people in many different countries and many different cultures, who have this vision of the nature of the transition through which we are passing and who are determined to devote their lives to contributing towards its successful fulfilment. Membership in this college is consistent with many different philosophical, religious and political positions. It is a college without a founder and without a president, without buildings and without organization.

So, what do social pioneers do?

BETWEEN THE NO LONGER AND THE NOT YET

The Institute of Cultural Affairs has found the following images helpful to represent the action of the social pioneer. D.H. Lawrence in "Song of a Man Who Has Come Through" speaks of "a fine, an exquisite chisel, a wedgeblade inserted." The wedgeblade can stand for the direction history seems to be moving in.

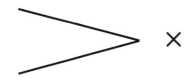

When we decide to act as a social pioneer, we put ourselves at the leading edge of the wedge. For example, if we decide to do something about the homeless, we find that old models of dealing with the homeless involved either dependence on the state or abandonment by it. If we are able to find new solutions for the homeless, we will probably be criticized both by those who are happy to have the homeless dependent and by those who want nothing to do with them.

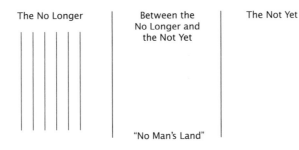

History is created out beyond what is past, between what is no longer and that which is not yet. Behind the No Longer are those who live contented with the structures that already exist. They are good people, but their care is directed towards maintaining things as they are. Somebody needs to do this, but there will always be enough people who want to devote their lives to maintaining what is. At the other end is the Not Yet: the future structures that will care for the coming generations; they exist only in someone's fertile minds. If no one envisions what the future needs to be and works to create it, the future—the Not Yet—suddenly arrives, the old structures no longer work, and people are uncared for, resulting in innocent suffering.

In World War I the area between the German and Allied trenches was called "No Man's Land." Anyone who ventured out there was likely to be shot at by either side. The future is built in a "No Man's Land" between the No Longer and the Not Yet. Here is where social pioneers work to create the new structures, patterns, and enterprises — economic, legal, health, educational, elder care, youth, environmental structures—needed for the arrival of the Not Yet. It is like trying to lay the railway track for the 21st century SuperFast Train when you can hear its whistle barely a mile away. Those who want to hang on to the past criticize their work and those who stand for a different future also negate them. Out on the point is a dangerous place to create the future.

So, assembling these lines and images, we get an overall image like this:

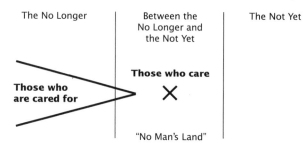

| The No Longer | Between the No Longer and the Not Yet | The Not Yet |

Those who care

Those who are cared for

"No Man's Land"

When we commit ourselves to creating the future, it is as if we laid our body down at the tip of the wedge to create the new that is needed. This deed of building the future is done not out of the desire to be recognized as a new Albert Schweitzer or Mother Teresa, but on behalf of all those who do not choose this path, and on behalf of the future generations. When we act as social pioneers, we wrestle with our own personal decision to create something on behalf of the future. In the process of doing the work, we will likely find others with a similar vision and band together with them as colleagues.

EXAMPLES OF SOCIAL PIONEERING

We are familiar with some of the names of those who have lived and died on behalf of the future: people like Martin Luther King, Rosa Parks, and Huda Ashraawi, an Egyptian leader for women's rights. These were people who said the un-sayable truth and did the un-doable deed.

In 1923, Huda Ashraawi committed an unthinkable act: as she disembarked from a train onto a crowded Cairo platform after returning home from a women's conference in Europe, she removed her veil. This was the first time any veiled woman in the Middle East had defied that tradition so publicly. When her veil was removed, at first there was shocked silence; then the women who had come to greet her broke into applause. Some tore off their veils too. For Huda, this signalled the final break with her old life as a protected woman in a harem and the beginning of her new life as the leader of a women's movement. Later that year, she founded the Egyptian Feminist Union which campaigned successfully to increase educational opportunities, improve women's health care, and raise the marriage age for girls to sixteen. She saw herself as not simply rejecting that tradition, but as upholding the original power of women in Islam,. Huda led delegations of Egyptian women to international conferences and organized meetings for Arab feminists from other countries. In 1944, she founded the all-Arab Federation of Women. She became a symbol of the fight for women's rights everywhere.

Rosa Parks grew up in the American Deep South with family stories about slavery which gave her a vigilant orientation toward racism. As secretary to the Montgomery, Alabama chapter of the NAACP (National Association for the Advancement of Colored People), she participated in daily protests at segregated drinking fountains and elevators in public buildings. On December 1, 1955, Parks recognized a bus driver as the very same one who had attempted to force her off the bus twelve years earlier. On this particular day, Parks had had a really hard day at work. Wearily, she sought a seat on the bus for the trip home. She even complied with Jim Crow laws by sitting in the "colored" section of the bus. When Parks refused to give up her seat to a white man who couldn't find a seat in the "white" section, she was arrested and convicted of breaking a city ordinance. Inspired by her courage, civil rights leaders asked her permission to organize boycotts in defiance of the Jim Crow law. The massive boycott, galvanized by the leadership of Martin Luther King, Jr., lasted 381 days and became the turning point of Civil Rights strategies to desegregate public facilities. Parks was eventually exonerated by a Supreme Court decision which ruled against segregationist practices in Montgomery. She went on to serve the civil rights actions of the Southern Christian Leadership Conference (SCLC), and to found The Rosa and Raymond Parks Institute for Self-Development, which aimed to empower young people between 11 and 15. Rosa Parks will always be remembered as the catalyst of one of the most significant social changes in American history.

Some readers will have heard of the work of Mohammed Yunus, founder of the Grameen Bank of Bangladesh. After the 1971 Bangladesh famine, Yunus left his teaching

in the U.S. and returned to his own country. He talked to local people in their own houses and saw how they suffered for lack of a tiny amount of money—even one or two dollars. He made a list of 42 people who together needed a total of only $27, less than one
dollar each. At first, he lent them the money himself, but, on reflection, he didn't see
that as a reproducible model. The banks refused to make loans to poor people for lack
of trust, Yunus tried offering the bank his services as a guarantor. He borrowed the
money from the bank, loaned it to the poor, and people paid it back. He did this in two
villages, then five, then ten, twenty, up to a hundred villages. Each time it worked. Each
time the bankers waited for the whole thing to collapse. It didn't. Finally, Mohammed set
up his own bank. His work was not just about loaning money and getting it back. He
also engaged his customers in discussions about the social problems that they faced
and the kind of solutions they imagined for themselves.

The Grameen Bank, as it is called, is now the largest rural bank in Bangladesh. It is
a model known worldwide for its innovative micro-credit program. It has inspired the
development of micro-credit in over fifty countries. The organization has gone on to
expand its services, moving into health care, finding markets for hand-loom products,
and investing venture capital in new small business. Grameen Telephone and Grameen
Cybernet now make rural telephone and Internet facilities available

Social pioneering happens in all kinds of social groupings. One of the most rigid
boundaries in the world today is that between management and workers in corporations
and agencies. Why can't some employees set production goals? Why can't employees
monitor plant efficiency? In an article in *Edges*, John Burbidge comments on what can
happen when a company decides to modify the pyramidal approach to employees:

> In Brazil, the Semco Company has already gone a long way toward more participa-
> tory management practices. Deciding that hierarchy was the single biggest contra-
> diction to participatory management, Semco replaced its cumbersome pyramidal
> structure with three managerial circles and just four titles—counsellors, partners,
> associates, and co-ordinators—which included everyone in the organization.
> Furthermore, the corporation insists that certain important decisions are made by
> a company-wide vote.

Such was the case when Semco needed a larger plant for its marine division.
Initially, it employed real-estate agents to search for possible plant sites, but the agents
were unsuccessful. So Semco's top managers turned the job over to the employees. In
one weekend, they came with three factories for sale near the existing plant. The company then stopped work for a day and sent everyone to inspect the factories. Next, the
workers voted and chose a plant the counsellors did not really want. Willing to trust the

workers' wisdom, the company bought the building. Workers designed the layout and hired a top Brazilian artist to paint it. The result? In four years, the divisions' productivity per employee increased 160 per cent and its market share jumped from 54 per cent to 62 per cent. Commenting on the experience, company president Ricardo Semler said, "We accepted the employees' decision because we believe that in the long run letting people participate in the decisions that affect their lives will have a positive effect on employee motivation and morale."

QUALITIES OF THE SOCIAL PIONEER

What does it mean to decide to put ourselves in the ranks of the social pioneers? First, we will find ourselves to be *solitary* individuals. We will find ourselves acting on our own. We will find ourselves confronted by moral issues only we have to deal with on our own. Nelson Mandela said, when in prison on Robben Island, "I feel like one who is on the sidelines, who has missed life itself." A colleague said to me once, "Stanfield, if you are the sort of person who needs friends and approval and lots of understanding, you better stay behind that line and keep off the point—you'll just be in the way; and if you need everyone's approval before you risk acting, better not even try." I learned that my decision to be a social pioneer is not contingent on anyone else's decision. If the rest of my family opts out of that decision, it doesn't excuse me.

We will be in situations where we don't know the full answer to where we are headed, and we'll be trying to get something done in a situation like Chinese baseball where the bases are being constantly moved around. In the midst of it all, the social pioneer needs to be the one who stands firm in the chaos, like an iron pillar of freedom. It is not that, as social pioneers, we don't have colleagues, but the people who show up with you to get a task done are never the ones you would have picked; and they tend to be a bit ornery, always throwing you back on your own decision, rather than trying to console you; in a strange way, they tend to emphasize the solitariness.

Those who have been social pioneers also speak of the experience of being *vulnerable.* Most people don't mind being solitary, if they just know that they are doing the right thing. But they don't want to be involved in the anxiety of actually making decisions—many of which have unknown consequences—in order to get something done. Between the No Longer and the Not Yet, there is no one around to lay it out for us, no trusted advisor to breathe the right answer in our ear. Courage here is the art of being the only one who knows you're scared to death. I remember, some years ago, a colleague and I approached a Canadian senator about funding a campaign for a series of community forums. He looked at the two of us, both under five feet-two, and said, "Are you sure you're up to this campaign?" And out of my mouth came, "Well, yes, of course, senator, we have a well thought-through plan." When you get home from an encounter like that, you find yourself saying, "Good God, do we *really* know what we are doing?" And you feel your vulnerability. Next day, when you get up to face the world, the question comes again, "Do I really know what I am doing?" You have to say to yourself all over again, "Of course I know what I'm doing."

Michael Ignatieff in *The Warrior's Honor*, speaks of the unjustified distrust of those who give their lives away in service to the world:

> The distrust is so deeply rooted that should a Dr. Albert Schweitzer expend his substance in some African bush hospital, or a Mother Teresa devote her life tending to the poor of Calcutta, an industry will surely be created to damage their repute. As soon as they become cultural icons, a counter-attack will be mounted: now it will be "discovered" that their methods and goals are authoritarian, even ethnocentric and eccentric, and therefore worthless. Should people devote their lives to caring for the children of the poor, it may even be hinted, or assumed, or expected, that they are also pedophiles abusing their charges. Such is the spirit of the times.

This is part of the reason why social pioneers prefer to work virtually invisibly, without fanfare.

Social pioneers have to live out of their own *interior resources*. Out between the No Longer and the Not Yet there are no rewards; no brownie points. As social pioneers, we are content with being nobodies. It is a strange interior reward. The peace of mind you get here is a peace that passes all rational understanding. It is a kind of problemlessness in the midst of trials. There is a kind of joy out on the point, but it is a joy unspeakable— the joy of sticking your fist into the deeps of life. As for honor, the people back in the secure structures of society receive honors: they get monuments dedicated to them and receive merit badges. Social pioneers are happy with being noble in their own eyes as the toilet cleaners of history, while the status seekers and celebrities take the honors.

The perpetual task of social pioneering takes *total commitment*. There are always new tasks there. There is no unemployment problem among social pioneers. We stay at it. Even when we are taking a vacation at the beach, we are conscious that we are taking it so we might be more effective at the task. Deciding to be social pioneers is a radical decision. It means deciding to be this social pioneer till you live to be 80, unless you live to be 99. It's no half-way decision. This is the vocation of vocations. The task is always there wherever we live, wherever we work, wherever we find ourselves. Retirement is for those who live in the established structures, behind the line.

A colleague of mine uses this story to describe the endless demands put on social pioneers:

> There is a tribe of Pygmies in the Kalahari Desert of southwest Africa. Their main source of food is giraffe meat. So picture yourself as the giraffe hunter for the tribe. When you get word that one is nearby, you collect your blowgun and darts and head off into the hunt. You carefully sneak out to the field where the giraffe is grazing, and very slowly and quietly creep into range. Then, just as you lift the blowpipe, the wind shifts, the animal gets a whiff of you and moves away. So you start all over again, this time circling around to get downwind. Finally, you get within range and let fly and score a perfect hit! You got him!
>
> Only the poison in the dart is slow-acting—it takes about three days. No self-respecting giraffe is going to stand around waiting to die. So it takes off running and you take off after him. Three days you go into the interior, chasing a doomed giraffe. Finally it falls down, exhausted and poisoned, and thrashes around. You creep up to deliver the coup de grace, but carefully, because those hooves are deadly. Finally you get in range and whack it on the head with a club, and it's dead. You've won.
>
> Except you look up to discover that here you are, a pygmy, with a dead giraffe three days' run from camp. What to do? So you begin carving up the carcass, and load yourself down with all you can possibly carry for the long march home.
>
> Just as you get a good start, you hear the lions roaring in the distance, and realize that you're carrying the bait! So you begin tossing pieces off the side, hoping to buy some time and distance to get the goodies home.
>
> After several days of this, you stagger into camp with what's left, and are met with a hero's welcome. People take the remaining meat and help you to a cool shady spot under a tree while the preparations for the feast begin.
>
> You lie there too tired to move as the faint aroma of barbecued giraffe begins to waft through the breeze and your mouth begins to water in anticipation. And you look up and the waitresses are bringing you, the hero, the choicest piece of medium-rare giraffe fillet, the smell of which has you in a dither of expected culinary ecstasy.
>
> Then, just as they set your plate before you, a scout comes in shouting, "There's another giraffe!" and you're off again to the hunt.
>
> You see, the secret of life that our friend has learned is that the fullness of life is not in the celebration: the fullness of life is in the hunt."

THE TASK OF THE SOCIAL PIONEER

Years ago, we might have been able to say that the task of the social pioneer is to *love*, to love all human kind. But *love* has become a puzzling word. We are never quite sure whether the one who uses it is talking about the experience of a recent infatuation, or some nice warm, fuzzy feeling. In this context its meanings are more like depth care, passionate commitment, structural justice, the healing of wounds, releasing people to live. The love we are talking about here is not making people feel good or buttressing their illusions. It is more like waking people up to their full possibilities, and recreating the structures of society so that everybody is cared for. This chapter describes two kinds of this deeper love: witnessing love and justing love. A third type, presencing love, is covered in the last chapter under "Signal Presence."

When we *witness love*, we communicate the images people need to be more complete human beings. When we look around at people, we see the crutches they walk round with: I'm not well, I'm too shy, I lack intelligence, I lack sophistication, I get stage struck, I get headaches. How do we communicate to each other that each of us has everything we need to be a full human being? We see the excuses for remaining unengaged in change: I'm too small, or too fat. When excuses are taken away, the freedom hiding behind them can be revealed. When we see unawareness or unconsciousness, we can call people to accept themselves just as they are, without pretenses. We can help them see that they are capable of extraordinary things. Some people respond well to directness; others prefer the indirect.

We can find in every situation ways to open people up to possibility, demonstrate that it is possible to love life, heal guilt and cynicism, and release people live to their full potential.

The word demonstration needs some attention here. The key to this is being or demonstrating the style of affirmation. I remember my first morning in India. Jeanette and I had spent the night on a mattress absolutely infested with bedbugs. No sleep. When I staggered out of the room in the morning to face my first day in India, and lusting for a cup of coffee, I encountered in the hallway the booming voice of Joe Slicker, the field development officer: GOOD MORNING, BRIAN! AND HOW ARE YOU TODAY? WOULD YOU LIKE SOME COFFEE?" My first internal response was: not quite so loud, Joe, please. But Joe knew exactly what he was doing—reminding me that, even with bedbug bites all over, life can be lived. With that greeting, I could remember again that life was good, just as it is, bedbugs, no sleep, and all.

When I speak of *justing love*, I mean creating or recreating structures of justice that care for people, including the structures of education, government, the economy, social services, health care, employment, or local community. These institutions move beyond individual caring to establish ongoing systems of care that do justice to people's needs. This kind of love seeks to renew these structures from within through the work of small cores of people operating as social pioneers, planning, strategizing, and carrying out their action plan.

When we decide to be social pioneers, we stay and confront the crisis with our lives. When communities are suffering in the wake of companies doing their layoffs, people rise up and create their own local economic vehicles, such as LETS (Local Economic Trading System) which allows people to trade their time and skills even when they are cash-poor. It was first founded in the Comox Valley of Vancouver Island and has now spread to many communities around the world. In corporations, many people are working at organizational transformation programs to flatten out hierarchies, to ease the innocent suffering of workers by bringing safety and a human working environment to factories, and to create opportunities for the full-scale participation of staff and workers in planning the future of these organizations. In many countries, teams of people are working to expand the right to vote and to get people out to vote, so there is a fuller accountability in government.

Social pioneers can also be found at any level in a group or corporation, even heading up a corporation as in this example, reported in *The Toronto Star*, a Canadian newspaper. Ray Anderson is managing director of Interface, a carpet manufacturer. His intent is to develop a management system so that his company fully embraces environmental sustainability. The first thing he did was give Interface a mission: To convert (itself) into a restorative enterprise; first, to reach sustainability and then to become restorative—putting back more than we ourselves take from the Earth—by helping others achieve sustainability, even our competitors. His vision embraced the conversion of linear to cyclical processes, so they would never have to take another drop of oil from the earth, and they could spend the rest of their days harvesting the carpets of previous years. They would recycle old carpets into new. At present, that's possible only with carpet backings. Research is continuing on how to recycle the face fibre. In the process they would convert sunlight into energy; with zero scrap going to the landfill and zero emissions into the ecosystem. Interface has already started renting, instead of selling, its carpet tiles. Under "perpetual lease" agreements with two separate companies in California, it has agreed to retrieve and replace tiles as they wear out. So Interface will no longer sell a product—it will sell a service. Ray Anderson and his team are forging the new sustainable face of an old industry.

For a very different example of making a radical change consider the ENF Housing Society in Vancouver, as described in Hubert Campfens (ed.) *Community Development Round the World*. (ENF stands for Entre Nous Femmes—literally, Among Us Women). Becoming a single parent changes many lives dramatically. For most women in Canada it means a drop in income, poor housing and increased responsibilities. A group of single-parents in Vancouver wanted a safe space where their needs as women and single parents were recognized and validated and from which organizing could take place. They undertook something that had never before been done in Vancouver—the planning, development, and management of affordable housing for single mothers, by single mothers. They had no previous experience in housing, but they also wanted to create an environment of opportunity and empowerment. To do these things, they had to overcome the scepticism of others, lack of interest and rejection. With persistence, they got funding from the government and the support of the local Member of Parliament. They took action on several fronts at the same time, nationally and locally. They decided to create a nonprofit system and insisted that half the units be subsidized.

The design for the Alma Blackwell housing community ensured a unique identity for each household while fostering interaction and communication among residents. Their building design included a community living room used for meetings, parties, workshops and craft fairs.

The journey toward completion was an intense and demanding experience; one of endless meetings and a constant search for consensus. Members steadfastly refused to give up on their vision despite external obstacles. "It definitely said that you can change the system," said one of the original ENF tenant board members. "It gave me a lot of hope, but I also became clear on the mountain of work involved." Two years after the project opened, more than half of the families originally dependent on government income assistance had become self-supporting. Ten years later, seven more such communities have been developed across Canada, demonstrating a remarkable integration of learning, empowerment and social action.

When we act like these single parents, we notice that other people find permission to do the same thing, and a trend gains momentum. What lights up the need for the new is the innocent suffering of people who, in this last case, were underfunded, overworked and trying to raise their kids in impossible situations. Innocent suffering is a key category for social pioneers. It always points to the need for change and new patterns. Everywhere we look, we see societal patterns that no longer serve people's needs. Society is full of situations where we can put our energy to create something more human that we care about.

HOW CAN I GET STARTED

Many of us hear of these problems every day. We feel deeply for the people who have to put up with these problems, and we would really like to do something about it, but just don't know what.

Sometimes, it just takes inviting two or three people for tea around the kitchen table to talk about an issue and see what happens. If we live in an apartment building and no one seems to know anybody on our floor, we could invite them all in for tea, so people can get to know each other better. In the process, we find out who needs special care, and how people can help each other. A senior who lives in an elder's center looks around and sees other seniors spending a lot of time complaining, and decides to do something about it. She organizes study groups, exercise classes, a band, a poetry writing contest and public speaking group, and soon the place is humming with creativity. If something in our workplace really bugs us, we can do something. We can explain the problem to the boss, and at the same time say that you are prepared to be on a task force to think through the problem.

Imagine the number of people who come home from work each day, really demoralized by a workplace problem which they unload on their partners—and that's where it stops. As social pioneers we can insist on doing something about it, determine who's prepared to take the time to think things through, ask what the real problem is, and organize a team to deal with it. Not knowing what to do is understandable. But, as the saying goes, it is always better to light a candle than to curse the darkness. When too much energy is spent on cursing the problem, there is too little energy left for dealing with it.

There is a simple one, two, three approach to doing the action of social pioneers when we see something that is causing trouble, a problem. First, we get a vision of what could be. Second, we see what is blocking the solution to the problem. Third, we come up with a three or four point plan to deal with it. Use this approach once, and we can use it for the rest our lives.

Finally, our decision to be a social pioneer is solitary. No one can make it for us. Those of us who so decide are no better than those who don't. Social pioneers are not necessarily the most intelligent, or anything like "born leaders." The only requirement is your commitment to changing people and social structures in a concrete situation of care.

Exercise A: Designing Your Tombstone

Imagine that you are dead, six feet under. Imagine an unknown visitor to your grave site. He is looking at the headstone on your grave. What words would you want the visitor to see on your tombstone (or the urn holding your ashes)? Do this little fill-in exercise and write your own epitaph: a short sentence or phrase that sums up what your life was about.

YOUR NAME: _____

BORN: (give the date: day, month, year) _____

DATE OF DEATH: (day, month, year) _____

YOUR EPITAPH: (brief)_____

_____

REFLECTION

1. What was the most difficult thing about this exercise?

_____

2. What happened to you in the course of doing it?

_____

Exercise B: Being a Social Pioneer

Try this simple one, two, three approach to doing the action of social pioneers. Name something in your organization, your neighborhood, or your building that you have noticed is a problem.

1. Write a vision statement of what the situation would look like if the problem were solved.

2. Ask yourself what is blocking the solution to the problem?

3. Come up with a simple three or four point plan to deal with it.

Make note of any allies or colleagues you might need to enlist to help you carry out the plan.

After you use this approach once, you can use it for the rest of your life!

CHAPTER 11

The Transestablishment Style

The Operational Approach to Social Pioneering

> The best leader does not ask people to serve him, but the common end. The best leader has not followers, but men and women working with him.
> MARY PARKER FOLLETT

> He who has a thousand colleagues has not a colleague to spare, and he who has one enemy will meet him everywhere.
> ALI IBN-ABI-TALIB

THE STANCE OF BEING FOR SOMETHING

As I wrote the first draft of this chapter, King Hussein of Jordan died, and the world watched his funeral on TV. Many people asked, "Why is this such a big deal? Why are all those heads of state there?" National leaders came from Russia, the US, Israel, many Arab states, and all over the world. Hussein was widely respected for many of his qualities: his statesmanship, his geniality, his peace-making abilities. He began by fighting the Israelis but gradually shifted to a mediating role which climaxed at the River Wye Summit in 1999. The older he got, the more he was able to stand above partisan rivalries and national hatreds to forge processes of conciliation. He was not always like this. There were times when he chose sides, but the longer he lived, the more he refused to be boxed into a position. For many people who simplistically equated the Middle East with terrorism, he put a human face on the Arab world.

Most facilitators would agree that one of the biggest difficulties to overcome on the path to real social change is the confrontational approach of partisan politics. We tend to think that, if we are on the side of social change, we are of necessity against something else, a certain political party or a corporation or an economic system. While we may deplore the innocent suffering created by these and other agents, the social pioneer always stands *for* something, namely, the creation of a more human future for everyone. To create that new future demands creativity, ingenuity, and the willingness to use whatever resources are around.

PRO-ESTABLISHMENT, DISESTABLISHMENT, TRANSESTABLISHMENT

Society has long used the word, "establishment" to describe the powers that be, and then coined "disestablishment" more recently to describe those who work against the establishment. There were no names for the other dynamics operating in society, so ICA made two up: *pro-establishment* and *transestablishment.*

As explained in Chapter 10, any agent of social change operates, at times, in a "no man's land," under fire from both sides.

The pro-establishment refers to those parts of society that guard the status quo. They work to preserve what is, guided by what has been. The pro-establishment is dedicated to maintaining familiar standards while resisting their disruption. As writer and philosopher John Cock puts it: "They are the bankers, lawyers, elected representatives, bishops, business leaders—the leaders and pillars of civilization." The disestablishment stands in opposition to the commonly accepted social structures and traditions of society; consequently, it is in tension with the pro-establishment. The disestablishment demands that the pro-establishment be accountable, and that it let no one fall out of the structures of community.

It is important to understand that both the pro-establishment and the disestablishment are really part of the "establishment"; they both sleep in the same bed. The proestablishment's concern is with the past, either attempting to keep the past and perpetuate it (the pro-establishment), or to destroy the past (the disestablishment).

The third pole of this triangle is the transestablishment, transcending both the pro- and the disestablishment to make a difference. While the disestablishment and pro-establishment argue over the shape of the present or the past, the transestablishment asks the futuric questions on behalf of everyone else.

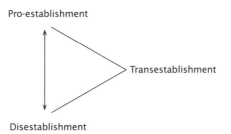

The intent of the transestablishment forces is to model and create the new while holding the tension between the pro-establishment and the disestablishment. It beckons the old to become the new.

For example, the disestablishment demands that the education system be torn down, so we can start all over again. The pro-establishment tries to maintain the structures that exist, while making cosmetic changes here and there. The transestablishment works *within* the structures to create the models that will change education from the inside out.

Society needs all three dynamics. Without the proestablishment, there would be no structures for the transestablishment to work creatively within or to engage the passion of the disestablishment. Without the disestablishment, the proestablishment would never be held accountable to the forces of change. Without the transestablishment or the disestablishment, society would stagnate and grow comatose.

THE TRANSESTABLISHMENT APPROACH

The transestablishment will work with anyone to create new responses. When we act as the transestablishment, we abandon the dualism of good people and bad people, of friends and enemies. As transestablishment, we assume that all players are potential allies. We seek collaboration, partnership and cooperation at every point. Abraham Lincoln declared: "I destroy my enemies when I make them my friends." Today he might have said, "...when I make them my collaborators."

Some years ago, government critics (disestablishment) decried the government apathy (establishment) about recycling glass, certain plastics and paper. Instead of writing more criticism, a transestablishment team gathered some resources and created the roadside Blue Box recycling campaign in a delimited area as a demonstration that said, "This can be done." The government saw the value of the Blue Boxes and decided to set up recycling in many Ontario cities and towns.

Perhaps nowhere is the transestablishment style more needed than in our communication processes. We are used to aggressive election campaigning, to investigative reporting, to change that involves criticism, to mutual recriminations, to public demonstrations, to arguments in meetings that try to demolish the opposition in one way or another. In the Western world, we tend to respond to social issues in very combative, judgmental ways. We tend to see our issues as an assault on our reason by the prince of chaos. The innocent suffering involved in many social issues gets lost in the torrent of argumentation. We do not have a vision of what could be. We are more concerned with how these issues impinge on our sense of order and personal comfort than with the damage they do to society as a whole and the people around us.

You may remember the bitter confrontation in Clayoquot Sound some years ago in British Columbia, between the timber giant MacMillan Bloedel and the environmental Greenpeace organization; but you may not have heard how this situation was turned around.

Company officials had been acting as if MacMillan Bloedel was stuck in a highly polarized ideological battle defending its logging practices as the right and only approach. Greenpeace, for its part, had decided earlier in Spain to use a protest over the company's logging in Clayoquot Sound to launch an international campaign against clearcut logging. The stage seemed to be set for permanent war between the two parties.

The company received advice from consultants that it needed to pay closer attention to its adversaries. Critical to the process was a re-imaging of the relationships between the parties as a marketplace where no one ruled. Certain visionary elements in the company began back-channel communications with Greenpeace. At a certain point, images shifted and the parties saw they could achieve more by working together than by confronting each other in the press at home and in the forest awaiting harvest. A genuine dialogue began, and, wonder of wonders, Greenpeace saw how they could influence MacMillan Bloedel"s policy.

Within the logging company, the Clayoquot protests had convinced its key executives that something had to change. It established an eight-member review board to develop a proposal for a new lumbering policy. These plans were shared with Greenpeace and government officials.

The new logging system leaves some trees on a logged site in groups, strips or islands to provide a habitat for wildlife and help regenerate a new forest. The company now logs more selectively; no longer do they do the massive clearcutting that had been its policy before this.

The results of the process are a testimonial to what can happen when conflicting parties put away their gloves and say, "Why don't we work together on this?" Because there were transestablishment people on both sides, and neither side sold out, they found a good neutral solution.

Subsequently, the company has been purchased by another company, but the story remains exemplary.

A number of other approaches flow from the transestablishment style for those attempting to bring about social change:

- We insist on being proactive, rather than reactive.
- We seek the collaborative and partnership mode, rather than the adversarial.
- Rather than alienating the powers that be, we seek their support through structural framing.
- We focus on the depth human problem.

PROACTIVENESS

Proactive is perhaps an overly used word, but it holds the sense of transestablishment style so closely, it is almost a synonym for transestablishment.. Its sense is forward, positive energy in contrast with the reactiveness of the distestablishment. A proactive stance involves doing a second take on our initial reflection, or re-reflecting. It is not enough for us to just be *against* something. The proactive one also builds a plan for dealing with it.

One of the first lessons I got in proactiveness happened when I was teaching school in Australia. I developed the habit of reporting issues I had observed round the school to the principal, Mr. Roberts. I got a certain sense of virtue out of it, each time I reported. One day, not Mr. Roberts' best, I approached him with yet another issue: the school toilets were running over. Something in him snapped. He said, "Stanfield, I'm tired of your issues. I want you to tell me what *you* are going to do about the issues. Next time you bring your issue to me, bring me your three- or ten-point plan for how it should be dealt with. Take responsibility, for God's sake!" I was greatly chastened, but the event stuck in my mind.

Stephen Covey's *The Seven Habits of Highly Effective People* contains a chapter on proactiveness that is a classic. "Highly proactive people," he says, "do not blame circumstances, conditions or conditioning for their behavior. Their behavior is a product of their own conscious choice, based on values, rather than a product of their conditions, based on feeling." The opposite of being proactive is being *reactive*. Reactive people may respond emotionally to a situation of great frustration by doing something, anything, to relieve the frustration, whether it is what is needed or not. It is the activity of just being busy. As Harrison Owen puts it in *Spirit*, "it appears that things are being done, but what things and to what purpose is not always clear. Carried to extremes, tempers become frayed and frustration mounts as action breeds reaction and then more action, all to no clear end." Then the blame game begins. Robert Theobald wrote shortly before his death in 1999: "I believe that moving from an adversarial to a dialogue stance is the core requirement if we are to move from co-stupidity to co-intelligence".

A citizen from Sudbury, Ontario, reports on the mind shift needed to get their Sudbury 2001 economic diversification project off the ground some years ago:

> We had to decide to take responsibility for our own history. We resolved to stop blaming other people, other governments, other solar systems for our problems. We did that because, back then, blaming others was our chief political sport. You can't really start to solve your problems until you are prepared to be accountable for fixing them. That realization was, I think, the beginning of Sudbury as a true city state....Taking charge of your future requires a certain level of suspended disbelief. You have to believe you can leap tall buildings with a single bound, you have to believe you can climb any mountain, ford any river.

"If we want to see more of the good news than the bad," says Charles Handy in *The Hungry Spirit*, "we will have to do it for ourselves. It's no good waiting for an unidentified "they' to fix our world for us. He goes on to cite the case of Helen Taylor-Thompson and the Mildmay Mission Hospital in east London:

> In 1982, the Mildmay, a district general hospital, was slotted to be closed down. Helen Taylor-Thompson, who had been involved with the hospital for thirty years, was determined that it would not shut. After a long campaign, she persuaded the government to allow the hospital to reopen by leaving the National Health Service and leasing the buildings on a peppercorn (nominal) rent.

> Before long the Mildmay had become one of the leading centers for AIDS care, with an international reputation for innovation. In 1988 it became the first AIDS hospice in Europe. It has thirty-two suites for the terminal care of people with AIDS, housed in the old Victorian hospital. In addition it has a purpose-built facility to treat parents with AIDS, without separating them from their children. This year it plans to open a treatment center in Kampala, Uganda. Mildmay is a world-class institution created from a hospital that was regarded as worthless fifteen years ago, born out of the entrepreneurial energy of one woman.

People of the transestablishment are the harbingers of change, devising new ways to provide support and development for those excluded from the opportunities of the new society. The transestablishment often learned more about themselves in the pursuit of something beyond themselves. Such people are not content to let the *status quo* be the way forward. They itch to make a difference.

Change agents are always on the lookout for any forces in the community or organization that have this quality of proactiveness. There is a story about a development agency that had an interesting method for locating proactive elements in the community. It was getting weary of the hand-out approach to development that did not elicit any engagement from the community. It decided to try something different. The agency had received a large amount of money for development efforts in a county-sized piece of geography. The agency staff decided to purchase a large number of concrete blocks with the money. They packed the blocks on trucks. In each village of the area a sizeable heap of blocks was dumped on vacant ground. Then the truck moved on to the next village and did the same. After a certain time, the development workers checked each village to see what had happened to the blocks. If the community had built something with the blocks, it became a number one priority for further aid. If an individual had stolen the blocks and built a home, he became priority two. If the blocks were still lying in a heap, the community was a low priority for further assistance.

COLLABORATION

When we work in a community to get something done, we are courageous when we act alone, but crazy if we think we can do it all on our own. We need a team—partners and allies. And yet, for some reason, people are skeptical or fearful of sharing their project with other people. These are some of the mindsets that have to be overcome if one is to work effectively with other people:

"I am an island"—Individuals and groups struggle to assert their own selfhood and identity. To this end, they develop their own sets of principles, values, approaches and solutions which can easily become rigid.

"Them and us"—We are not trained in the mental agility that is able to see two, three or four sides of an argument at the same time. Society is poor in processes that unite rather than divide. We have developed the tension between opposites into a high art form. We see ourselves as right, and others simply as wrong, or at best, inadequate.

"Let's get together and fight"—Any interchange over any topic is traditionally approached as a debate. Trying to resolve a dispute with another dispute, even disguised as mediation, is not likely to create lasting solutions. It often just ups the ante.

"I heard what I said."—We report on many conversations by telling people what we said. Truly hearing a different perspective is not easy when the roar of our own thoughts drowns everything else out.

"Who's got the power?"—Our relationships and social systems are based, all too often, on power relationships. Resolving difficulties and making decisions has become a

matter of gaining or manipulating enough power to have one's own way.

"We need to find a solution and I've got it."—We tend to approach a lot of our work with our positions blazing. As Colonel Potter reminded us all in *M*A*S*H*: "Just remember, there's a right way and a wrong way to do everything and the wrong way is to keep trying to make everybody else do it the right way."

Working against those mindsets, the transestablishment style consistently demonstrates its willingness to work with many different kinds of people. When meetings are held, transestablishment leadership is open and accepting of people's participation. Such a leader accepts every piece of information offered or question raised as valid, coming as it does from authentic life experience. Everyone in the group is understood to have a piece of the puzzle. The whole picture is obtained, not by selecting the information that makes good sense to the leader, but by hearing and understanding all the perspectives. Most conflict assumes two opposing sides to an issue. Recognizing the many possible perspectives involved in any one topic takes people beyond a dualistic worldview and allows them to see a larger picture. When the problem is reframed, the possibility for effective solutions increases.

In 1998, a Lotteries and Gaming Conference in a Canadian province, concerned about some negative public reaction, asked ICA to conduct two workshops—one on the positive and negative impacts of lotteries and gaming on the province's communities, and another on what could be done to accentuate the positive impacts and lessen the negative.

These two questions set up the expectation that people would deal with the whole picture, and this is key. The first workshop got out all the perspectives at one time, put them on cards and then arranged the cards on the wall in front of the group. The process acknowledged that there are positive and negative impacts, so there was no defensiveness or arguments about the negative. Then the process asked people to bring their creativity to bear on the whole issue rather than just fighting for one side or the other. It moved the outcome from being controlled by the loudest or most politically astute lobby to turning all the interest groups' energies to finding the best solutions. People were astounded at their own creativity and that of others. Everyone's contributions went up on the wall. Everyone said yes to the solutions. Some people were disappointed because the ICA method did not allow them to control the outcome of the meeting. Most were delighted to see everyone's contribution received.

The people who stand with the transestablishment leader to form a group to work on an issue are probably not the ideal group that the leader envisioned. It may be like the odd collection in *The Dirty Dozen* or the even weirder combination in *Trading Places*. The struggle for us at this stage is to believe that the group we have is the right group to wrestle with the issue at this time. In this awareness, we know we do not have to call in experts. We trust that the people in the room, at the particular meeting, have the answers and are capable of wrestling with the issues.

FRAMING

A key method of the transestablishment is framing, or establishing a framework of support and authorization for a change project. While some people launch their effort by criticizing, confronting or attacking the powers that be, those of the transestablishment stance take the opposite tack—we seek their support and blessing, then move beyond them. "Acknowledging the powers," says Walter Wink in *The Powers That Be*, "is an indispensable part of social action." Or, as a native proverb puts it, "If you live in the river you should make friends with the crocodile."

These powers can stop any social change project dead in its tracks. If we can get the powers on our side, they are capable of smoothing the way into the future quite remarkably. At minimum, we need just enough of a "yes" from the powers to be able to go forward.

This does not mean getting in bed with the establishment. Framing appeals to the self-interest of those with power and even enlists them in particular aspects of the task, thus turning them into collaborators who see they are making a difference. For example, when ICA conducted community forums and town meetings across North America some years ago, we called on the mayors to let them know what we were planning, but also to invite them to give the opening address. Invariably they felt honored and empowered.

Every community or organization or social structure has these powers present. Things just do not happen in any community unless certain channels, such as the mayor, are honored. This is a fact of life. However, the real power may not the mayor or the board, at all. Some organizations, for example, are run by a little old lady from behind her knitting needles, rather than by the official board. In a corporation, no matter how much sanction you have from the higher-ups for some creative change project, unless you get the finance office or the technical expert or the mailroom on side, your project will get stalled and you will never know it. You will think it is someone on the board or some middle manager who's blocking your efforts, but it won't be them at all. Any community or organization is like that. Your task is to find out what authorization is needed, both silent and overt. It is important that they know what you intend to do, so it is strategic to set up some visits to go see them.

In one community where I worked, the "power" was another change agent. Her name, ironically enough, was Felicity. Felicity had been working in the community for 20 years. She was a very down-home person; everyone knew her. She was passionate about making things better. She also didn't like a whole lot of other people around meddling with her turf. It was as if she sat at the center of a very large spider web. of social relations. You would not get anything done in that community unless you got her on your side, or at least in the communication loop. You could fret and fuss all you liked at the situation, but it did no good. It was just a fact of life that you needed to check what you intended to do in the community with her. Otherwise you were stymied. So you'd catch Felicity as she came out of the community centerand ask for a minute of her time, and tell her the plans for a big workday on the park. Felicity would just nod and say, "Sounds like a good idea." And that was that. I also remember a time when we tried to do a workday to tidy up a vacant lot without checking with Felicity. For some reason, none of the usual volunteers showed up and we were unable to borrow the usual tools from the local parks supervisor.

Jo Nelson tells about two communities in Texas with two quite different approaches to developing their communities. One community's approach was to fight the Anglo landowners; then they began fighting each other. They got nowhere. The other community enlisted the landowners' support in developing their community. Their community project is still going strong.

CONTRADICTION-ORIENTED

"Without vision," goes the adage, "the people perish." Social change always begins with looking at the desired future. The orientation is toward the positive—the situation we want to create and develop. The local pioneer is constantly engaged in creating or returning to the practical vision which helps them see the whole in a new way, while doing the nitty-gritty practical tasks. Some organizations or parts of organizations have no vision at all. Others do only what the boss says. You can usually locate the vision by asking people what they hope and dream for; what they need or long for, what they look forward to.

But vision is not enough. The minute we attempt to implement our vision, we run into *contradictions*: things that block us from our vision. It is like a log jam on a river where logs are coming down the river from the cutting area to the mill. A few logs get stuck on rocks or a bend in the river, and before long, there is a log jam across the whole width of the river. No logs will move on that river till that log jam is broken up. So it is with contradictions.

Working with the contradiction is the opposite of dealing with symptoms. Lederer and Burdick's book, *The Ugly American*, contains a letter written on behalf of the old people of Chang Dong to "the wife of the engineer." The seniors in this village traditionally suffered from bent backs. They had always thought this was part of growing old, and it was one of the reasons they dreaded old age. The wife of the engineer did not get the elders doing physical exercises. She used her observation and common sense. She noticed how the people of the village did their sweeping bent over with short brooms in their hands. The engineer's wife introduced the village elders to long-handled brooms and a new way to sweep. The letter said, "you will be happy to know that there are few bent backs in the village of Chang Dong." Getting the villagers to do exercises to deal with their back problem would have been dealing with the symptoms. The engineers' wife dealt with the underlying problem: short-handled brooms.

No matter how powerful our vision is, it will go nowhere until the contradictions are dealt with. How we deal with contradictions "separates the serious change agent from the dabbler. Most of us go along fine, as long as we don't encounter any blocks in our path. But as soon as we meet a block, or contradiction, some of us come to a grinding halt. We then are likely to go round in circles, or perhaps we go to take a nap, or play golf, hoping the contradiction will go away or be dealt with by the time we get back. Most often, it's still there, growing larger in our minds by the moment. If we rebel against it and spend our energy railing at how hard it is to get anything done because of all these problems we are encountering, we waste our energy and miss the point, because, strategically, the contradictions are the doorway to the future. Like a nettle plant, a contradiction must be grasped firmly, and moved against with great energy.

Although a contradiction can be the source of great pain for many people, a contradiction is not negative. In fact, it can become the doorway to the future for us. Paul Hawken, in his *Ecology of Commerce*, tells how this worked in Curitiba, a city in southeastern Brazil:

> When architect Jaime Lerner was appointed mayor of Curitiba, Brazil in 1973, it was a rapidly growing town of half a million with sprawling slums (favelas). These favelas had many problems, not the least of which was garbage that could not be collected because of narrow or non-existing streets.
>
> Since trucks could not get in, and because the garbage was attracting rodents that could carry disease, Lerner's solution was to pay people for their garbage by placing recycling bins around the favelas and giving the people tokens to the city's transport system for the separated and therefore recyclable garbage. For organic waste, which was taken by farmers and made into fertilizer for their fields, he gave chits that could be exchanged for food.
>
> The strategy has worked spectacularly. Kids scour the favelas for garbage, and can spot the difference between polyethylene terephthalate and high-density polyethylene bottles. The tokens give the poorer citizens the means to get out of

the favelas to where the jobs are, while promoting cleanliness, frugality and the reclaiming and recycling of waste.

When we come to terms with a contradiction, it can leverage our organization or a whole society into the future. A "vicious colonial salt tax" was the doorway to Gandhi's Indian revolution.

The problems are not the real problem. When we look more deeply, we find that these problems coagulate into clusters of related blocks and issues. These clusters give us clues to the underlying realities of our situation which prevent us from moving effectively toward our vision. When we can recognize the causes that sustain these barriers, we have discovered an underlying contradiction. But we have to dig for these contradictions. When we encounter a cluster of problems and name them, we have to keep asking, why is this in being?

For example, a brainstorm of obstacles in a mid-sized company yielded this cluster:

- Hard focus on financial resources

- People unsatisfied with work experiences

- Laborious implementation of financial and accounting controls

- Rigid bureaucratic environment

- Abuses of managerial power

- Inhibited initiative on the job

- Absenteeism

These problems in the brainstorm showed up in a cluster. The group working on the problems kept on asking "Why?" and came up with a deeper contradiction which they named, "ignoring human resources as assets." The contradiction, if properly named, says what needs to be done to deal with it. In this case, the company had to find ways to treasure its human resources as its primary asset. Some very radical change was needed if the company planned to be around in five years and realize its appropriate market share.

FOCUS ON THE DEPTH HUMAN PROBLEM

The transestablishment focuses on the depth human issues facing a structure or community rather than surface or single issues on the surface. We know that if our efforts are not directed toward the depth human issues in the life of a structure or community, we cannot bring about substantial social change. If, for example, housing and health services are improved while nothing is done to alter a deep-seated sense of self–depreciation within the citizenry, the gains will be short-lived. To address the depth human problem, we cannot define change solely in economic terms, although local economics are really important. In planning, it is important to discern the block to change that lies deep within the structure itself. Often the block is a mindset, a perspective of impossibility because of external factors. It is often a resignation to defeat, reinforced by generations of futile efforts. Sometimes it is an embarrassment over some aspect of the past that prevents full exploitation of its unique gifts.

The contradiction in one American community was stated as "demoralizing images of civic identity," or as one person put it, "bright past, no future." Until they overcame their belief that their town was a dying community, not much could happen to ensure its future. They went on to create common symbols for the town, regular town festivals, essential public works, cultural clubs for the citizens, and systematic neighborhood maintenance, among other efforts. These initiatives directly and indirectly began to counteract the image of "bright past, no future." The depth human problem had been addressed.

Dick Richards in *Artful Work* points to this focus on the depth human problem as what is most needed in corporations today: "Our familiar beliefs," he says, "cause us to embrace a never-ending procession of techniques. We have tried managing by objectives, searching for excellence, creating vision statements, self-managing teams, instituting notions about quality and service, and now reengineering. We spin from one solution to the next, and our solutions are too often ineffective because they address the symptoms rather than the causes. The problem is that we change our ideas and techniques without changing our beliefs."

ICA's 5th City Community Reformulation Project offers a prime example of dealing with the depth human problem. This was a comprehensive community development project in a ten block area in the black ghetto of Chicago's West Side. It was launched in 1962 and still continues today. Its comprehensiveness was based on dealing with all the people; all ages from preschool to elders and all the problems, economic, political and cultural, including the depth spirit problem which in this community was the victim image—a sense of overwhelming powerlessness. Fifth City and its preschool (see Chapter 10) became a symbol of possibility in many countries for everyone who visited it or heard of it. The community reformulation project became a model for many who tried the approach in their own community.

Exercise: Thinking About Your Community

These questions can get you thinking about your local neighborhood or community:

1. Get out a street map showing your local community on it, and a piece of paper. Draw a quick picture of your neighborhood, showing its north, south, east and west boundaries—look for things like creeks, rail lines, arterial roads, high tension power lines, green strips, a ridge.

2. Around the map, write answers to these questions: What are the nodes or gathering places of your community—where do people stop to talk? the town square? the chestnut tree? the pub? the waterfront?

3. What do you know of the demographics of your community? Is it mainly elders, leading-edge baby boomers, later baby boomers, Gen-Xers? What are the main cultures represented?

4. What part of your community would you talk about as "on the other side of the tracks," whether there are railways tracks there or not.

5. See how many separate problems you can list for your community or neighborhood. Think of economic problems; political problems; problems related to health, education, or well-being problems related to youth, families, seniors; symbolic problems related to meaning, level of engagement, values.

6. What, do you sense, is the area of the depth human contradiction?

7. What is one step that *you* could take to begin to deal with any of these problems?

CHAPTER 12

Signal Presence

Demonstrating Radical Living

And if, as we work, we can transmit life into our work,
life, still more life, rushes into us to compensate, to be ready
and we ripple with life through the days.

D.H. LAWRENCE

No pressure, no diamonds.

MARY CASE

MAKING A STATEMENT ABOUT LIFE

Larry King has hosted CNN's highest rated show, *Larry King Live* for nearly 14 years. In a recent book, *Powerful Prayers*, he has a wonderful story of an interview with Swami Satchadananda, founder of the Integral Yoga Institute in Virginia. The swami got his lick in first. He asked Larry what comes into his mind when he gets out of bed. Larry indicated not much. The swami replied with some surprise, "You don't even say a thank you?" "No."

The swami continued by pointing out that a thank you would have put him in tune with the day. Larry would be a participant in the day, and not just an observer. "Let's suppose," the swami proposed, "that at the deli you order toast and you get burnt toast. How would you respond?" Larry replied that he would create a scene because he had paid for the toast, and making a scene would produce better toast. The swami admonished Larry, asking him why he wouldn't express his appreciation for the burnt toast to the cooks. Swami added that afterwards Larry might ask them for any toast that has escaped burning, and volunteer also to accept the bad toast to ensure there is no waste.

Larry was speechless before the swami's suggestions. Those in the control room could not contain their mirth. Finally the swami pointed out that when Larry yelled and screamed, he poisoned the atmosphere between him and the one making the toast. Swami asked Larry what if, instead of making a scene, his concern was to offer a suggestion, and leave the deli in a better state than when he came in. That would be participating in the life of the deli, rather than just showing up and leaving.

The quality of our presence can make a difference, even on a visit to the deli. *Signal presence* is being present in such a way that we make a statement about life. We ourselves become a sign of what we stand for. In the 19th century, the red coat of the Northwest Mounted Police was a sign of law and order in a rather chaotic period of Canadian history. To describe this signal presence adequately, we would really need to bring before us some of the people mentioned in this book, and have a conversation on what becomes clear to us as we look at their physical presence and the spirit presence that shines through them: people like Martin Luther King, Aung San Suu Kyi, Mahatma Gandhi, Eleanor Roosevelt, Indian village leader Choka Baba, or the leader of the Californian grape pickers, Cesar Chavez. It is a presence that becomes a sign of what is possible for other human beings. The preceding eleven chapters have built up a basic profile of the substance of this presence. In this chapter, we will spell out the interior patterns and some external dynamics that lead to this kind of presence.

PRESENCING LOVE

In Chapter 10, we called it *presencing love*. This kind of presence tends to make an impact. I remember when I was a boy in my parent's hotel, a guest I admired a great deal visited every year during the school holidays. Bert Thorsby came as a guest and friend of our family. When Bert and his wife went fishing up the river, they always invited me to go with them in the boat. He, unlike many of the other men I encountered, was very gentle. He spoke in a quiet voice, and seemed to be at home and at ease with himself and life. And he seemed to attract the fish. A stretch of the Hastings River called the Hatch was our favorite place to fish. We always returned with scores of whiting in the gunny sack whenever we went out. He reminded me to treat the small fish gently and to ease them back into the water so they could grow to the legal size and beyond. I always felt richer from being in his company. He had qualities that did not readily show up in other men I knew. In retrospect, what I experienced in him was a particular kind of presence. Today, I would call it centeredness. The centered person breathes deeply and processes the happenings of life so they don't storm in to block being present to what's going on in the moment. The centered one knows that people need to encounter energy that gives life rather than energy that saps life.

To be this presence of love in the world, we project a style that is a sign of possibility. It is a profoundly human presence beckoning others to become profoundly human also. It is the presence of an awesome decision about life that is visible to others, and calls to them. It is as if reality or being is revealed through the body of a human being. This presence has nothing to do with our attempts to be somebody or to win acclaim in the world. It is the impact of the person between the no longer and the not yet, working to create the new structures and images that are needed. Celebrities do not tend to hang out there.

People with signal presence give others the possibility of standing before the human condition as it is. They push in front of other people's noses the truth that no one escapes being responsible for life. They show how ordinary people can stand with the weight of care and see it as a gift.

The aliveness of being that allows us to be a presence flows from more than an abundance of vitamins, sleep or exercise. It wells up from another place, the point where you have given of yourself and then given some more, and, strangely, more life rushes in. Retired master teacher Joseph Slicker describes the experience:

> I remember the first race I ever ran in school. They put me to running the mile, of all things. On my first race, I ran and I ran and I ran and I ran and I ran and I ran. I didn't know the proper way to run the mile, but, thank goodness, the other people running didn't know either. After running and running and running, the pains began to come. I began to hurt all over, I was short of breath—I did not know what was going to happen, and yet I kept running and running and running. I think all of us about tied, for it seemed that we all fell down on the finish line. Suddenly a great aching elation came over me. I knew that I had run the race and more than that I knew I was alive. Power was there in the midst of my tired aching being.

We know that when we cease to cling onto our life, when we quit boxing it off or trying to protect it, and give our life up—then, life begins to flow into us. Energy is unleashed. Life flows on. And we remember the poem of D.H. Lawrence which witnesses to the fact that "life still more life rushes into us to compensate, to be ready, and we ripple with life through the days."

It's as if a strength not our own comes out of the bowels of the universe and flows into our life. It is an eerie sort of strength. A strength that seems to come up out of nowhere bubbles up in the midst of you. And when you become the nothing that you are, then life flows in with greater strength.

You might, with some justification, ask how this expenditure of life is any different from the life of the workaholic? The social pioneer expends her life getting things done in society, pushing through a contradiction on behalf of the future generations. The capacity to relax, to let go, is equally important. This expenditure pauses regularly to reflect and celebrate. The workaholic cannot afford to stop because the work is filling up the vacuum in his or her life. If a stop is made, there is a danger that the emptiness at the center might be revealed. Then the game would be up, and the workaholic would have to change or find another addiction—or wake up to her real life.

SOCIAL DEMONSTRATION

Signal presence is also a sociological category. It can refer to organizations or communities that become signs and demonstrations of possibility.

The "sign" aspect of presence is critical. In a world where image matters so much, we learn much faster about what it means to be a human being from seeing others exemplify it than from reading about it in books. What we need today is a lot more people willing to be, in their own persons, demonstrations of the humanness they see as possible for humans today. They become signs of possibility, just as Gandhi was for India in his time, or Martin Luther King was for North America.

The same dynamic happens for organizations, where a group or organization offers to the world a new way of operating, and becomes a demonstration of what is possible. Elliot Leyton in his book, *Touched by Fire*, describes the work of Doctors Without Borders (MSF) as they operate in war-torn situations. Doctors Without Borders is an international association made up of doctors, nurses, water and sanitation specialists, logistics specialists and administrators, founded by a group of disillusioned French doctors and journalists who returned to Paris from a Red Cross mission to the Biafran War. It quickly became the worlds' largest private, independent emergency medical relief organization. Thirteen nations, including Canada, have affiliate status. MSF is the "smoke jumper" among international aid organizations. While others are often stymied or delayed by bureaucratic red tape, the men and women of MSF move in. MSF can place its emergency medical teams and equipment anywhere in the world within 24 hours. They provide food and clean water. They dig latrines. They set up first-aid stations and field hospitals. They treat all-comers according to need. Often they are the last to remain in situations abandoned by others as too dangerous. They can be found in most of the world's hot spots: Ruanda, Burundi, Sudan, Afghanistan, Central America, Somalia, Bosnia, and others.

These women and men routinely go where modern armies and their political masters fear to tread. If staff are at home on leave, a packed suitcase sits ready by the door, because they can be recalled at any time. If a million refugees are pounding down the road in Rwanda, the MSF stance toward everybody else is: "We can handle it. Don't panic! Everything is fine, at least until tomorrow morning." MSF aims to establish a fresh, unbureaucratic way of responding to crises. Where other organizations are slow, cautious, heavily bureaucratic, and quick to pull out in the face of danger, MSF takes risks, can respond rapidly, and seems to thrive in the face of danger. The staff are also clear on the terrible ambiguity in which they operate, as they attempt to heal people who may be murdered the next day or die of starvation, because of the extreme instability of the environments in which they operate. The world needs more organizations like this that can demonstrate a different approach to caring for human suffering. Of course, it also needs organizations that are more cautious.

There are many other groups that try to demonstrate a different approach and a different kind of presence in the world. The Body Shop, founded by Anita Roddick, is often quoted as an example of a corporation that tries to market its line of body-care products with respect for the environment, the Body Shop employees, and the indigenous peoples who provide many of the raw materials.

LETS (Local Economic Trading System) demonstrates a new approach to economics. It is a type of barter system that was first developed by Michael Linton for the Comox Valley, British Columbia, in 1983 and has since spread around the world. LETS works on the principle that we all have skills to offer, but at times the cash economy doesn't give us enough opportunity to use them. When you 'sell' goods or services to another LETS member, you earn a credit in a community currency called Green Dollars (g$). You can then use this credit to buy whatever you want from any member of the system. Participants are free to trade their skills and meet their needs even when cash is in short supply.

The system works like this: Alicia is a carpenter and Rezaul a gardener. Rezaul wants to buy a small table, but doesn't have enough extra money. In a cash system, the trade would not happen—both sides would lose. Alicia doesn't need gardening, so there is no possibility for a straight barter between them, either. But if both were members of LETS, they could trade!

All LETS accounts start at zero. Each new member gets an interest-free line of credit in LETS dollars (g$). (Currently, the credit limit is g$500 for individuals and g$1,000 for businesses, but exceptions may be negotiated with the manager.) Most transactions are settled partly in LETS and partly in Canadian currency. The total price usually equals the going rate on the regular market. So Alicia and Rezaul settle on, say, $20 and g$80. (The currency is handled in the usual way. Then Alicia either arranges to have the g$80 transferred to her account from Rezaul's by phoning the LETS banker, or, Rezaul simply hands her g$80 in LETS banknotes.

Today, hundreds of LETS systems are operating in Canada, the U.S., the U.K., Australia and New Zealand. LETS is a significant experiment in a highly replicable local economic vehicle. It takes the mysticism out of money, and in a time when money on the international markets is reduced to an electronic blip, LETS regrounds the money concept in the value of products and services. The LET System demonstrates that local people never need to become victims of recessions or global capitalism.

Is ethical investment possible? Well, look at the ethical investment funds around and see for yourself. Can you produce wood pulp without cutting down trees? People are doing it, using hemp instead of the forests that are needed to maintain healthy ecosystems. Do local people have the savvy to transform their own fading communities. Well, look at what happened here and there. This is why demonstration efforts are needed in every part of the social process. They create signs of possibility that others can come and look at, and go away saying, "Well, blow me down. Look at that. They've gone and done it. We could do it, too!"

QUALITIES OF PROFOUND PRESENCE

This section describes five qualities of this signal presence as it shows up in human beings.

Presence is constantly *showing up.* "80 per cent of success," said Woody Allen, is just showing up." One basic aspect of presence is showing up on time, where your calendar or timeline says you need to be. Crossing guards have always fascinated me. Every day I pass a Chinese crossing guard on the corner of Main and Swanwick, when I make a trip to the library. We nod to each other. He is always there, doing what crossing guards do, holding up his red flag, blowing his whistle, beckoning the school children to cross or telling them to stop and wait. With his orange garb, his flag and his whistle, he ensures safe passage across Main Street for the kids in the nearby school and anyone else. He or she also becomes a local symbol of structural care. He gives no evidence of pleasure or pain in what he is doing. He is just there—every school day—without fail. That is basic presence.

Tom Washington was part of the leadership of the 5th City Community Reformulation Project on Chicago's West Side. Tom was a very ordinary man, but he had decided to be a caring presence in his community. Every morning at five a.m., he would make his cup of coffee and set out to walk the streets of his community. He kept up a steady pace, pausing only to note something that needed to be dealt with later on: an abandoned car, some youngsters heading home too late, some spilt garbage. People getting up early recognized Tom on his beat, and understood what he was doing. Tom showed up on his beat every day of the year, year after year, until he was too old to do it. He was a sign of care for that community.

Presence is *interior discipline.* Some people equate presence with charisma, that extraordinary power in a personality that attracts people and support to certain leaders. That can be a great gift, but the kind of presence described here is based on interior discipline, not charisma. This is the way Joseph Mathews put the difference:

> I get awfully angry when people talk about charismatic leadership, as if charisma were something that certain of us were born with, something that some have, and others don't. For years I've been saying that the source of charisma is the capacity to stand day after day after day in the waterless desert. While this one falls over and that one fades away in the strain, you just *stand* day after day after day after day. *That* is charisma. If some of you young ones think it would be fun to have a dose of charisma, then it is very simple: you just stand day after day after day with the shells falling all around you while this one starts bitching and bitching and bitching, but you give up the luxury of bitching and grind away at the task. It is just that simple. This is interior discipline.

In other words, presence is not some special external cachet that people like Paul Newman or Princess Diana had, and the rest of us don't and can't. For presence is a result of enduring despair, rejection, disappointment and betrayal and still deciding to stand in the desert day after day. It is a result of getting up early in the morning, dealing with family, task, people and contradictions one after the other and coming home at night only to find oneself trying to figure out how to deal with the next day's problems and the kids at the same time. In other words, presence comes from engagement in one's mission up to the elbows, day after day—like the Doctors Without Borders. It comes from travelling the distance through the journey of consciousness and care. It comes from the experience of always going through it and never going under. It comes from the decision, made day after day, to affirm and live life as it comes; to deal with the complexities that life puts in our way; to accept the constant experience of having bitten off more than we can chew. Doing that for 20, 40 or 60 years leaves a mark, the mark of presence, the kind of presence which beckons to others.

Although people who care always work to affirm life as it is and to demonstrate the joy there is in service to the world, there is an *inevitable sadness* underneath that affirmation and joy. The sadness comes from knowing that millions upon millions of people in the world will never realize their potential, let alone have enough food, clothes or shelter. In other words, it comes from knowing life's inescapable tragedy. Those who care tend to speak out of the silence, which is the experience of internalizing the suffering of the world. This kind of presence is light years beyond the spontaneous bubbling and burbling away of some effervescent personality. This is not to say that this profound presence is humourless. It's not. But it cannot forget the innocent suffering of the world.

Problemless living flows from the decision to serve the world. It is trusting that the way life is is how it is, and, therefore, you do not have any problems anymore. What you used to call problems is just the way life comes at you. Caroline Myss, in her *Anatomy of Spirit*, talks about the syndrome she calls "woundology", or hanging on to the wounds one has sustained from life, long past what is normal:

> We've lost the courage to be what we think we want to be. We've lost our backbone and replaced it with wishbone. We need the courage to be able to say: "I've turned my wound into street currency. I like the mileage I'm getting and I'm afraid to let go of it." We've got to be able to say to someone we love: "I've witnessed your wound long enough. Knock it off, because at this point it's costing you your cell tissue and I am not helping you. You're not progressing in your life. You're indulging in self-pity and I don't think this is support." We've got to recognize that healing is the courage to let go of those wounds, not to sink into them and not to turn your entire lifestyle around being wounded and weak. That is not healing.

As social pioneers, we have given up the luxury of advertising and licking our wounds, knowing that we cannot care adequately for the world if our care is locked into our own suffering. Daily reflection on life gives us time to absorb and digest those "dark night attacks" that life puts in our way. It helps us deal with the woundings of the day— disappointments, the insensitive words of others, the pain of realizing one's own mistakes and blunders—to own up to them, learn from them, and put them behind us. Without this constant reflective process, our unhealed wounds accumulate and link up, until we seem to be one vast wound. Social pioneers give up the luxury of despair, hurt and hostility.

Barry Denenburg in his biography, *Nelson Mandela: No Easy Walk to Freedom*, describes how Mandela transcended his own suffering in prison and found time to care for other inmates:

> He continued his habit of exercising every morning. By day the prisoners dug out limestone slabs and loaded them onto trucks. In the evenings he studied. He was

studying law through the mails as well as educating himself about Afrikaner history and language. At one point permission to study was withdrawn for four years. This was particularly difficult for him. He would not give in to the monotony of prison life. Each day was treated as a new opportunity. Friendships were made and renewed. Experiences were shared and old stories told yet again. Plans for the future were discussed. Mandela helped many survive behind bars. He encouraged them to educate themselves.

On another occasion, Mandela remarked, "As we let our own light shine, we unconsciously give other people permission to do the same. As we're liberated from our own fear, our presence automatically liberates others."

Those who have travelled a long way on the journey of the spirit often develop a certain enigmatic presence. They may grow a pigtail, or start wearing purple, or ask people they encounter strange questions. In so doing, their presence points to an increased depth within themselves.

CLASSIC ROLES

Most people live out of the context of "What's in it for me?" But, as social pioneers, our concern is what we can give to the situation to make it more human, more alive, more caring. You have to be able to picture yourself walking into a dentist's waiting room or some such place, noticing the air of silent gloom, and saying in your most cheerful voice: "Good morning! How are we all today? What a beautiful day!" Sometimes the magic works, and people come alive, and sometimes it takes a lot more work than that.

Being the presence of love seeks to release others to their greatness. Four classic roles enable this release:
- The Sage
- The Poet
- The Saint
- The Leader/General
- The Wise Fool

The Sage: There are times when we encounter the wisdom of the sage in our lives, but there are also times when we put on that role. The sage is like a shaft of light that illuminates realities formerly hidden in the darkness of illusion and confusion. Sages watch for the undeniable truth in a world of uncertainties, knowing how to turn bewilderment into common sense and indifference into passionate conviction. They can use the wisdom gained from past experience to unlock the secrets of the present and read the signs of what is to come. Their wisdom gives back to us the depth and breadth of our own life understanding, calling us in our turn to be the sage.

I remember a tough time when I had reached a certain stage in teaching high school. There were piles of kids' homework on my desk awaiting marks, my university assignments were stacking up, and I was involved up to my armpits in other aspects of the school. My being was strung so tight, one more thing would have snapped it. As I was sitting at my desk in the staff room, with brow furrowed, an older teacher sidled up alongside me and said, "You know, you may not believe it, but there is more to life than this school. You need to take a break, get out more, go to the movies, and not be so hard on yourself." Well, that advice was my salvation. I did go to movies, I began to relax, and my perspective on life improved dramatically. That intervention reminded me that giving of yourself 100 per cent every day means burnout unless you recharge your batteries. Everyone needs this kind of mentoring from a "sage" at certain times in life. At other times you experience yourself as the wise one.

Deciding to be that kind of presence is a risk—you never know how people are going to take it. Are they going to say, "Look, this is none of your business. Keep your big nose out of this!" Or, they may say nothing, and you wonder if you have been heard at all. In either case, it's not a good idea to hang around and try it again. Just deliver your message and get out of the way, giving the person time to struggle with what you've said, without trying to justify your intervention to yourself. Being this kind of wise presence demands a certain nonchalance. People generally don't change overnight. It might take them ten years to finally hear what you say to them. The sage understands this. He also understands the power of repeated messages over time.

The Poet. Presence can also be like the energy of the poet. In a general sense, poetry is like music that evokes the deep insights existing in every consciousness. Poets use whatever language they can find to express the truth that is beyond language. They enable a group to transcend the tyrannies of time and space, both by dreaming new dreams and by turning abstractions into living realities. Their images replenish the wellsprings of wonder and creativity in our lives and call us in our turn to be the poet.

One of my ICA colleagues tells the story of putting on a cabaret in an elders' home. The elders' home staff asked ICA to do something that would breathe new life into the institution. There was a great deal of bickering and criticism going on, people were unhappy with the staff, and the staff were unhappy with the bitching of some of the seniors. Something needed to happen to lift the spirits. At the time, ICA had been experimenting with the cabaret as an art form of awakenment for rousing people out of their torpor and despair. We had come to see that release from despair is one of the primary elements in the creation of the cabaret, which can re-awaken the hope that is already latent within people, even if it has been stifled for years. We saw that creating a cabaret-type event could be an instrument for encouraging people to participate in the wonder and the miracle of life. So, the elders jumped at the possibility; while some of them trained to be the dance troupe and sewed their dancing–girl outfits, others created the satirical skits about life in the seniors' home, and still others prepared the lights and stage settings. They selected a master of ceremonies, everyone rehearsed and practised, and finally, the night came to stage the cabaret. It was a howling success. When the music struck up, and this troupe of "girls" in their seventies and eighties came out in their colourful outfits and did the opening cabaret dance, the place just exploded in glee and excitement. Then, as the show developed, and many of the facets of the senior's home were held up for satire, people alternately laughed and cried at the parade of human folly and greatness.

These seniors and their home were never the same again. They heard and saw the truth that is beyond language; and the wellsprings of wonder and creativity were replenished in their lives. The poet at work did a job on them all.

The Saint. A third role of this signal presence is that of the saint (with a small "s"). Secular saints can be found in any walk of life, among nurses, bus drivers, office workers, police officers, and street sweepers. Sainthood is like a fire of vitality that blazes till it has nothing left to expend. Through being what they are, saints reveal to others the way of fulfillment, problemlessness and meaningful existence. They see a world of wonder in the midst of everyday labor and a world of hope in the midst of impossible problems. By living the style of possibility, embracing life's pain and suffering, they embody the option of glorious living and call us in our turn to live our own possibility.

Bev Parker was one of the founders of ICA in Canada. In her later years, she saw herself as an enabler. She prepared wonderfully appetizing lunches for the ICA Board when it met, paying special attention to individual preferences and diets. Several times a week she went to a senior's apartment to do all her housework and cook her a square meal.

Bev knew that life is good. And that death is good. She also knew that those two truths were not glib utterances but insights derived from struggling authentically with life as it happens. I think it was this sense that life is good just as it is that made Bev Parker such a good storyteller. She made a news event of everything going on in her life. If you asked Bev how things were going, she would talk of her garden, the shawl she was knitting, how her grown-up children were doing, her walk along the boardwalk with a friend, the Chinese woman she was helping with English, or her conversation with the manager of the health food store that was in danger of going bankrupt, or the purple beans that were growing like topsy in her tiny vegetable garden, or the eggs she had got standing on end at the equinox—Bev was always very much in tune with the earth. All the corners and edges of her room were filled with rocks.

To chat with Bev was to talk about the nitty gritty of life. The more mundane her life became, the more she seemed to relish it and consider it newsworthy. For Bev, life's significance was in the here and now. Some people make a vocation of the reverse Midas effect: turning the gold of their life into garbage. For Bev, every part of her life was a media event. And all of life was intensely fascinating and invested with great significance. After all, it was her life, she was talking about, and it was good. Beverley Parker always seemed to me to be saint Beverley.

The Leader or General. A fourth role is that of the leader or general (although not in a military sense). Leadership can be a fresh wind that awakens the life of honor and confidence within a team. Leaders take responsibility for the whole situation. They sustain and symbolize the whole group's conviction that the success of their enterprise is not only possible but a historic necessity. Alert to the implications of every action, aware of the dangers and opportunities at each point of the task, they call us in our turn to be the leader.

Burmese popular heroine and Nobel Prize winner Aung San Suu Kyi has been struggling on behalf of a more democratic future for her country. It brings her to frequent grips with the government. One day, as she was walking down the street with some followers during a campaign visit, six soldiers under the command of an Army captain jumped down from a jeep, assumed a kneeling position, and took aim at her. She motioned her followers to wait on the sidewalk, and she herself walked down the center of the road towards the soldiers. "It seemed so much simpler to provide them with a single target than to bring everyone else in," she said. It was at this point that a major ordered the captain to revoke the shooting orders. Her leadership has always exhibited a rare kind of courage.

Of course, leadership can also have a very "down-home" side to it. When Mrs. Brown phones some of the parents in her son's school and invites them to afternoon tea at her kitchen table to talk about drugs in the school, she is also taking responsibility for the situation—as she does when she convinces the parents that something, indeed, can be done about it and they are the ones who can do it. That is also leadership, or generalship.

The Wise Fool. Finally, one more role or archetype, I want to throw in: that of the *wise fool*. This is not the same as the idiot. It is more like the fool found in several of Shakespeare's plays, who keeps the King from going off the rails or getting too big for his boots. The Wise Fool exemplifies the wisdom found at the end of the journey which allows us to get the great cosmic joke. One form of the wise fool has always been the madman or madwoman. In Jane Wagner and Lily Tomlin's *The Search for Intelligent Life in the Universe*, Trudy, the bag lady, tells how she experienced the "kind of madness Socrates talked about, a divine release of the soul from the yoke of custom and convention." Trudy is a modern-day Wise Fool, whose loss of sanity opened her mind to the cosmic:

> The human mind is kind of like…
> a piñata. When it breaks open,
> there's a lot of surprises inside.
> Once you get the piñata perspective,
> you see that losing your mind
> can be a peak experience.

The fool helps us laugh at our own over-seriousness about all kinds of things: our own virtue, our sense of importance, our great deeds. It's the fool who allows us to laugh at our own ridiculous *hubris* for taking on impossible tasks, like writing this book. But also, when things get rough and everyone gets worried and anxious, it's time for the Fool to illuminate the situation in a way that makes the load seem lighter and our own anxiety a lack of basic trust in the universe. Carol Pearson in *Awakening the Heroes Within* throws more light on the role of the fool:

> The lowest-level comics use humour to degrade. The highest, most ennobling comics help us to test the fool's perspective by causing us to chuckle in sympathetic enjoyment and celebration of life's most difficult moments and to enjoy the common bond of our fallible humanity, even with people who are ordinarily seen as "others"….The wise fool allows us to enjoy life, the moment and each other without judgment but also without illusions.

> Without the fool around, we tend to get psychologically bloated through constant feeding on our self-importance. The fool has to be around to prick illusions, remind us of our contingency and mortality, and with a light touch, keep our spirit moving forward.

Mahatma Gandhi summed up signal presence when he remarked, "We must *be* the change we want to see in the world."

The Final Exercise: Creating Your Own Style

Now that, perhaps, you have read the whole book and done a few of the exercises, you might be asking the question, "What difference is this book going to make in my life?" The issue here is putting on a new style that incorporates some of what you have read.

Externally, style is the organization of space and time. Internally, style is writing the poem of your relation to the mystery of life. In the last half century, we have seen the rise and fall of several styles: the slate-grey, briefcase-carrying "organization man" of the fifties; the flower-child hippie of the sixties, the "me-generation" self-centeredness of the seventies, and the Wall Street financial piranhas of the eighties and nineties. Life style is very practical, utterly unavoidable, and very profound in the sense of tying together the art form and specific presence that your life is in history.

1. Style makes most sense in the context of your vocation. You might want to flip back to the exercise at the end of Chapter 6, and either do the exercise or, if you have already done it, review your responses. Remember that style is a missional creation that has to do with your life purpose.

2. Fill in the chart below with examples of your self-image and the stylistic qualities that support it—in the past, currently, and the ones you sense you need for the future.
   Examples of images: man or woman about town, recluse, mouse, housewife, village idiot, playboy.
   Examples of stylistic qualities: Teflon suit, confidence, gentle patience, winning decisively.

	PAST STYLES	CURRENT STYLE	FUTURE STYLES
IMAGES			
STYLISTIC QUALITIES			

3. Style shift is a sign of resurgence, a kind of re-incarnation of the self in history.

Changing styles is awkward at first. We have all come across examples of a sudden shift in style. For example, Uncle Broderick who has always been a slob, comes late, his clothes are mussed, his hair unkempt, and he talks like someone from the backwoods. The next time you see him at a relative's wedding, he is first inside the church, is immaculate and dressed in a tux. When you talk with him, he has acquired an educated accent. That's a style shift. Or at work there might be someone who is loud-mouthed, arrogant, domineering, and a real pain to work with. He gets a job in an Asian country. When he returns, he is soft-spoken, considerate, flexible and a delight to be around. That's a style change. You feel like asking the person, "What on earth happened to you?"

When styles change, there is an interior transformation, but with visible signs: voice, hair, dress, walk, glasses, etc.

Look back at what you wrote about the images and characteristics related to the style you want to become which is related to your mission in history, your life purpose.

4. List 15 concrete things you need to do to create your new style and image:

_____	_____	_____
_____	_____	_____
_____	_____	_____
_____	_____	_____
_____	_____	_____

5. Create a timeline for accomplishing these 15 things.

	MONDAY	TUESDAY	WEDNESDAY	THURSDAY	FRIDAY	SATURDAY	SUNDAY
WEEK 1							
WEEK 2							
WEEK 3							
WEEK 4							
WEEK 5							

Reflect on this exercise.

What discoveries did you make about style?_____

_____

_____

How did you feel as you did the exercise?_____

_____

_____

What are the implications of the exercise for you? _____

_____

_____

_____

CONCLUSION

Summoning the Will and Courage

Now it's time to ask, "Well, so what? When a group of us at the Canadian Institute of Cultural Affairs (ICA Canada) sat down months before publication to decide on the title for this book, we came up with *Authentic Leadership from Your Own Backyard.* We wanted to convey that leadership begins where everyone is, whether it's a backyard, an office, a community meeting, a kitchen table meeting, a PTA meeting, or the conversation you are having. That title bit the dust, one of many. Finally, *The Courage to Lead* got nods from all around.

"Courage," said Winston Churchill, " is rightly esteemed the first of human qualities because it is the quality which guarantees all others." So, none of the twelve standing points described in this book will really catch fire for us without the courage and will to implement them on the firing line, in real-life situations. What is demanded is more than a knowing about these stances. We need to be able to summon up the will and energy to operate out of these stances in spite of the situation. Eleanor Roosevelt used to say, "You gain strength, courage, and confidence by every experience in which you really stop to look fear in the face."

It takes courage to live life as given without complaint or criticism or trying to protect ourselves from the pain of life through drugs (illegal and legal), alcohol or other addictions. It takes double courage to decide to lead: to say what needs to be said without being wishy-washy. Sometimes, all it takes to be a leader is to ask the right question at the right time: Is this what we had in mind when we launched this project? What would it take to really go for broke on this plan? Is there any reason why we just can't go ahead on this? What's the block here? How are we going to fund this?

Most of us manage to relate well to life when we are frisky and energetic. But when we get really tired, and our care is still needed, it is easy to collapse. We need the courage to keep on keeping on when we get tired and stressed. It is important to distinguish this kind of perseverance from the workaholics who do not dare stop working lest they have a moment to reflect on their lives. When we decide to say yes to the fatigue and to continue in spite of everything, we can often find a strength and energy that seems to come out of nowhere, that allows us to persist in the task until it's done—even when completing it feels like swimming upstream in molasses. (It is also true that some people can get so stressed out they should be sent home to rest.) However, we all rely on doctors, nurses, teachers to keep going in spite of weariness. Robert Frost described well the situation of many care-givers:

> The woods are lovely, dark and deep
> But I have promises to keep,
> And miles to go before I sleep,
> And miles to go before I sleep.

It takes courage to persist in doing our own journey work, so that, whatever our task, our being is open and in balance to receive what's happening. In fact without the centeredness that comes from doing our journey homework, operating effectively becomes very difficult. Our interior gets so cluttered with our mental baggage that it affects how we relate to everyone else. Courage here becomes a matter of scheduling when we do our journey work, and sticking to it. It is also easy to lose our sense of wonder in life when we become overly preoccupied with efficiency and "pushing things through." Rachel Carson used to say, "If I had influence with the good fairy who is supposed to preside over the christening of all children, I should ask that her gift to each child in the world be a sense of wonder so indestructible that it would last throughout life." Equally important is staying open to our intuition and and trusting it to let us know when something needs to be said or some intervention needs to be made. There are times when things just gnaw at our insides. We wake up in the middle of the night, and we just can't get this thing out of our mind. We can try to use our rationality to dismiss those interior promptings, but when they persist, then we have to trust those intuitions, and say, "Rationality, be damned. I really care about this, and I'll take the consequences."

Another aspect of courage is the power of persistence. Calvin Coolidge had a good word about the refusal to give up: "Nothing in this world can take the place of persistence. Talent will not; nothing is more common than unsuccessful people with talent. Genius will not; unrewarded genius is almost a proverb. Education will not; the world is full of educated derelicts. The slogan 'press on' has solved many problems of the human race."

Sometimes the task we have taken on turns into a swamp. A voice inside nags, "Drop it, Jack! It's simply not worth all the trouble. Life should be simpler than this. I don't need all these bosses nipping at my heels. I'm out. This project is over." At this point you have to ask yourself the question, and answer it honestly: "Was this project worth my life when I initiated it?' If the answer is yes, then it is only the next step that is required. Pick up the phone one more time, call one more meeting, go on one more funding call. Those moments when we are in the bottom of the barrel, in the greatest despair, are often the times of breakthrough that encourage us to keep moving. Persistence is often omnipotent. We just have to get over feeling silly about being persistent.

Life is always asking for our YES. What might happen if one fine morning, we decided to live the life style of YES: yes to the way life is, yes to myself and my mistakes, yes to life, yes to the future, yes to the needs of my family and colleagues , yes to the needs of society? Jean Anouilh has a great passage in *Antigone* about saying yes and no:

> It is easy to say no. To say yes, you have to sweat and roll up your sleeves and plunge both hands into life up to the elbows. It is easy to say no, even if saying no means death. All you have to do is to sit still and wait. Wait to go on living; wait to be killed. That is the coward's part. No is one of your man-made words. Can you imagine a world in which trees say no to the sap? In which beasts say no to hunger or to propagation?

What if we decided to plunge both hands into life up the elbows? Listen one more time to this pearl from Nelson Mandela's inaugural speech:

> We are born to make manifest the glory that is in us.
> It's not just in some of us, it's in everyone.
> When we let our own light shine,
> we unconsciously give other people permission to do the same.
> As we are liberated from our own fear,
> our presence automatically liberates others.

Appendices

The History of ICA

Bibliography

The History of ICA

The life stances portrayed in this book arose from the work of the ICA over half a century. ICA is truly a learning organization in its ability to evolve, learn from, and meet the needs of changing times.

In a nutshell, the journey of the organization took place in five phases:
- The Fifties: University community of study;
- The Sixties: The inter-faith dialogue, teaching and community demonstration work of the Ecumenical Institute ;
- The Seventies: The formation of the Order: Ecumenical and the global expansion of the Institute's work;
- Late Seventies and Eighties: The global development work of ICA with its local awakenment and demonstration projects;
- The Nineties: A period of facilitation, training and publication.

The twentieth century presented humankind with profoundly new times, affecting every social institution. Major shifts in society were precipitated by nothing less than revolutions in our scientific understanding, urban living and secular style. With the dawning of this new age came a profound new consciousness of social interrelatedness and resurgent human spirit. Along with other institutions, the church also found itself responding to the radically new times. Renewal took place through a ground swell of theological writings and study, lay participation and visioning, and ecumenical dialogue and coordination.

After World War II, both the Second General Assembly of the World Council of Churches and Vatican Council II began to review the critical issues then facing the

FIVE BROAD PHASES OF ICA'S HISTORY				
1952-1960	1961-1968	1969- 1976	1977-1988	1989-2000
LOCATION	LOCATION	LOCATION	LOCATION	LOCATION
Christian Faith and Life Community, University of Texas	West Side of Chicago The Ecumenical Institute The Order Ecumenical	101 locations globally headquarters in Brussels, Hong Kong, Bombay, and Chicago	Working in thousands of villages around the globe The order destructured	ICA offices in 34 nations
Study, research, community living	Teaching, 5th City community reformulation, research	Social research, teaching and broad-based programs globally	Local awakenment and demonstration	Facilitation, Training and Publication

Christian Church. The 1954 meeting of the World Council of Churches in Evanston, Illinois made a resolution to begin a center for the training of lay people in North America, taking as an example the Ecumenical Institute of Bossey, Switzerland. In 1956 Christian businessmen in Chicago founded the Evanston Institute of Ecumenical Studies and invited Dr. Walter Leibrecht to come from Germany to be the director.

During the same period, a group of students and staff at the University of Texas began to research the practical relationship of their faith to contemporary life. This group called itself the Christian Faith and Life Community and was founded by a former Naval chaplain, Rev. W. Jack Lewis. Drawing from the experience of experimental lay communities in Europe such as Taizé and Iona, the Christian Faith and Life Community evolved a common life of worship, study and mission and was recognized as a significant pilot project in forming a Christian community. It designed a curriculum for students and laity under the direction of Dr. Joseph W. Mathews, formerly an associate professor of Social Ethics at Perkins Theological Seminary in Dallas, Texas. The curriculum included courses in systematic theology, Old and New Testament, and Christian ethics. The community began to turn their attention to the role of the local congregation in society and they developed a week–end residential seminar, known as Religious Studies I (RS-I) for local congregations and student groups.

When Dr. Leibrecht returned home to Germany in 1962, the Ecumenical Institute— by then a training division of the Church Federation of Greater Chicago—appointed a new Dean, Dr. Mathews of the Christian Faith and Life Community. He brought with him a staff who had been experimenting in methods of concentrated theological training for laity and clergy and in forms of disciplined corporate life and mission, emphasising a corporate life–style of worship, study and service.

THE SIXTIES

This period was the origin of the Order: Ecumenical. These families were volunteers without a salary. They continued to develop the curriculum for local congregations while researching the form and meaning of contemporary Christian community. After studying the forms of corporate life of the historical religious order, the staff began to model the community after family orders.

The Ecumenical Institute is an outgrowth of a groundswell of church renewal efforts particularly in Europe—theological writings and study, lay participation and visioning, and ecumenical dialogue and coordination. Staff members studied, visited and participated in many of these pioneering church renewal movements including the evanagelical academies located throughout Europe, the Taizé Community in France, the Iona Community in Scotland, the House Church movement and Sheffield Industrial Mission in England, as well as Vatical Council II in Rome. The Institute was deeply indebted to the life and work of all these renewal forces within the church.

The training dimension of the Institute's work was balanced by an emphasis on practical research and demonstration. When the seven families of the Ecumenical Institute moved to Chicago, they undertook a practical experiment in comprehensive community development. From the premise that local communities constitute the basic building block of society, the Institute began working in a ghetto neighborhood on Chicago's west side, which became known as 5th City. Door-to-door interviews and neighborhood meetings provided a way for the local residents to review their many problems and to begin to design practical solutions.

The early training of the Institute encompassed a comprehensive set of religious studies courses, both theoretical and practical. From 1962-1964 these courses were taught in the Chicago area. A corresponding curriculum focused on depth understanding of the times grew out of a seminar entitled, "The 20th Century Cultural Revolution." The inclusive cultural curriculum was designed to present models of the edge thinking and issues in the cultural disciplines and social structures. The Institute undertook a systematic training across North America. Some 20,000 people participated in Ecumenical Institute seminars between 1964 and 1967. In 1967, a team of four faculty taught courses in Asia and Australia. Similar trips followed in Latin America, Europe and Africa.

The Institute's curriculum evolved into two distinct branches, on branch focusing on biblical, theological and religious dialogue courses and the other on contemporary society and changing attitudes in the family, community and world. The religious seminars presented people with an opportunity to rediscover the meaning and relevance of the Christian message in the modern world. The cultural seminars provide a way to understand the basic dynamics of society, the current issues, and new trends of thought within various disciplines. Since the first seminars were taught, many hundreds of lay people and clergy have attended them in many countries.

That seven families could develop a national education program taught throughout the nation and the world out of nothing was an absurdity. Yet it happened. That twenty individuals working full-time could build a community organization where agencies with ample resources had often failed was also absurd, but true. And all of it had come about as the result of a thousand miracles, no less astonishing for their comparative importance in the total picture. Festivals for thousands, world teaching tours, stood side by side with what was literally a hand–to–mouth financial situation.

By 1964 the Ecumenical Institute began working closely with groups of people who had found the seminars relevant to the needs of their own churches and communities. At their request, the staff developed more advanced research and training programs. In 1965 the first annual summer research assembly was organized. Some of these research assemblies drew 1,000 people from around the world. Their research creates and refines the practical methods and design through which both the Institute and many other groups have sought to serve the needs of local communities.

TRAINING CURRICULUM

The original curriculum created in the 1950s and 60s for the training of Christian lay people and community leaders globally, included courses that were both religious and secular. The first of these courses, Religious Studies I, focused on the twentieth century theological revolution and grounded the insights of Bultmann, Tillich, Bonhoeffer and Niebuhr in the lives of participants. This was the basic and introductory course. Another introductory course, Imaginal Education, aimed to equip educators with new images of education and new methods for teaching. The rest of the courses were intended to convey a comprehensive overview of the key disciplines of our times as a context for engagement in reformulating society.

Complementary to these were the methods courses: Intellectual Methods, Social Methods, and Personal Growth Methods.

Intellectual methods include: the conversation method, the charting method, the seminar method, the lecture building and presentation methods, curriculum planning method, and corporate writing.

Social Methods include: the workshop method, community gridding, strategic planning, frameworking and community development.

The *Personal Growth Methods* include: solitary reflection, depth conversations, the Other World mythology, studies of classical spiritual writers such as the psalmist, Teresa of Avila, John of the Cross, and the phases of the human spirit journey as in Nikos Kazantzakis, Hermann Hesse, and Joseph Campbell.

ICA'S CLASSICAL CURRICULUM	
RELIGIOUS COURSES	CULTURAL COURSES
Theological Revolution	Cultural Revolution
New Testament	Psychology and Art
Old Testament	Science and Philosophy
Church History	Sociology and History
Ecumenics	Nation and World
The Missional Congregation	Community and Polis
Ur Images (World Religions)	Individual and Family

In the 1970s we added to these personal growth methods systematic studies of the dark night of the soul, the long march of care, Castaneda, the Sufis, Lao Tzu, Chuang Tzu, Sun Tzu, and Miyamoto Musashi. In the 1980s, personal growth studies included: Jean Houston, Willis Harman, insight meditation, and experimentation with several other methods such as visualization, DMA, and NLP (Neuro-Linguistic Programming).

During the 1970s, two extensive training programmes were developed using this curriculum: the Global Academy, an eight week course of religious and cultural seminars, and a six-week International Training Institute (ITI), with a greater emphasis on practical field work. The first ITI was held at Trinity College in Singapore, in 1969, and was attended by 102 people from 23 nations. Since then the ITIs have been held in multiple locations around the world.

THE EARLY 70S

The Order: Ecumenical in the 70s was a family order of 1,400 adults and 600 children of 23 nationalities. The Order formed the permanent staff, first of EI, then of ICA. The creation of a family order was based on the presupposition that renewal of the social order in the light of the family crisis of our times depended on the demonstration of missional families operating within a covenanted community. The Order members staffed the institute, lived in "religious houses" whose task was to do the institute's work in the region around the house.

One of the essential characteristics of the order was the disposition of economic resources. The order operated under the principle of total self-support, which meant that all donations for the work of the Institute went into the mission rather than for staff salaries. Half the members worked in different occupations as lawyers, doctors, businessmen, teachers, social workers, etc. Their income, after taxes, was pooled, using part for stipends and part for corporate funds for health, travel, special celebrations, children's education and annuity. The family stipend was below the actual poverty level in most countries where the order worked.

The growing acknowledgment of both the 5th City experiment and the seminars led to a number of invitations for the Institute to work in other countries as well. In 1968 there were just over 100 people on the staff, all living in 5th City. By 1974, the number of staff had grown to 1,400, working in over 100 offices in 20 nations with a large percentage of the staff coming from countries where offices had been newly established. Co–ordinating centers were established in Bombay, Hong Kong, Chicago, Brussels and Kuala Lumpur.

After careful research and analysis of the methods and programs that had been successful in 5th City, the Institute accepted invitations to begin similar projects in Australia and the Marshall Islands. These projects were viewed as experiments to test the applicability of the original methods developed in 5th City in the radically different cultural situations of a remote Aboriginal settlement and a South Pacific Island.

Many professional and business people took part in all three development projects as voluntary consultants. They asked the Institute to design a seminar to demonstrate the relevance of the project planning methods to other groups in different circumstances. This led to the development of LENS (Leadership Effectiveness and New Strategies), a seminar which has since been used by social agencies, government offices and private businesses around the world.

As the Institute's work came into close contact with people from other religions, especially Hindu, Islamic and Buddhist peoples—to say nothing of the highly secular concerns of people in corporations—it became clear that the churchy title, Ecumenical Institute, was not an adequate banner to work under as they moved into working with both secular corporations and non-Christian villages. In 1973, the Institute of Cultural Affairs (ICA) was incorporated as a charitable organization in Illinois and in Canada in 1976. Other offices in other nations followed suit.

By 1974, the many aspects of the work of the Institute were grouped into three major ICA programs: Human Development, Community Forum and Research, Training and Interchange.

THE LATER SEVENTIES

In 1975, ICA wanted to inaugurate a system of demonstration community projects around the globe to apply the Fifth City model. The criteria for these projects were:

- Comprehensive distribution pattern across the world. They decided to have one "Human Development Project" (as they were called in every time zone, making twenty-four in all.) The idea was that as demonstrations they had to be accessible to anyone anywhere who wanted to go and see them.

- The villages had to be reasonably accessible to international or feeder airports, so they could serve the demonstration function.

- "The band of 24," as the social demonstration projects came to be known, would follow the Fifth City model and be pioneers in comprehensive village development: each would have economic, social and cultural programs dealing with all the problems in the village, and somehow engaging all the people in the process.

Around the same time ICA askeditself how it might carry the message of local development to many more villages and towns. Development was not just for the developing countries, but for the first world as well. The Town Meeting or Community Forum was a one-day meeting of presentations, planning and celebration intended to wake up local communities. During the late 1970s, one such forum was held in every county in North America, resulting in 5,400 events. Over 1,000 were held in 13 countries in Europe.

The Human Development Programme was designed for use by a particular local rural or urban community. It was based on the methods researched in the first three projects. Since 1975 pilot projects were begun in over 300 communities in 25 nations. Each project sought to demonstrate effective social and economic development that could be applied to its region and nation. The starting point was a week-long consultation where a broad cross-section of the community, voluntary consultants from both public and private sectors, and ICA staff worked together to design an integrated four-year plan for comprehensive local development. In India, the original pilot project sparked off development across 232 villages in Maharashtra state. This development effort was known as the "New Village Movement" or *Nava Gram Prayas*. An even more extensive village movement involved 1000 villages in Kenya. Less extensive replication experiments were also carried out in Indonesia and the Philippines.

The Community Forums used simple workshop methods in a community meeting that helped clarify community concerns and created practical plans to tackle local problems by using the community's available resources and cooperative effort. The methods were also adapted for use by groups whose particular concerns often required a special approach. These include the Global Women's Forum and the Community Youth Forum.

ICA staff, voluntary consultants and local people from around the world did extensive research, training and interchange. The Human Development Training Institute was a direct result of this work. It was used extensively to train community leadership, village volunteers and government field workers.

THE EIGHTIES

In the early 1980s, the regional consultation was developed as a tool to link the work in local communities into a wider geo-social context. While community forums continued to wake up local communities in many parts of the world, a series of 62 regional consultations were held while Human Development Training Institutes continued to train more local leaders for community development. The European volunteer movement gathered strength, continuing to send many young people to work in village projects in many parts of the world.

Training, Inc. was first launched in Chicago as a 13-week program to ensure job training and placement. The training was tailored to those who had their high school certificates, but were unable to find a job. The program gave them rapid-fire effective training in computers, accounting, billing, sales, reception, word processing and data entry. The program focused on changing the foundational images and behavior of the students. In the eighties, similar programs opened in several other cities and gained an awesome reputation—both for the depth of their training and their success in job placement.

In 1982, work on the International Exposition of Rural Development (IERD) began to occupy the attention of ICA offices. Co-sponsorship by several UN agencies gave the program additional cachet. Workshops were held to document the keys to success in hundreds of projects run by many different organizations around the world. 800 representatives from the projects gathered in New Delhi, India, in February 1984 for the central IERD conference to share their projects. A series of books were published to hold the insights of the conference and ICA began to publish, starting with three books of learnings from the IERD conference and the years of social work in rural villages.

As the 1980s continued, ICA began to build partnerships and share experience with other caring organizations around the world. A wide variety of presenters took part in summer research assemblies; some, like Jean Houston, became colleagues. In 1986 Donna Marie West published *What More Can We Ask For* about her experiences in a Human Development Project in Guatemala. Laura Spencer published *Winning Through Participation,* about ICA's methods of participation, shortly after in 1989. It focused on

ICA's Technology of Participation ToP™ methods of facilitation. The publishing continued in the 1990s with books on business and the civil society, facilitation and
foundaional understandings.

TRANSITION FROM ORDER TO ICA

At a conference in Oaxtepec, Mexico, in November 1988, ICA made the painful decision
to destructure its family order dimension. It had become so diverse with so many cen-
trifugal pulls, that "the center could not hold." But what was really happening, in retrospect, was the Institute's transition from being dependent on the order community to
striking out on its own as a non-profit organization. Suddenly ICA had to really think
about hiring staff, paying salaries, and rewriting its mission and philosophy statement
to fit the new times.

THE NINETIES

In the 1990s, partnerships continued to be key. The International Association of
Facilitators (IAF) was a joint venture of former and current ICA staff and many practicing
consultants. Membership has been growing rapidly among professionals who sense
something unique in the contexts and the combination of ICA's rational and spirit methods with the knowledge and experience of many facilitators. Consultants have taken planning, problem-solving and personal growth skills into many business, government and
non-profit venues. Training in ICA's methods and contexts has grown. Colleagues in several countries have done research on the Technology of Meaning. With the proliferation
of e-mail, it has become easier to involve disparate groups in such tasks as planning the
major conference in 2000 in Denver on shaping profound social change.

With the IERD there was a shift from Global Research Assemblies to international
conferences. Building upon the comprehensiveness of the social process work and the
impetus to reach out to many partners, a series of global conferences in the 1980s and
90s have been signs of hope, toward enabling care for all of creation and full human
lives for every person. The conferences and their themes have ranged from Our
Common Future in an Environment of Change (Taipei, 1990) to Exploring the Great
Transition to Our One World (Prague, 1992) and The Rise of Civil Society in the 21st
Century (Cairo, 1996).

ICA's work continues through its institutes in 34 nations and focuses increasingly
on facilitation, consultation, training and research. Each institute operates autonomously,
but under the guidance of a Board of Directors. A degree of coordination among the

national offices of ICA International (ICAI) is exercised from a secretariat in Brussels. Cooperation and partnership is increasingly the preferred mode between offices; courses and methods are shared between institutes and new ideas and experiments made available. Further details can be obtained from ICAI's Web page at htpp://www.icaworld.org.

SOURCES

Where did the wisdom in this book come from? The short answer, already described, is from the lived experience, research and reflection of the staff of the Institute of Cultural Affairs and its predecessor, the Ecumenical Institute.

Religious Studies I. For its first 20 years, the Ecumenical Institute (EI) was concerned with the kind of adult education that would wake people up to the limits, possibilities and purpose of life. EI's primary instrument was the Religious Studies I course (RS-1), a non-denominational approach to the theological revolution of our times. It was taught all over the world to at least a million people. Chapters 2, 3, 9, and 10 of this book are derived directly from this course.

Research. The Institute of Cultural Affairs (ICA), has always described itself as a research, training and demonstration organization. A major instrument of its research was the summer assemblies and conferences. These large meetings created many of ICA's basic designs, tools and societal maps. The comprehensive models in Chapter 7, such as the global grid, the social process triangles, the comprehensive life curriculum, and the Other World charts in Chapter 5, were created through these research efforts.

Demonstration. Early on, the ICA saw that it is not enough to teach what is possible; it has to be demonstrated sociologically, on the ground. In ICA's first social demonstration, Fifth City, a ten-block community in Chicago's West Side., ICA staff worked with community leaders to create a plan for the revitalization of this inner-city community that includes new housing, health care, early childhood education, a shopping mall, and programs for youth, adults and elders. The story of this effort spread across the city and around the world as a sign of what was possible for local communities everywhere. ICA applied these learnings working with local people in the global village demonstrations to improve the local economy, health, education and well-being. This experience is reflected in chapters 10, 11 and 12.

Training and Facilitation. ICA's courses, academies and trainings schools developed since the 1950s grew out of a comprehensive curriculum model, described in Chapter 7. Beginning around 1988, the focus shifted to facilitating and training in methods of participation. Wisdom from the ICA staff and network since 1988 has been focused on building up a culture of participation in local communities and all kinds of organizations. The wisdom from this phase shows up particularly in Chapters 1, 4, and 11.

Over the years, ICA has relied on wisdom from many sources: theologians, philosophers, sociologists, psychologists, artists, popular songwriters and local people. In this tapestry, the discerning reader will notice threads from several 20th Century movements,

1. The 20th century theological revolution, found in the work of the "German theologians": Rudolph Bultmann, Paul Tillich, Dietrich Bonhoeffer and H. Richard Niebuhr. (Theology here means something like "a study of the depths of living" rather than the more doctrinal overtones of the word).

2. The phenomenological process, developed by Edmund Husserl, Rollo May and others, provided a process for continually deepening our appropriation of life as it happens. Aspects of this process show up in chapters 4 and 5.

3. The existential philosophers:, especially Jean-Paul Sartre and Albert Camus, and, Sören Kierkegaard. The combination of the new theology with the existential thread grounded the truth about life in a way that nothing else could have. The reader will find traces of this thread in Chapter 2 on disciplined lucidity.

4. The education revolutionaries, especially Jean Piaget, Jerome Bruner, Paul Goodman and Kenneth Boulding, who changed the meaning and methods of the educative process. They have had an indirect influence on the way this book is written with a heavy emphasis on images, illustrations, stories and experiences.

5. Key exponents of social philosophy and social anthropology: Karl Deutsch, Jean-Jacques Servan-Schreiber, Mircea Eliade, Lewis Mumford, Franz Fanon, Kevin Lynch, Joseph Campbell, Riane Eisler and many more. They contributed immeasurably to ICA's work on the Social Process, and the key role of culture in social transformation.

6. Studies of great minds and spirits from diverse cultures such as Lao Tzu, Sun Tzu, Musashi, Buddha's Eightfold Path, Carlos Castaneda, the Sufi stories, Confucius, Rabindranath Tagore, Octavio Paz, Hermann Hesse, Teresa of Avila, John of the Cross and others ensured that the spirit winds of many cultures blew through ICA's life and work. They are quoted throughout the book.

7. Radical empiricism:, the wisdom, compassion, and "on-the-ground savvy" that comes from living and working in the urban ghettoes of Chicago or Calcutta and rural villages of the world, sleeping sometimes on cowdung floors, or in the open air, drinking from the village well, eating what the local people eat, and trying to figure out with the local people every single day how to work through whatever contradiction it was that was blocking development, by standing in, seeing through, and acting on the situation.

These days, ICA staff in 34 nations are reinventing how the organization will face the challenges of a new millennium. Research, training, demonstration and facilitation will continue to be major tasks, whatever new programs are developed.

◈ BIBLIOGRAPHY

Allenbaugh, Kay: *Chocolate for a Woman's Soul*, Simon & Schuster, New York, 1997

Anderson, Laurie: *Stories from the Nerve Bible,* HarperPerennial, New York, 1994

Anouilh, Jean: *Antigone*, Methuen and Co., London, 1956

Arendt, Hannah: *The Life of the Mind*, Harcourt Brace and Co., San Diego, 1971

Arnold, Roseanne Barr: *My Life as a Woman*, Harper and Rowe, New York, 1989

Ashby, Ruth and Gore, Deborah: *HerStory: Women Who Changed the World*, Viking Penguin, New York, 1995

Aung San Suu Kyi: *The Voice of Hope, Conversations with Alan Clements*, Seven Stories Press, New York, 1997

Aung San Suu Kyi: *Freedom from Fear*, Penguin Books, London, 1991

Beckett, Samuel: *Waiting For Godot*, Grove Press, New York, 1965

Belden, Hyatt & Ackley: *Towards the Learning Organization: A Guide*, ICA Canada, Toronto, 1993

Bellah, Robert, et al.: *Habits of the Heart: Individualism and Commitment in American Life*, Harper & Row, New York, 1985

Berger, Thomas: *Little Big Man*, Dell Publishing Co., New York, 1964

Blackburn, Simon: *The Oxford Dictionary of Philosophy*, Oxford University Press, Oxford, 1996

Bly, Robert: *The Kabir Book: Forty-Four of the Ecstatic Poems of Kabir*, The Seventies Press, 1971

Bonhoeffer, Dietrich: *Ethics*, SCM Press, London. 1959

Boorstin, Daniel: *The Seekers*, Alfred A. Knopf, New York, 1999

Boulding, Kenneth E.: T*he Image*, University of Michigan Press, Ann Arbor, 1966, Brown, D. Mackenzie: *Ultimate Concern*, Harper & Row, New York, 1965

Bultmann, Rudolph: *Essays: Philosophical and Theological*, SCM Press, London, 1955

Burbidge, John (ed.): *Beyond Prince and Merchant*, Pact Publications, New York, 1998.

Campbell, Joseph: *Hero With a Thousand Faces*, Princeton University Press, Princeton, New Jersey, 1958

Campfens, Hubert (ed.): *Community Development Around the World*, University of Toronto Press, Toronto, 1997

Camus, Albert: *The Myth of Sisyphus and Other Essays*, Vintage Books, New York, 1955

Canfield, Hansen, Rogerson, Rutte, and Clauss: *Chicken Soup for the Soul at Work*, Health Communications Inc., Deerfield Beach, Florida, 1996

Casteneda, Carlos: *The Journey to Ixtlan*, Pocket Books, New York, 1981

Cock, John: *The Transparent Event: post-modern Christ images*, tranScribe books, Greensboro, NC., 1999

Csikszentmihalyi, Mihaly: *Creativity: Flow and the Psychology of Invention*, HarperCollins, New York, 1996

Cummings: *Collected Poems*, Harcourt Brace, San Diego, 1979

Dalla Costa, John: *Working Wisdom*, Stoddart Books, Toronto, 1995

de Chardin, Teilhard: *The Phenomenon of Man*, Harper Collins, New York, 1980

Denenberg, Barry: *Nelson Mandela: No Easy Walk to Freedom*, Scholastic Inc., New York, 1991

Dershowitz, Alan M.: *The Abuse Excuse and Other Cop-outs, Sob Stories, and Evasions*, Little, Brown and Company, Boston,

Dewdney, Christopher: *Last Flesh: Life in the Transhuman Era*, Harper Collins, Toronto, 1994

Dineen, Dr Tana: *Manufacturing Victims: What the Psychology Industry Is Doing to People*, Robert Davies Publishing, Montreal, 1996

Eliot, T.S.: *The Complete Poems and Plays: 1909-1950*, Harcourt, Brace, Jovanovich, Orlando, Florida, 1950.

Fox, Matthew: *Confessions: The Making of a Post-Denominational Priest*, Harper, San Francisco, 1996

Frankl, Victor E.: *Man's Search for Meaning*, Washington Square Press, New York, 1993

Fulghum, Robert: *Words I Wish I Wrote*, Harper Collins, New York, 1997

Goold, Douglas and Willis, Andrew: *The BRE-X Fraud*, McClelland and Stewart, Inc., Toronto, 1997

Grun, Bernard: *The Timetables of History*, Simon & Schuster, New York, 1975

Hammarskjöld, Dag: *Markings,* Faber and Faber, London, UK, 1963

Handy, Charles: *Hungry Spirit*, Random House, London, UK, 1997

Harrison, Paul Carter and Duke, Bill: *Black Light: The African American Hero*, Thunder's Mouth Press, New York, 1993

Hawken, Paul: *The Ecology of Commerce*, Harper Business, New York, 1993

Henderson, Hazel: *Building a Win-Win World: Life Beyond Global Economic Warfare*, Berrett-Koehler Publishers, San Francisco, 1996

Hesse, Hermann: *Journey to the East*, Noonday Press, New York, 1954

Hillman, James: *Kinds of Power: A Guide to Its Intelligent Uses*, Doubleday, New York, 1995

_____: *The Soul's Code: In Search of Character and Calling*, Random House, New York, 1996

_____ and Ventura, Michael: *We've Had 100 Years of Psychotherapy and the World is Getting Worse*, Harper, San Francisco, 1993

Houston, Jean: *The Possible Human*, J.P. Tarcher, Los Angeles, California, 1982

Hubbard, Barbara Marx: *Conscious Evolution: Awakening the Power of Our Social Potential*, New World Library, Novato, California, 1998

Ignatieff, Michael: *The Warrior's Honor: Ethnic War and The Modern Consequence*, Penguin Group, Toronto, 1998

Jaworsky, Joseph: *Synchronicity: The Inner Path of Leadership*, Berrett-Koehler, San Francisco, 1996

Jenkins, John C. and Maureen R.: *The Other World...in the midst of our world*, Imaginal Training, Groningen, The Netherlands, 1998

_____: *The Social Process,* Imaginal Training, Groningen, The Netherlands, 1997

John of the Cross: *The Dark Night of the Soul*,   Doubleday, Garden City, New York, 1959

Kastenbaum, Peter: T*he Heart of Business: Ethics, Power and Philosophy*, Saybrook Publishing Company, San Francisco, 1987

Kazantzakis, Nikos: *The Saviors of God*, Simon & Schuster, New York, 1960

Kesey, Ken: *One Flew Over the Cuckoo's Nest*, Viking Press, New York, 1962

Kierkegaard, Sören: *Despair: The Sickness Unto Death*, Princeton University Press, Princeton, New Jersey, 1980

Killen, Patricia and de Beer, John: *The Art of Theological Reflection,* The Crossroad Publishing Company, New York, 1994

King, Larry with Rabbi Irwin Katsof: *Powerful Prayers*, Renaissance Books, Los Angeles, 1998

Lawrence, D.H.: *Selected Poems*, Viking Press, New York, 1959

Lawrence, T.E.: *Seven Pillars of Wisdom*, Cape, London, 1948

Leyton, Elliott: *Touched by Fire: Doctors Without Borders in a Third World Crisis*, McClelland & Stewart Inc., Toronto, 1998

Maslow, Abraham: *Toward a Psychology of Being*, D. Van Nostrand, New York, 1968

Moore, Thomas: *Care of the Soul: A Guide for Cultivating Depth and Sacredness in Everyday Life*, HarperPerennial, New York, 1992

Myss, Caroline: *Anatomy of Spirit*, Harmony Books, New York, 1996

Needleman, Jacob: *Consciousness and Tradition,* CrossRoad Publishing Company, New York, 1982, p. 13

Niebuhr, H. Richard: *Radical Monotheism and Western Culture*, Westminster John Knox Press, New York, 1993

_____ *The Meaning of Revelation*, MacMillan, New York, 1960

Owen, Harrison: *Spirit: Transformation and Development in Organizations*, Abbott Publishing, Potomac, Maryland, 1987

Ortega y Gasset, Jose: *Man and Crisis*, Norton Library, New York, 1962

Otto, Rudolph: *The Idea of the Holy*, Oxford University Press, London, 1923

Payne, Robert: *The Life and Death of Mahatma Gandhi*, Konecky & Konecky, New York, 1969

Pearson, Carol: *Awakening the Heroes Within*, Harper, San Francisco, 1991

Pozzi, Doris and Williams, Stephen: *Success with Soul*, Dorian Welles, Pty. Ltd., Melbourne, 1997

Rees, Nigel: *Sayings of the Century*, George Allen and Unwin, London, 1984

Remen, Rachel Naomi, MD: *Kitchen Table Wisdom: Stories That Heal*, Riverhead Books, New York, 1994

Richards, Dick: *Artful Work*, Berkley Books, New York, 1997

Rifkin, Jeremy: *The End of Work*, Tarcher/Putnam, New York, 1996

Robertson, Edwin: *The Shame and the Sacrifice: The Life and Martyrdom of Dietrich Bonhoeffer*, Macmillan, New York, 1988.

Russell, Peter: *The Global Brain*, J.P. Tarcher, Los Angeles, 1983

Saul, John Ralston: *The Unconscious Civilization*, House of Anansi Press, Concord, Ontario, 1996

Serling, Rod: *Requiem for a Heavyweight*, Bantam Books, New York, 1962

Stanfield, R. Brian (ed.): *The Art of Focused Conversation*, ICA Canada/New Society Press, Toronto, 1999

Seuss, Dr.: *I Had Trouble in Getting to Solla Sollew*, Random House, New York, 1965

Sewall, Gilbert T. (ed.): *The Eighties: A Reader*, Addison-Wesley, New York, 1997.

Shah, Idries: *Tales of the Dervishes*, Penguin, New York, 1993

Singer, Peter (ed.): *Ethics*, Oxford Paperbacks, Oxford University Press, Oxford, 1994

Stephenson, Jay: *The Complete Idiot's Guide to Philosophy*, Alpha Books, New York, 1998

Sun Tzu: *The Art of War,* translated by Thomas Cleary), Shambhala, Boston, 1998

Tannen, Deborah: *The Argument Culture: Moving from Debate to Dialogue*, Random House, Toronto, 1998.

Tarnas, Richard: *The Passion of the Western Mind*, Harmony Books, New York, 1991

Taylor, Charles: *The Ethics of Authenticity*, Harvard University Press, Cambridge Massachusetts, 1991

The New English Bible with the Apocrypha, Oxford University Press, New York, 1971

Team Tech, Inc.: *The Everyone a Leader SmartWare System*, Team Tech, Inc., Olathe, Kansas, 1998

Teresa of Avila: *The Interior Castle*, Doubleday, New York, 1985

Thompson, William Irwin: *The American Replacement of Nature*, Doubleday Currency, New York, 1991

Tillich, Paul: *The Courage to Be*, Yale University Press, New Haven, 1959

––––––– : *The Shaking of the Foundations*, Scribner, New York, 1948

Toffler, Alvin: *Future Shock*, Random House, New York, 1970

_____ : *Ecospasm Report*, Bantam Books, New York, 1973

_____ : *The Third Wave*, Morrow, New York, 1980

_____ : *Power Shift*, Bantam Books, New York, 1990

Troxel, James P. (ed.): *Government Works: Profiles of People Making a Difference*, Miles River Press, Alexandria, Virginia, 1995

Tuchman, Barbara W.: *The March of Folly: From Troy to Vietnam*, G.K. Hall & Co. Boston, Massachusetts, 1984

Vaill, Peter B.: *Managing as a Performing Art*, San Francisco, Jossey-Bass, 1989.

van Oech, Roger: *A Whack on the Side of the Head*, Warner Books, New York, 1985

Vardey, Lucinda (ed.): *God in All Worlds: An Anthology of Contemporary Spiritual Writing*, Vintage Books, New York, 1996.

Wagner, Jane: *The Search for Signs of Intelligent Life in the Universe*, Harper & Row, Publishers, New York, 1986

Wepman, Denis: *Desmond Tutu*, Franklin Watts, New York, 1989

Whoopi Goldberg Book, Rob Weisbach Books, New York, 1997

Wheatley, Margaret: *Leadership and the New Science*, Berret-Koehler, San Francisco, 1992

Wilder, Thornton: *Our Town*, Harper and Row, New York, 1957.

Williamson, Marianne: *The Healing of America*, Simon and Schuster, New York, 1997

PERIODICALS, PAPERS AND MANUSCRIPTS

Burbidge, John: "The Semco Story," *Edges*, September 1993, ICA Canada

Barlow:, Maude: "Seed Keepers" in *Canadian Perspective*, The Council of Canadians, Winter 1999, Ottawa

Epps, John L., Review of Ken Wilber's *A Brief History of Everything*, manuscript, 1997

Epps, John L.: "Strategy: Perspective, Process and Practice" *LENS International Newsletter*, Kuala Lumpur, 1998

_____ : "Debunking The Promotion Myth: Finding a Destination for the Career Path", *Edges*, December 1998

_____ : "Strategic Thinking", *LENS International Newsletter*, Kuala Lumpur, 1998

Griffith, Beret: *A Chronological History of the Ecumenical Institute and the Institute of Cultural Affairs*, San Carlos, California, 1992

Havel, Vaclav :"The Need for Transcendence in the Postmodern World", Transcript of a Speech made at Independence Hall, Philadelphia July 4, 1994

ICA:*Estimates,* Vols. I and II, Chicago, 1976-77

Lush, Kay: "Profound Humanness as Care", a Talk at Global Council, Chicago, 1977

Mathews, Joseph Wesley: "Transparent Being," *Golden Pathways CD-ROM*

_____ : "Meditation," in *Selected Talks*, ICA Chicago, 1980

_____ : "The Recovery of the Other World," in *Selected Talks*, ICA Chicago, 1980

_____ : "Human Motivity and Reform of New Community," in *Selected Talks*, ICA Chicago, 1980

_____ : "The Substance of Taking Care of Yourself," in *Selected Talks*, ICA Chicago, 1980,

Ray, Paul H.: "The Rise of Integral Culture," *Noetic Sciences Review*, Sausalito, California, Spring, 1996

Roddick, Anita: "Finding Spirit Through Service," in *The Image*, Issue 32, March 1998

Stanfield, Jeanette and Barkony, Barbara (eds.): Fifth City Preschool Manual, 1976, *Golden Pathways CD-ROM*

Ventura, Michael: "Revisioning Psychology: An Interview with James Hillman," *L.A.Weekly*, June, 1990

Ward, Larry: "The Wheel of Change," *Edges,* August 1998, ICA Canada

Wiegel, James: "The Indicative Battle Planner," *Golden Pathways CD-ROM*

ICA AS ORGANIZATION

The Canadian Institute of Cultural Affairs is a unique facilitation, training and research organization providing effective participatory skills to hundreds of individuals, communities and organizations across Canada. With 40 years of experience in 32 nations, The Canadian Institute of Cultural Affairs is on the leading edge of change and consistently delivers quality programs and resources.

ICA Canada licences ICA Associates Inc. to use its training and facilitation methods.

OUR MISSION

Our mission is to promote, develop and enhance people's capacity to participate in the creation of a more human world through:

Training in group facilitation and change management methods,

Consulting in individual, community and organizational development,

Research in trends affecting society and the positive responses to them,

Delivery of social transformational knowledge on multiple platforms.

HOW TO CONTACT US

BY MAIL: The Canadian Institute of Cultural Affairs
579 Kingston Road
Toronto, Ontario
Canada M4E 1R3

BY TELEPHONE: In Toronto 416-691-2316
In Canada outside Toronto: 1-877-691-1422
Outside Canada: 416-691-2316

BY FAX: 416-691-2491
BY E.MAIL: ica@icacan.ca
WEB SITE: http:// www.icacan.ca

ICA INTERNATIONAL WEB PAGE: htpp://www.icaworld.org

New Society Publishers' mission
is to publish books that contribute in fundamental ways
to building an ecologically sustainable and just society,
and to do so with the least possible impact on the environment
in a manner that models that vision.

If you have enjoyed *The Art of Focused Conversation*,
you may also want to check out our other titles
in the following categories:

Progressive Leadership
Ecological Design & Planning
Environment & Justice
New Forestry
Accountable Economics
Conscientious Commerce
Resistance & Community
Educational & Parenting Resources

For a full list of NSP's titles,
please call 1-800-567-6772,
or check out our web site at:
www.newsociety.com

NEW SOCIETY PUBLISHERS